DEDICATION

I take great pride in dedicating this story, of the first part of my life, to my wonderful children and grandchildren. Most of all to my daughter Heidi, who has spent many years interpreting my awful scribing, typing, researching, editing and proofing!

Thank you.

William Mansfield

Chapters

DEDICATION 1
ONE 5
TWO 21
THREE 40
FOUR 48
FIVE 61
SIX 68
SEVEN 77
EIGHT 90
NINE 97
TEN 106
ELEVEN 116
TWELVE 129
THIRTEEN 139
FOURTEEN 154
FIFTEEN 166
SIXTEEN 182
SEVENTEEN 199
EIGHTEEN 215
NINETEEN 234
TWENTY 254

ONE

I was born a Scouser, a Liverpool baby, probably of Irish descent. It was the time of the great depression in the middle of the 1930s, when most of the world was in turmoil: Wall Street in America was in crisis causing banking systems in the United Kingdom to fall apart; businesses failed; jobs by the million were lost; people committed suicide and the country was in dire straits. Obviously not the best time to enter this world and certainly not to be born in what was already the most depressed part of Liverpool.

Mainly colonised by Irish families, both Catholic and Protestant, who had arrived over the years looking for a better life, they were now back to square one - or at least their descendants were.

My mam and dad and their parents and siblings, all born in Liverpool, were some of these descendants; Mam was of the Protestant religion, Dad was a Catholic. I learned that Dad, or at least his family, would only allow what was known as a mixed religion marriage so long as any children of the marriage were christened Catholic. Ironically, I decided to convert to the Church of England religion, but when I married a Catholic girl, I could not then object when I was told I would have to take lessons from a Catholic priest on the Catholic religion!

As I grew up, I learned that the house we lived in was situated in Plumpton Street, a downtown and rather seedy district of Liverpool. To a small boy it seemed enormous, and climbing the linoed stairs to the two bedrooms with whitewashed walls was great fun. Falling down the stairs, which I frequently did, was no deterrent and neither were the smacks I got after being examined for broken bones. I used to wonder why Mam and Dad were so concerned about injuries from my falls when they were intent on injuring me anyway!

Downstairs was the room Mam called the parlour; it too had whitewashed walls and a lino floor. I remember the lino was always wrinkling and coming up in a blister; when Mam would ask him to do something about it, Dad would reply there was nothing to be done, it was from the damp underneath the old stone slabs. He would then walk around the room stamping on the blisters, which would invariably crack open as Mam called him names.

The other room Mam called the scullery; these walls were also whitewashed but it had no lino, just cold stone slabs. When Mam was busy and couldn't pay me any attention, she would sit me in a chair in the scullery with a butty, usually a bit of jam on bread; I would sit there dangling barefoot and my toes would turn blue with the cold in winter. Around the walls were bare wooden shelves where Mam would place and hang pots and pans and dishes; most of the dishes were a browny-white and full of dark cracks. She did have other dishes that had flowers and leaves and things painted on them, but these would never be used, as they were only for display in the small wood and glass cabinet which was the centre-piece of the parlour.

The great cracked white sink under the small window, which had no curtains, was fed by a single tap, and had lots of uses – doing the dishes and the pots and pans, washing clothes, for holding water to mop the floor with, and as a bath for me. Dad would wash and shave in it; Mam would strip and douse herself down in it. I once saw Dad, after arriving home drunk, wee in it! My childish glee and remark of Daddy weeing in the sink brought Mam running out of the parlour and Dad desperately trying to get out to the yard where the closet was before she could get to him.

The closet at the bottom of the yard next to the high wall surrounding it was a dark and sinister place to me; the plank of wood with a hole in it was scrubbed constantly, though I was never allowed to use it; the hole disappeared into a stained white bowl and then vanished into the ground. Mam would say, 'You're too young to use it; you could fall down the pan.' This always puzzled me; I used to think all the pans were in the scullery! Anyway, when I looked down the closet hole, I definitely couldn't see any pans!

In our winters there, Dad would take jugs of boiling water and pour it over the pipes and what he called the cistern. 'Bloody frost, bloody ice, bloody winter!' he would constantly repeat as Mam brought out more hot water. The ice in the yard caused Mam to burn her feet when she spilt the hot water one day when she slipped. 'Bloody ice!' she said, 'and the bloody drain's frozen up as well!'

In the house in winter, the only warm room was the parlour, because it had what Mam called a 'range' that filled one wall. It was all brick and iron and contained the oven, which had a big iron door, and a fire gate underneath it; opposite the oven, was a wide iron shelf. Mam would stand the big kettle on the shelf, when it wasn't hanging over the open fire which would be roaring up the chimney. When she had some money, she would buy flour and apples and bake apple pie on one of the old plates in the oven. We ate it with Bird's custard; Mam was an expert at mixing the powder with milk at just the right temperature. This was the best food that I ever had.

Our cat, Blackie, named because he was the same colour as the range, used to like to keep warm, either curling up on it, or in the oven after the fire had gone out each night. But one freezing cold morning, Dad lit the fire. He lit it in a hurry, forgetting to look inside the oven. We didn't discover poor Blackie until the evening, and it was weeks before a devastated Mam would bake another apple pie.

Mam loved that range; she would polish it with what she called 'blacking' every day, until all of it was a shiny black. Everything on it was also polished black with the exception of the big brass latch; the iron mantle above the range was filled with useless bits of pottery and old brown photographs and would not escape the blacking. After replacing everything, which had been dusted and cleaned, Mam would stand back and admire her handiwork before starting the next chore or attending to Lillian, my younger sister.

I really don't know why, but Lillian is not really part of my memories of that time. At only fourteen months younger than me, she was always present, but she cried a lot and Mam paid her a lot more attention than she did me, and yet somehow she was a faint background figure, of no interest to me at the time.

Sometimes, when Mam was mangling the washing in the backyard, I would help her turn the handle. I would turn it and it would revolve the big heavy rollers, which would squeeze all the water out of the washing making everything as flat as an iron would have done; that didn't stop Mam taking the hot flat-iron off the grill above the fire and ironing them in the evening once everything was dry. Occasionally, a neighbour would come to the backyard door on these wash days, for a jangle. With the back door open and them talking, I was able to slip out unnoticed to the jigger.

The jigger, or back alleyway, separating the two rows of houses backing onto each other was a place of mystery to me. Long and narrow it had two gas mantles, one at each end, which were lit up at night. I'd hear Dad saying on a few occasions to Mam, 'those bloody courting couples have broken them again; why can't they find somewhere else to play around?'

I used to wonder what it was that they could be playing in the dark - perhaps hide and seek? - I couldn't think of anything else!

He would also moan constantly when 'drunken sods', as he called them, used the alley after closing time as a 'piss house'; Mam would remind him that at least they didn't piss in the sink!

The high wall separating the jigger from the yard and the houses either side belonged to the moggies; the cats, which every house owned, used it exclusively. Blackie used to be up there most of the time; that was until the accident when silly Dad stopped Mam making apple pies. Dad would say we'd have to get another cat to keep the mice down. We used to have lots of mice, but Mam said no, she couldn't go through losing another cat like that again.

On a couple of occasions I remember Mam shrieking and shouting, and when I ran into the parlour, she would be standing on one of the chairs with three or four mice running between the legs of the chairs. She would yell for Lilly and me to get up on one of the other chairs, but I always thought it was more fun to chase the mice.

All of the closets in the yards on both sides of the jigger had cats lying on the roof, whilst others would be taking walks along the wall; Mam, Lilly and I had one heck of a laugh one day when the moggies started shooting off in all directions, even knocking each other off the walls in their panic. The reason for this soon appeared; someone had lifted a scruffy dog onto the wall and Mam said it must have been a dog's heaven as there were more cats to chase than he would have ever seen before. Tail wagging and tongue hanging out, he was as good as the cats at keeping himself up there as he raced the whole length of the alleyway and then back again, still keeping his balance on the wall.

When Mam told Dad about it, he said that if he could find a dog like that, that was half a monkey, he'd get one; I couldn't wait for him to bring one home, but he never did.

I had lots of aunties and uncles, as Mam had six sisters and four brothers, and Dad had seven brothers; both families had originally come from Ireland and settled in Liverpool. Dad's parents lived in Plumpton Street, like us, and Mam's were in Catherine Street, which was just a short walk away.

Mam would tell stories of when she was little. My favourite story, because it always made me laugh, was about her father, my Grandad; I don't remember him at all, or perhaps I never even met him, as he probably died before I was born.

Grandad worked, when it was available, on the docks in Bootle. One day, he had come home from work with a box under his arm and gathered all the kids and Grandma around the kitchen table. With everybody present he gently opened the box and out stepped a little duck. To the squeals of delight from around the table it waddled about, and everybody tried to touch it. Grandad told them that somebody in a truck in the docks had given it to him and he would make a little pen for it in the yard. Every day the kids, including Mam, would go to feed Quacky, as they named him, bits of anything that was left over. Quacky thrived on what Grandad would call 'non-duck food' and Quacky would chase them around the yard looking for more. He, or she, nobody ever knew what sex it was, got fatter and fatter.

As winter approached and with it Christmas Day, the possibility of Father Christmas bringing them something and having a party took their minds off the duck; it was left to Grandad or Grandma to look after Quacky and feed it. When the great day arrived, sure enough Father Christmas came and went leaving Mam a lovely comb, and everyone was given a job to do in preparation for the great dinner. Mam and her sister Eva had to peel and wash the potatoes; there were always dozens of these at every dinner and twice as many on Christmas Day. There would be cabbage and dumplings and, wonder of wonder, sausages, and after this there would be Christmas pudding which Grandma had made and boiled over the range.

When everybody was seated, Grandad had, on this particular Christmas, disappeared into the scullery and emerged with the unbelievable sight of a turkey on a plate. They knew it was a turkey as they'd been told it was what you should have at Christmas, and everybody cheered and clapped as they'd never had anything like it before. Grandad put it in the middle of the table and Grandma began to dish out the food.

Suddenly, Lillian, my youngest aunt, after whom my sister Lilly had been named, shouted 'Wait, what about Quacky?' She ran out into the yard and she came back in tears. 'Quacky's gone, Quacky's gone; there's only feathers left!'

Mam and all the older kids turned and looked at the turkey on the table and then looked at Grandad.

'He's killed Quacky!' Mam's brother Charlie shouted, and everybody started crying; none of them would have any part of Quacky despite Grandad lying that a cat must have got the duck.

'This,' he insisted, 'is a real turkey!' But nobody ever forgave him.

Mam said they never saw anything of the turkey-duck again, but they were all sure that Grandad and Grandma had eaten the lot!

One day, I saw Dad coming home bruised and bloodied and learnt from Mam that he had stood in for a boxer who hadn't turned up for a match at Liverpool's boxer's stadium and, win or lose, he would get a payment of a few pounds. He would get that payment for volunteering to stand in for anyone who needed to be replaced. I learned eventually that all my uncles used to do the same thing. He would come home and hand the purse to Mam who would then patch him up. Mam had a number of purses. Dad also played a banjo and after he'd joined the Royal Engineers Territorials, or the Terries as Mam would call them, he'd entertain his fellow soldiers at various rallies; he could also sing.

By trade Dad was a blacksmith, but in the 30s there was little work due to the worldwide depression, so a combination of blacksmith's jobs, a small amount of pay from the army and the boxing winnings, or losses, put bread on the table. To supplement things even more, he would busk; for many people busking was very commonplace.

There were buskers who would be escape artists, working on street corners, tied up in chains and put in a sack from which they had to escape in a very short time; people would then throw money down onto his coat or hat that he'd left on the pavement. Others would do similar things, but they would lie on the pavement and put paving stones or such like on their chests and then an accomplice would smash the slabs with a heavy maul or hammer.

Dad would find a queue for the cinema and play the banjo and sing. He'd wear his uniform and cap and before the queue of people would disappear into the cinema, he would walk up and down the line offering his cap for what would only be pennies. Mam would allow him to keep the odd one or two for a pint of ale.

His brothers would all take a turn at the Boxing Stadium to earn some extra money. According to Mam, none of them could knock the skin off a rice pudding, but they still went, whether to win or lose, just happy to have a go and earn a couple of pounds. 'It's their bloody Irish blood,' she would say. 'They'd go anywhere for a fight.'

It was 1939 when kidney problems, derived from his boxing, ultimately resulted in Dad's untimely death. Dad's coffin was laid on a couple of chairs against one of the walls in the parlour in our house in Plumpton Street; the coffin lid was left off in order for friends and mourners to still see him when they came to pay their respects. Mam had somehow managed to scrape funds together to make sandwiches, which filled our only table. The family friends and mourners brought with them bundles of beer or spirits and these were handed to Mam with the usual words of condolence and then stacked under the only window.

It wasn't long before the beer supply was swiftly disappearing, and all the reminiscing and jokes about Dad were making for a jolly occasion. Then, out of the blue, a sound came from the coffin and one of Dad's arms raised up and appeared to wave. Pandemonium ensued. The women screamed, Mam included; the talking stopped and some of the more devout were ferociously crossing themselves. Then, with another wave,

Dad's arm fell back into the coffin. The only people in the room not in a complete panic were Dad's brothers; they'd managed to keep straight faces but now they were bursting a rib with laughter. George, the only brother who had not been in the room, came down the stairs laughing, saying between guffaws, 'It worked! Bloody brilliant, it worked!'

He then explained that they'd bored a small hole in the bedroom floor above when Mam wasn't in the house, then they'd put a thin piece of fishing line through the hole and tied it to Dad's wrist. Nobody had spotted it. George had been given the job of 'hand raiser' and was given a glass of whisky as a reward, as everybody said that Dad would have loved the joke - and he probably did.

As time went on, everybody seemed to get happier and merrier the more they drank and it all ended with singing and dancing; Dad would have loved that as well.

The advent of the war, when my uncles joined the forces like thousands of other Scousers, ended the tradition of boxing. Some years later my uncle Charlie, my Mam's elder brother, took me to see a boxing match at the stadium.

Sitting watching the fight my uncle leaned over and whispered, 'Your dad used to fight here, Billy.' I was so proud.

It was shortly after Dad died that we found ourselves living in Bootle, close to the docks. In those days, midnight flits were commonplace to avoid paying any rent due, and so Mam moved us whilst Lilly and I were sleeping. Because people were so poor, they would have to find somewhere else to live or end up in the local Workhouse. The Workhouse was the last resort; cold and damp from Victorian days, they would allow destitute families, in the main women and children, to stay a while; dads weren't very often allowed to stay with them. Everybody hated them and did everything possible to avoid ending up there; Mam and her brothers were of the same mind.

My uncles must have borrowed a handcart and moved our belongings to our new home at Coffeehouse Bridge, pulling the cart all along Scotland Road, known as 'Scotty Road', with a pub on almost every corner. Then along Stanley Road, through Kirkdale and on into Bootle. In all, probably about six miles; a hard trek with all our meagre belongings. Whether they stopped at any of the many public houses on the way is anyone's guess.

My new home was set in the dock area of Bootle, known as Miller's Bridge, very close to Huskisson Dock; it was much bigger than Plumpton Street and seemed warmer. Mam and I were very pleased with our new home.

We had not lived at our home for very long when what was known as the Phoney War from 1939-1940 came to an end and the real war commenced. I would have been five and a half at the time, and it soon became apparent that our luck, or whatever it was that had brought us to Bootle, was about to run out.

Mr Brown was a tall, slim man with dark hair and a neat moustache on his pockmarked face; he was either the owner or the lodger of the house we lived in and he would allow Mam, Lilly and me to listen to his radio. It was here that we heard Winston Churchill really declare war on Germany.

Mr Brown said to Mam, 'That's it, the balloon's gone up.'

Lilly and I were left wondering where the balloon had gone up and why it was on the news. Later, Mam explained it was just an expression people said and not a real balloon; Lilly and I were very disappointed!

It was not long before we saw many monstrous balloons.

The move from Plumpton Street to Coffeehouse Bridge was the beginning of my life as I would understand it and remember it. My life was completely turned around; I had to go to school and I naturally rebelled as school was not for me. Mam thought otherwise and dragged me screaming to St Mary's. It was within easy walking distance from our house and Mam frogmarched me in through gates that led into a graveyard, which naturally didn't do anything to alleviate my terror.

St Mary's looked just like a church complete with a steeple and somewhere in the bowels was the classroom complete with desks for infants in my age group. A lady teacher, after a brief conversation with Mam, took charge of me. By now I was just sniffling but after seeing Mam leaving, my previous screaming protest was nothing to that which now took place. A rather stinging smack on my bare leg, followed swiftly by another, raised my yells another octave. And only another couple of even harder smacks persuaded me that I had better not continue. As I stood sniffling in the classroom, other children filed in and stood at the desks grinning at me.

By now, the war had more or less started and everybody had been supplied with gas masks. Mine and Mam's were the same, grown up ones as I called them. Lilly's was known as a Mickey or a Minnie Mouse one, because it had a floppy mouse-like nose on the front that was pink and the rest of it was red and black, unlike ours which were just black. These were issued with memories of the Germans' use of gas in the 1914-18 war, which was still in living memory of most adults.

Mam would march me down to St Mary's each morning, on the odd morning stopping to buy me some sweets, usually dolly mixtures. My gas mask was in a box with a piece of string to carry it over my shoulder. On reaching the classroom, our masks were put alongside our desks and we would say prayers, sing 'All Things Bright and Beautiful' and learn to read. Around midday the teacher would lay out small mats in rows and we would have to lie on them and go to sleep. I was never able to fall asleep. I did receive a smack now and again from the teacher for not sleeping and I never really understood why.

In our new home we had two bedrooms and Mr Brown's part of the house was completely separate to ours. Mam and Lilly had one bedroom and I had the other; at Plumpton Street we had all slept in the same bedroom and even in the same bed. Mam had got another bed for the house at Coffeehouse Bridge and so I now had my own. I really did like that.

Every morning we would have the same routine; Mam would bang open my door saying, 'School time, get washed!' This house had an inside toilet and a little room with a sink; I could now use this and not have to wash in the kitchen. I'd splash water on my face, dry it on an old towel and go and see what there was to eat. Mam would check my neck, whirl me round and send me back into the toilet saying things like, 'What about the tidemark around your neck, you scruffy little get!' She would scrub my neck until it was sore before allowing me back in for breakfast. Lilly, of course, was already there; how I detested her!

Breakfast would consist of either Connie-onnie on bread, or bread and margarine with a sprinkle of sugar over it. On a good day, if we'd had some meat to eat the day before, we would have bread spread with dripping - that was my favourite. Connie-onnie was very sticky, sweet milk in a tin.

Whilst I ate my breakfast, taking my time in the hope that I would be too late for school, Mam would spend the time on Lilly's hair. Shirley Temple style was all the rage, so naturally Lilly's had to be the same. She would tie Lilly's hair in ringlets, telling her when she did it how lovely she would look. When she took the rags out, Mam couldn't see what Lilly was doing, which was making awful faces at me; I thought if this Shirley Temple was anywhere near as ugly as Lilly, the people who went to the pictures to see her must have been mad!

Mr Brown continued to let us listen to the radio and it was here that we heard about Dunkirk, how there had been a terrible battle and people had been taking boats of all sizes over to a place called France to bring our soldiers home. They'd even taken one of the ferries from the Mersey. I asked Mam where this place called France was and why were our soldiers there? Mam didn't seem to have any interest in it so couldn't explain to me what was happening, but she was to become very interested indeed when she learnt more things were to be rationed. All our food and clothing was to be cut and we were to be issued with ration books. These books contained coupons that were taken to the shop when an item was bought.

The coupons had to last each week and after they'd been used up, there was nothing to be had. The pain for Mam became even greater when the food that she'd always found available, like bananas and oranges, weren't there anymore.

It was to be over five years before we were to see a banana or orange again.

At the same time, the Blackout started; after dusk no lights were allowed to be shown. Black blinds had to be bought or made for every window so no light could be seen. Air Raid Precautions, ARPs or Air Raid Wardens, as they were called, would check every house in every street and you would hear them knocking heavily on doors and shouting, 'Put those lights out!'

Mam moved us into her bedroom and we all slept in the same bed. Mam explained we then only had to light the gas lintel in one room instead of both rooms. We also had an oil lamp for when the gas was cut off or when the lintel which was very delicate, would break. When lit by a match or a piece of paper you had to be really careful as the mantle would break and you wouldn't have a light.

The only heating was wood or coal and this would be delivered by a man either in a truck or in a horse-drawn cart. The coal man would put a sack of coal on his back where it would rest on a leather harness that was fastened around his waist, then he would lift the round steel grid in front of the house's front door and flip the sack of coal over his shoulder and down into the cellar. I used to love watching this as he never missed and he was always black from the coal dust. Mam would give me a bucket which I would have to fill and carry up from the cellar; I hated this job but then when Mam lit the fire I loved it. Of course, Lilly never had to do any of this.

It was some time after rationing and the blackout laws came in when our war really started. We'd heard and been told all about the air raid warning signs and of the all clear signal, so we knew what they would mean. We didn't know what was to come and the nightly terror we would all suffer. I am sure Mr Brown knew. He was very keen on following the war's progress to the point where he had a large map of Europe pinned to a wall in his room. He had flags dotted all over it; most of these flags were Swastikas, and he would move them around the map daily. Having been told that Swastikas were a symbol of the Germans, I was convinced that he was a spy. I wasn't really sure what a spy did, but I knew it wasn't very nice for our country so one day I decided, with Lilly's help, to move all of his flags. The hiding I got from Mam when Mr Brown told her didn't really change my mind about him, although it did stop me from doing it again. Needless to say, Lilly didn't even get a smack!

Mr Brown would listen constantly to all the war news on his radio; he would let Mam, Lilly and me listen as well, explaining what everything meant. He was especially keen to listen to Lord Haw-Haw, a man named William Joyce, a British traitor as Mr Brown explained to me, who would be on most nights broadcasting from Germany, boasting about German advances on the continent and which cities the Luftwaffe, the German air force, were going to bomb that night.

Most of the time the targets seemed to be in countries I'd never heard of, until London became Haw-Haw's main choice. He always seemed to be right.

It was some time before it became Liverpool's turn and he would tell of the hundreds of planes we could expect each night. Mr Brown explained our puny air defences were useless against the mighty Luftwaffe and that our docks and the ships docked in them would be obliterated. It wasn't until the first raid occurred that Lilly and I realised what it all really meant. When they did come, they were indeed mainly at night and I can still hear the siren warnings and then the deep drone of aircraft engines in their hundreds. Up and down, rising and falling, the sound was then drowned out after the first explosions. How I came to hate the drone of the planes which to me sounded like the hum of millions of bees, wishing they were, but knowing they probably meant death.

For the first months of 1940, everything in Bootle seemed to be quiet; we used to watch the barrage balloons on their long steel cables sent up all over the docks. Mr Brown said this was to stop the bombers flying low and seeing the targets more easily. He said he had been in the Great War and so knew all of this. Our army would have guns all around Liverpool and Birkenhead called Ack Ack guns; keeping the bombers high in the sky would allow our search lights to find them easier so that the guns could shoot them down. Mr Brown seemed to know everything - just like any good spy would. And though he seemed to enjoy telling Lilly and me how our guns would shoot the bombers down, I knew he was just pretending to enjoy the thought of the British killing his German friends.

Mam decided I was big enough to walk to St Mary's and back on my own. 'Don't think I won't know if you don't turn up,' she told me. 'The teacher knows to come and tell me, and you know what you'll get for that!'

    I'd heard that the bombings in London meant schools had closed; boy, would that make me happy! One afternoon I was walking back from school when I heard an aeroplane engine quite close and then gunfire. The bombers had finally come. It was a Nazi plane trying to shoot some balloons down; I watched as another plane, a Hurricane, came out of the sky with his guns firing, trying to get the Jerry.

I immediately tried to make my way home. I recognised the Hurricane as their pictures, as well as those of Spitfires, were in lots of books that some of the other kids at school had. I was so happy to be seeing this, I was jumping up and down and shouting when I suddenly felt a wallop on the back of my head and a hand grabbing hold of my arm; it was Mr Brown.

'Get home to your mam, you silly little sod!' he said. 'Are you trying to get yourself killed?' and he pulled me all the way back to the house. Naturally, when Mam heard all about it, I got another hiding, whilst Lilly looked on smirking.

Weeks went by and except for the occasional sound of an aircraft engine which Mr Brown said were Nazi snoopers figuring out where to bomb, nothing happened. It was very disappointing as I still had to go to St Mary's.

Then, in the July, Old Haw-Haw said on the radio that we were next. The first raids were usually early evening and we could hear the constant explosions in Liverpool and Birkenhead. There weren't many in Bootle at the time, but even so the good news was that Mam had decided there was to be no more school for me. It made me very happy.

Not so Lilly, who made it very clear that she would prefer me to be anywhere but home, so occasionally I'd give her the odd clip, despite knowing full well that she would switch on the tears, even if it was hours later in order that I would get the usual clout from Mam.

I always thought it was worth it!

A few more weeks went by and then bombs started to fall on Bootle; the first one was on the 15th July, 1940 - my sixth birthday.

TWO

Two weeks earlier, Mam had gotten herself a job after getting her younger sister, Lillian, to look after me and Lilly; this arrangement was great as far as I was concerned as Auntie Lilly was very nice and never smacked me. She obviously considered Lilly her favourite and I was probably still a naughty child, but nonetheless, with no smacks and no school it was a pleasant time.

Mam's job was at the Huskisson Docks in Bootle as a trucker; women were taken on for this heavy work as obviously there was a great shortage of men. As well as the men signed up to fight, many other men were signed up as police constables, auxiliary fire servicemen, Air Raid Wardens and bomb removers. Many did these jobs as well as their day work. Women played their part too; they were employed as auxiliary nurses, ambulance drivers and, like my Mam, truckers.

The truckers' work was loading and unloading cargo from ships, for which they had a small hand-truck to move heavy items. For the women it was very hard work, but Mam seemed to love it. She went to work in overalls, boots and a peaked cap – she looked ridiculous. Up until then I always thought I had a beautiful mam, but now I wasn't so sure.

Not long after Mam started work, Auntie Lilly suggested that we go and visit her at the docks. It was a lovely day and the walk to Huskisson Dock was not very far. Lorries of every size were waiting on the Dock Road to load and unload the ships.

A policeman on the Dock Gate told Auntie Lilly there was no way we could be let in to see Mam, for several reasons. 'One, there are too many trucks around, and one of you could have an accident; two, if there's an air raid siren you wouldn't have a clue what to do here; and three, there's a ship full of ammunition in the dock. If anything goes wrong and it blows, half of bloody Bootle will go with it.'

'In that case, it won't matter if we're in the dock or not, will it?' Auntie Lilly stated crossly. 'We live so close we'd be blown up anyway!'

'The answer is still no.'

The raids really began in earnest in July 1940. Initially, they were sporadic; three or four planes dropping bombs during daylight. At night, they would return with a small number of planes and the air raid warnings would sound, sending us all to our shelters or basements with the full blackout rules applied. Sometimes the second waves would last into the early mornings.

Mr Brown would make constant suggestions as to how many planes were coming and which buildings they were hitting. Docks, hospitals, town halls and houses were being demolished night after night, yet somehow they hadn't touched us – obviously they knew where Mr Brown lived. As we sat waiting for the all clear, I kept my thoughts to myself, for I knew he must have had some way of being in touch with his German friends who had told him where they were going to bomb. I sat staring at him and he would grin back at me, obviously reading my thoughts.

I would spend sunny days scouring bombed buildings looking for pieces of exploded bombs; it was always a challenge to try and find the biggest piece and have the biggest haul. We couldn't get into a bombsite until the emergency services had cleared it of any unexploded bombs, and anyway, we were always warned to stay away, but as soon as the bomb removers left, we kids moved in.

I had a large collection but my prize piece was an incendiary bomb which had just burnt itself out and was totally intact. I could have swapped it for any number of pieces from the other kids, but it was my pride and joy. I couldn't keep the pieces at home, and if Mam had known what I was doing I would have been in real trouble. Underneath Coffeehouse Bridge, alongside the canal, I found a big old rusty tin box where I kept all my shrapnel. I then hid it in the undergrowth beside the canal. I'd spend hours looking at my haul and picking out pieces, trying to guess how big the bomb had been and how many people it might have killed.

How I wished a Jerry plane could be shot down near us and I could find a piece of it, but it never happened.

The cellar, or as Mr Brown called it, the basement, in our house was very big – or so it appeared to me. It had a very rickety wooden staircase leading down from the hallway, which Mam said a few weeks earlier would definitely collapse if we weren't careful. Mr Brown had volunteered to fix it and he'd made it very strong with large timbers of wood retrieved from bombed houses which surrounded us. He'd also built a wide bench under the stairs which he said was for us children to lie on, as it would be the safest place in the house. As well as fixing the stairs, he'd put wooden forms, like they have in church, all round the walls. I was sure he must have got them out of St Mary's Church when it had been bombed. Mam said Mr Brown would never do such a thing, but when I argued, 'Yes, he would – 'cos he's a *spy*!' I got a slap for my trouble and told never to say such a thing again.

After that, I never said anything to Mam about him, though Mr Brown insisted on talking to me all the time. I'd see him looking at me with a grin all over his face and what puzzled me more was that Mam would also be grinning and they would whisper to each other. I was very puzzled.

In the wall of the cellar was a window and outside on the pavement was a big grille of steel. You could look through the grille and see people walking past on the road. An Air Raid Warden told Mam that the window could be very dangerous if it shattered from a bomb blast and she should block it up. Instead, she asked Mr Brown to nail boards across, but he said that wouldn't be a good idea as it would mean we couldn't open it to let fresh air in when there was no bombing going on. Next thing, he'd come back with a large door complete with hinges, probably from another bombed church, or even the same one, I secretly suspected. He cut it to size and fitted it, but put it on hinges so we could open it. He was very clever, as spies always are.

Every night, when the sirens sounded, we would go down to the cellar and make ourselves comfortable. Mam would bring sandwiches and drinks because it was usually morning before the all clear sirens wailed and we would all get very hungry, especially Lilly and me.

Some nights, friends of Mam's or Mr Brown's would come and stay with us in our cellar rather than go to one of the above ground shelters. They'd all insist that our house was safer than theirs, but I thought it was because all the other houses around ours had outside toilets, whereas ours had an inside lav. Some of the raids would last for hours, especially when the bombings grew nearer and louder and became more frequent, which was when our inside lav came into its own. Lilly and I were well catered for with a gazunder, which was a pee-pot, and the kids from the other families used it as well. A bucket in the furthest possible corner of the basement was used to empty the gazunder into. Mr Brown said it was to be hoped a bomb wouldn't come and hit the bucket as we'd all be covered in shit!

When the basement was full we'd all have a sing song, my favourite being 'Roll out the Barrel'. During the singing, Mr Brown would hand out beer, and although we knew hundreds of people had been, and were being killed, the singing would almost drown out the sound of distant bombs so that we could forget about it for a time.

One set of friends was the Gallaghers; they lived round the corner in a house which also had a cellar, but they thought ours was much safer. The Gallaghers were very nice people. Mr Gallagher and his son Duncan were both dockers and most of the time they didn't come; they would be working at the docks and helping with fires that lit up the whole sky and turned it into a beautiful orange ball every night. Mrs Gallagher was a woman who talked and talked and made a joke about just about anything. Mam said, 'That's because she's Irish.'

'But Grandad and Grandma were Irish, so why isn't she like they were?' I asked.

'Because she hasn't kissed the Blarney Stone,' was the answer, which left me very confused because what the heck was the Blarney Stone? And why, by kissing it, would it make you different? If that were true, I wished I could get Lilly to kiss it.

The three Gallagher daughters were all grown up; at least, they were as far as I was concerned. Rachel, at eighteen, was like her mother; she never stopped talking. She had black hair like Mr Gallagher and very dark eyes; I wasn't sure whether or not I liked her. Violet was the middle one at seventeen; she never said anything, just smiled or nodded when spoken to, and she had shiny hair – Mam said it was peroxide hair and that her real hair was as black as Rachel's. I never really understood how she could have two separate heads of hair! Annie, who was my favourite, was the youngest at fourteen; she had shiny hair too, but blue eyes. She looked like a princess in a book I had seen in school, and the prince in the book also had shiny hair. When she came into our cellar I would imagine I was the prince, as I had shiny hair as well, and I would ride away with her. Annie would let me sit with her and hold her hand as she told me stories.

Secretly, I wondered if she pinned her knickers up to her vest like the girl next door in Plumpton Street had. That girl had asked me to undo her pin once and I had a very funny feeling when I was doing it. Mam had come up the street to where we were sitting on a step. She had grabbed my arm and began hitting me as she spun me round at arm's length, telling me what a dirty little beggar I was. I don't know why the girl had asked *me* to do it. Anyway, I knew that for some reason six-year-old boys definitely didn't do that, so I never asked Annie.

The Gallaghers had a pet parrot, a very large Macaw with beautiful colouring, and when they came round he came with them in his large cage. He was a very good talker, and his favourite sayings were, 'F**k off, Hitler!' and 'Bugger the Jerries!'

One evening, as usual, we were getting ready to go down to the cellar; I couldn't wait for the Gallaghers to come round. Mam said Mrs Gallagher and the family would not be coming tonight because Mr Gallagher and Duncan were not working that evening and she and the girls would be staying in their own cellar making dinner for the men. I felt strangely sorry that Annie would not be coming, and I didn't know why I felt so sad.

The air raid siren was later than usual that night and, for a while, we thought the Nazis would not be coming. We'd actually both, Lil and I, been put to bed when the siren finally wailed. Mam shouted, 'Come on, come on,' pulling me out of the bed and picking up Lilly.

'Get your trousers on!' she shouted as she pulled me down the stairs. 'What are you doing, you little sod?!' she shouted as I found I could not run.

She dragged me down to the cellar where Mr Brown had already lit the lamps. 'You little get!' said Mam. 'We could have been killed if they'd started bombing!' She was busy getting Lilly settled under the stairs when Mr Brown started laughing. 'You know why he couldn't run, Bella?' he said. 'He's got both legs in the same trouser leg!'

They couldn't stop laughing even when the aircraft drone that sounded like giant bees hummed up and down and the first bombs began to fall.

As always, the rising and falling deep hum of the bombers indicated how far away they were. Mr Brown, importantly, would say things like, 'Probably King's Dock,' or, 'That's down the south end near Herculaneum Dock.'

Of course, I knew how he knew. Lord Haw-Haw was on the radio every night and day from Germany telling us how hard the Junkers were going to hit us that night. Some of this would be code for Mr Brown so that he'd know exactly where the bombs were to be dropped and he could get out of the way. I was never scared of the bombs, as our house would never be hit whilst he lived with us. That's why I didn't tell anyone, just in case they took him away.

On this particular night, the bombing was very hard and coming very close to us. Mr Brown sounded worried when he said, 'They're a bit close to us tonight.'

Suddenly, there was a tremendous explosion and Mam and Mr Brown looked at each other.

'Oh, God!' exclaimed Mr Brown. 'That's either the ammo ship or a mine.' Mr Brown explained that a mine was normally dropped by parachute and could wipe out whole neighbourhoods.

Another huge bang blew open the door over the window and smashed it against the wall opposite. Luckily, we were all sitting under the stairs so we escaped the effects of the blast. Lilly started to cry and Mam quickly comforted her and then held my hand, squeezing it tightly.

'That's from that big explosion we just heard,' said Mr Brown calmly. 'Lucky the Gallaghers didn't come round; they'd have been sitting there and caught the lot.' He moved quickly to put out the lamp, remarking, 'Bloody Air Raid Warden will be on us in a minute.'

They usually were if even the smallest chink showed through the blackout blinds. I remember watching Mr Brown that night and thinking, 'That was *very* close; I wonder if the Jerries think he's not here tonight?'

The bombing continued, but not too close to us, when there was a hammering at the front door.

'I told you that bloody Air Raid Warden would be here!' said Mr Brown as he ran up the stairs.

Mam and I listened but could only hear odd words: 'Mr Gallagher', 'the girls', 'Mother'.

I asked Mam what was happening.

'Shush' she replied, but she sounded worried.

The cellar door opened and Mr Brown came down the stairs. 'Help me get this blind into place, Bella,' he said to Mam. 'We need some light down here.'

When it was done, a torch appeared at the top of the stairs. I saw it was the Air Raid Warden and behind him a fireman holding something with both hands. As they came down I could see it was a stretcher. I knew because I'd seen some a few days ago when a shelter had been hit and they were bringing dead people out. Mam, after giving me a belt for 'standing gawping' as she'd put it, had told me what they were.

As they brought the stretcher down another fireman appeared, then another stretcher and another fireman.

'Oh God!' Mam exclaimed.

They put the two stretchers on the floor and the Air Raid Warden started talking to Mam.

'It's Mr Gallagher and Duncan,' he explained. 'The whole block has gone; a parachute mine did it. We're digging who we can out, and Tom and Duncan were two of the first.' He paused then continued shakily, 'We couldn't get to the girls. Tom and Duncan were upstairs eating; they'd just got home from work.' He stopped for a moment and gulped. 'The girls were in the cellar, getting it ready.'

'What about the girls' mother, Gladys?' Mam asked in tears.

'She was down there as well,' said the Warden.

Duncan was crying.

'How's Annie?' I asked him quietly, and he was still crying as he answered me.

'She was lighting the cellar fire and she was thrown into it; I could hear her screaming for me to help, but I couldn't move!'

I got frightened because now he was screaming, 'She was burning and I couldn't help my Annie!'

As the light was so dim, it was only then that I realised he was covered in blood. I started to cry.

The Warden spoke again, 'Tom's unconscious, but I think he's got a broken back. Duncan's lost an eye and has other injuries.' He stopped talking and looked at me. 'Don't cry, son, I'm sorry to have scared you.'

How could he know it was my Annie I was crying for and it was all Mr Brown's fault? I was going to kill him.

The Warden, speaking again to Mam, said it was Duncan's idea to bring him and his dad round to us; they couldn't get an ambulance to take them to hospital until the raid was over. The fireman had already left, gone back to carry on digging people out.

The Warden then said, 'I'll get back there myself,' and Mr Brown added, 'I'll come with you.'

The Jerries were still dropping bombs when they went up the stairs. Still crying for Annie, I suddenly began to doubt that Mr Brown was a spy; after all, a rotten German wouldn't go and probably get himself killed to help us, would he?

Mam was doing her best to comfort and console Duncan; Mr Gallagher was still unconscious. There was a knocking at the door, so Mam went up to answer it. She returned with two ladies who she said were volunteer nurses. They immediately set to work trying to make the two men comfortable.

'I'll make some tea,' Mam offered and started up the stairs.

Lilly started screaming as Mam ascended the stairs; bombs were still falling and Lilly was obviously frightened.

'You look after your little sister, Billy,' Mam said to me. My mam was very brave; it was obvious to me how dangerous it was for her to go upstairs, but still she went.

It was almost daylight before the all clear siren sounded, and shortly afterwards an ambulance arrived to take Duncan and Mr Gallagher away. When Mr Brown came home, he was covered in dust and dirt and both of his hands were bandaged. It was daylight and we were preparing to leave the cellar. Mr Brown was completely exhausted and sat on one of the cellar steps with his head in his bandaged hands.

'We were just going upstairs,' Mam said. 'I'll make some tea.'

Mr Brown took his head out of his hands and looked at Mam, his face full of grime and rivulets of white showed beneath his eyes. 'You've been crying,' I thought, and I was amazed. I could never imagine Mr Brown crying.

'Thanks, Bella,' he said. 'You wouldn't believe what has happened out there; whole streets of houses have been blown apart. God knows how many have been killed.'

He put his head back into his hands and Mam began to cry.

'Did you manage to get anybody out?' she asked.

'Only about half a dozen,' Mr Brown replied quietly. 'In the street where I was helping, we got some Irish Paddies out, but there must have been dozens dead and goodness knows how many still missing.'

'Is that the street the Gallaghers lived in?' whispered Mam.

Mr Brown nodded. 'Yeah, and all the other streets around them as well. Lots of volunteers turned up and told me to go home and get some rest.'

Mam offered to look at his hands, but Mr Brown said no and that a volunteer fireman had looked at them and bandaged them up after he'd seen them bleeding. Mr Brown had been using his bare hands to try to find people in the wreckages.

Could Mr Brown really be a German spy?

The same day, after a Connie-onnie breakfast, I couldn't wait to go out and see the bombed streets. But it was awful. Most of the houses had been completely flattened, and some were still on fire. Ambulances were still there, ARPs and firemen were trying to put out fires, and nurses and policemen were running up and down the crowded streets. It was a terrible sight. However, it didn't stop me deciding there must be lots of shrapnel around, so I started to look. Some other kids turned up at the same time, intending to do the same. Nobody seemed to have noticed me, but now with the others arriving, a policeman spotted us and came running, shouting at the top of his voice as he jumped and stumbled over debris.

'I'll put my boot right up your arses when I get over there!' he shouted.

We all swiftly scarpered in different directions.

I later found another street that had been cleared of most of the debris, so I did add to my collection.

The next day, there was a knock at the door. Peering out of the window I saw it was an ARP and a Police Warden. Mam went to the door and invited them in, and I was terrified that they had seen me and come to tell Mam what I had been up to.

I needn't have worried; they asked Mam if they would be able to install a Schoolboy Emergency Rider with us each night before the air raids started. I knew about these as most of the kids I knew had brothers who were doing this job. The lads were usually fifteen or sixteen years old and had bikes; during raids where there was damage to communications, they would take messages on their bikes to the different locations. They did this night after night and some were killed, but it didn't stop them volunteering.

Reg, the lad the ARP was discussing with Mam, had stayed in a house that had just been bombed and needed somewhere else to stay. Mr Brown had joined the conversation and immediately said yes. I was so pleased; I would be having a hero staying with me.

On the night he came round, Reg brought his mam and sister and brother; his dad was in the army away fighting. Reg was very funny and kept everybody laughing; though his younger brother was very sulky He was too young to be a dispatch rider and was obviously jealous of his brother.

Whenever the ARP called on Reg to take a message somewhere, everyone became very worried, but when he returned safe and sound we all relaxed with relief.
One night, during a very heavy air raid, Reg was called out and after an hour or so he came back. We were all sat in the cellar and after hearing him at the door, Mr Brown shouted, 'That you, Reg?'

'Yes, help me!' was the reply.

Before Mr Brown could move, Reg's mother shot up the stairs and screamed as she saw Reg.

In the cellar we were all terrified. Reg came down the stairs; his arms, chest and head were heavily bandaged and saturated with blood. Mr Brown helped him down the stairs whilst his mother cried hysterically behind him.

'It's alright, everybody,' Reg said. 'I've got a few wounds, but nothing too bad; except your bike's gone,' he added to his brother.

Through tears, his brother shook his head and said, 'I don't care about me bike!'

Reg accepted a cup of tea from Mam and then suddenly started laughing; he stood up as we all stared at him and he started to pull off his bandages.

'What are you doing?' his mother screamed, but he carried on.

Still laughing, the bandages all came off with not a wound in sight.

'Just a joke!' he laughed. 'Some of the lads at the station bandaged me up and put red ink all over me.' I didn't understand some of the words his mother, brother, Mr Brown and Mam called him, and I was surprised to see that even Reg could get a slap for his trouble from his mam, but eventually relief caused everyone to laugh as well.

'Oh, by the way,' Reg said to his brother. 'Your bike's outside the front door – unless someone's swiped it!'

During the remaining months of 1940 we had weeks of light and then heavy air raids and up to the Christmas period we even had occasional lulls in the nightly raids. However, in the week before and after Christmas Day, including Christmas Eve, one hundred or even more planes bombed us constantly. Probably because of this I don't remember that Christmas at all, but I'm pretty sure I never received any presents; perhaps Father Christmas was too scared to travel on his open sleigh.

From January through to May of 1941 the raids were fairly constant, culminating in what I was later told was known as the May Blitz when 1,000 people were killed and injured.

A few days later on the 3rd May 1941, The Malakand, the ammunition ship that was in Huskisson Dock, caught fire and despite all the emergency service efforts, eventually it blew up. Mam said the whole of Huskisson Dock area was flattened but luckily there were only a few casualties as far as she knew. Fortunately, Mam hadn't been trucking at the time.

The bombing of our house was a day or two after the tremendous blast of the ammo ship. We had endured many heavy raids, during which Reg still did his dispatch riding; after another night of heavy bombing I went upstairs with Mr Brown whilst Mam tidied up the cellar.

We were both shocked to find the house had no roof! It was absolutely devastating. Mr Brown decided to look at the house from the road outside and when he opened the front door, there, on the front step, were two unexploded incendiary bombs, which he immediately kicked into the middle of the road.

'Bloody good job they were duds,' he remarked.

We went outside to look at the house and found the outside walls still intact except for a few cracks.

Mr Brown said, 'Let's look upstairs,' so up we went. There was so much debris from the roof everywhere; I went into my little bedroom at the back of the house and could now see all of the ruins of the streets around us.

I found Mam in the scullery talking to Mr Brown; she turned to me and said, 'Well, that's it, son, we'll have to find somewhere else to live.'

She packed up our few belongings that we still had, and taking Lilly, she went to find us somewhere to stay, leaving me with Mr Brown. Eventually, Mam came back and said the Emergency Services had found us somewhere to stay in a nearby school that was still intact.

Now I had a new worry. Now that we were going to be living in a school, did that mean I'd be having teachers and lessons again? If so, I'd rather live in a house with no roof, but I was never given the option.

As it turned out, being allocated a section of a large area comprising of a number of classrooms separated by concertina doors, worked quite well. We had two-tiered steel beds and communal tables and chairs to sit and eat at; best of all there were other families like ours which meant other boys to play with. We were always being punished by our mams!

At this time, all children in Liverpool were allowed free bottles of concentrated orange juice – just add water. Lilly and I loved it! We were also given malt, which was spooned down our throats with the largest spoon available, but this treacle-like potion was nowhere near as nice as the orange juice. We also received free milk, a small bottle for each child each day. But the one freebie everybody hated was the castor oil; bottles handed out to all the mams for us kids to be forced to swallow a large spoonful every day.

'It'll do you good,' Mam would say as she forced it down my throat. Even Lilly had to take it, which pleased me no end as the tears streamed down her face.

During the daylight hours I was still allowed to play outside and I would spend my time sneaking out of the playground with a few other boys to search for shrapnel in some of the bombed areas nearby. I now had quite a hoard and it looked as if I was going to have to find another box to keep it all in.

Each night before a raid, as we no longer had our cellar to go down to, we all had to be taken to an air raid shelter, specially constructed supposedly to withstand the bombing. People from other buildings, who also had nowhere to shelter, came to ours, making it extremely crowded and sweaty. Mam tried to make Lilly and me as comfortable as possible with blankets so that we would sleep, but the noise was always immense with people talking and babies crying.

In a small space, no larger than three foot square, we would have to try and sit or lie down until given the all clear.

As well as all the local people, the shelter had to house the odd soldier, sailor or airman on leave and quite a number of merchant seamen. Two of these became my friends, and they were black men. Mam said they were from Africa and they were called Lascar Seamen, but she didn't seem to like them very much; probably because they were black and, anyway, they didn't speak much English.

We were in the shelter for about a week, and though the people in the shelter changed by the day, probably finding other places to stay, my Lascars, as I called them, were there all the time. Mam said they were waiting for their ship to be ready to leave; I didn't want them to as they were my friends and I liked them. Although they spoke a different language, I learned to understand them and we would somehow talk.

Lilly and I didn't have anything to play with; my soldiers and her doll were still in our house, so the Lascars gave me two small pot dogs. Mam said that the men were very kind but that I couldn't keep them, as they were presents for when they went back to Africa. Lilly and I were playing with the dogs, pretending they were real, when I suddenly didn't feel very well. The bombs were still falling that night, so I just lay down and went to sleep.

I awoke and didn't know where I was and I felt very sick. I didn't know the room or the bed that I was lying in. Pillows propped me up and I could see somebody standing at the bottom of the bed; a soldier was looking at me.

'Hello Billy, you're awake,' he said. He had on a big army coat and a peaked cap with a beautiful shiny badge; the buttons on his khaki coat were also lovely and shiny in the dim light.

'Come on Billy, you'll be alright soon,' said the soldier. I suddenly realised who it was.

It was my Uncle Eddie who I hadn't seen for a very long time; why was he here?

He kept talking. 'I've come to see you because you're not very well and your Mam can't get here tonight. Do you like my uniform?'

I tried to talk but no words would come out so I pointed to his buttons, waving my right arm up and down. Weirdly, my other arm wouldn't move.

'You like my buttons, do you?' Again, I couldn't answer, only stare and wave, 'Well you can have them,' said Uncle Eddie and pulled all the buttons off his coat, placing them on the table beside the bed.

'You can have this as well and you'll be better in no time.' He took the beautiful badge off his cap and placed it beside the buttons. Uncle Eddie was still talking to me and I could hear the booming of bombs as I fell asleep once more.

I woke up feeling much better and realised I was in a hospital; there were no other beds in the room and it was dark. The nurse explained that I was in isolation.

'Where's Uncle Eddie?' I asked her, and then, 'Where's my mam?'

The nurse laughed and told me it'd been a week since my uncle came to see me but I'd been improving ever since.

'It must be those buttons and his badge that he left for you,' she said, laughing. 'Look, here they are. Your Uncle Eddie was very brave to give you them; he won't half be in trouble when the army finds out.'

'Where's my mam?' I asked again. She told me Mam had been here every day and night, walking the huge distance even when the bombs were falling.

'She'll be here soon,' she promised, and she was.

Mam told me later that I had caught diphtheria, meningitis and scarlet fever, probably from people in the shelter. The doctors had told her one day that I would probably die within a couple of hours and, as she had so far to walk to the hospital, could she sign my death certificate; which she duly did. The doctors, nurses and Mam were amazed at my 'miraculous recovery' as Mam kept calling it. I just wondered what all the fuss was about.

The shelter received a direct hit two days after I'd been taken away, but as Mam had been so worried that Lilly might catch something too, she and Mr Brown had moved back into our cellar, even though we didn't have a roof.

Everybody in the shelter had been killed.

How funny, I thought. If I hadn't been so sick, we would all be dead.

'What about the Lascars, my friends?' I asked anxiously.

Mam said they'd left the day after I'd been taken to hospital; they had returned to their ship, but they'd left the pot dogs for me. Mam had been worried in case the dogs still had the germs on them, so she'd thrown them away.

'Where did they sail to?' I wanted to know.

'Africa,' she answered.

'And where's Uncle Eddie?'

'Africa as well; he was posted last week.'

I hoped he'd meet my Lascars.

Funny, though, how the shelter got bombed only after Mr Brown had left it. I expected he had got a message to Germany and they'd said it would be alright to go back to our cellar. I decided I'd let him stay there to keep Mam and Lilly safe, but when the bombing stopped, I'd kill him.

It was some time before I was allowed to leave the hospital, but eventually I was allowed to go to our new home; Mam and Lilly were staying with Mam's brother, my Uncle Charlie. My left arm was in a sling, although it caused me no pain as it was paralysed. Mam said the doctors thought it was something going wrong in my head because of the meningitis.

Uncle Charlie had a modern home in Clubmoor, which was considered a posh part of Liverpool. He had a small garden at the front and a slightly bigger one at the back; it was very nice but I wasn't happy. I often wished we were back in Bootle. I missed my friends and I missed my shrapnel. I even missed Mr Brown.

After a while at Clubmoor, my arm suddenly came back to life, although it seemed to me to be thinner and very withered-looking.

The bombing had become less frequent and Uncle Charlie would state that the Jerries had obviously realised they couldn't beat us Liverpudlians.

THREE

Almost a year earlier, even before the Blitz on Liverpool had really started, I'd heard of kids being sent away or, in some cases whole families, with the exception of fathers who were required for work in Liverpool.

Now, having survived what turned out to be one of the worst parts of the bombing war in Liverpool, the authorities decided to evacuate me and Lilly. Though I knew what evacuation meant, I had no idea just how it worked and how many other kids would be going with us.

Lilly and I were told by Mam that we were being sent to a very nice place called Lancaster and then she dropped the thunderbolt that she would not be coming with us. It seemed her trucking job on the docks was deemed important war work and she was required to stay. I was very shaken by Mam's news, but the more I thought about it, the more I saw it as a great adventure. Until then I had never left Liverpool, not even to go to New Brighton across the River Mersey, and I most certainly had never been away from Mam except when I was in hospital.

Lilly, however, was still the world's biggest whinger and spent the days before we left crying non-stop. Then the big day arrived and a bus pulled up outside Uncle Charlie's house.

Mam had obtained a small suitcase in which she had packed what little clothing Lilly and I had; our gas masks were in their boxes and strung over my shoulder.

Uncle Charlie came over to me and said, 'You're a big boy now, Billy, so make sure you look after Lillian,' and he held out his hand. 'Shake,' he said. I shook his hand and felt quite strange doing it but also a little proud. I felt very grown up.

Mam gave me a hug and a kiss and said through her tears, 'I'll come and see you as soon as I can.'

I climbed into the bus. Lilly was clinging on to Mam and crying, but Mam prised her away and passed her to me on the bus. Lilly had begged Mam to come to the railway station with us, but it wasn't allowed. As I had the suitcase and the gas masks, I struggled to keep hold of Lilly too; I decided that as soon as we were out of sight she could carry her own gas mask box.

There were other kids on the bus all a similar age to me and Lilly; some were still crying but others, mainly the boys, were looking quite happy. I suppose for them, like me, it was an adventure. As the bus set off, Lilly and I waved to Mam and Uncle Charlie and I could but wonder if I would ever see Mam again.

'Where are you two off to?' one of the lads asked me.

'We're going to Moorfields train station to get a train to Lancaster,' I told him although neither he nor I knew where that was.

'I'm going to Wales, I don't know where. I don't actually know where Wales is,' he said sadly.

Lilly and I were the last ones on the bus. The bus had stopped at Lime Street Station and all the other kids got off; I supposed they were all going to Wales and I wished Lilly and I were going there too. The bus finally took us to Moorfields station where a man stood outside the station, busily shuffling papers in his hands.

Lilly had eventually stopped crying and as we stepped down from the bus, the man came over to us.

'Billy Mansfield?' he asked. I nodded slowly.

'How old are you, son?'

'Seven, sir.'

'And this must be Lillian.'

'Yes, sir.'

'Good!' he proclaimed and he led us into the station.

'Not long now until you'll be on that train going to your new home. Lancaster is very nice, I've been there. It has a very old castle which you can play in,' he said, looking at me. This cheered me up no end. He seemed a very nice man and was wearing a very nice suit; much nicer than the one Dad used to wear on Sundays. Bending down, he pinned a label to my jacket with my name and a number on it, and turning to Lilly he did the same. Then, opening the gas mask boxes, he examined them and put them back.

'Let's hope you won't need these where you're going,' he said. 'I'll be back in a minute; just you two wait there.' Off he went, and being a very tall man he walked with long strides, showing what he meant when he said he wouldn't be long.

Lilly, at only five years old, didn't see this as an adventure at all, but I was just happy she had stopped crying.

'When are we going home?' she asked me, her big eyes boring into mine.

'After the war, maybe next week,' I replied taking hold of her hand. 'It's just like going on holiday, I think,' I added. I wasn't very sure as I'd never been on holiday, but I'd heard about them.

'Well, where are we going now?'

'Lancaster.'

'Who was that man?'

'I don't know, do I? He'll be back soon and you can ask him.'

'No, I can't!' she shouted and started crying again. 'We can't talk to people; we're not allowed to talk to strangers.'

'OK! I'll talk to him,' I said wearily. 'Just stop crying.'

The man reappeared and handed me two packages. 'Sandwiches for the train,' he said. 'Now, follow me.' And he led us along the platform.

A train was pulling into the station and, as we climbed on, I looked to see if any other kids were being evacuated but it looked like it was just Lilly and me.

'You'll be met at Lancaster,' the man said to me. 'I'm sure you'll be well looked after; see you after the war!' he laughed, and slammed the train door.

'Look after your sister!' he shouted and was gone.

I looked around the carriage we were in. It was a scruffy carriage just with seats and a rack for luggage, but as we only had the little suitcase, we put it on the seat next to us.

The journey was exciting, for me, anyway; fields, cows, sheep and what looked like mountains passed us by. Of course, I'd seen all of these in books, but *these* were real. Lilly started to cry again, and she said she needed to pee, but as there wasn't a corridor on the train, there was obviously no toilet.

Eventually, she had to do it on the floor of the carriage. As it swilled around to the motion of the train, I began to panic at the thought of the trouble we'd be in when someone found it. But fortunately it had dried, leaving only a small stain, as the train pulled into Green Ayre Station in Lancaster.

Stepping off the train at Green Ayre, we realised we were the only two children there. A lady came up to meet us; she was tall and slim with a thin face. She looked at us, looked at the labels on our coats and, without as much as a hello, said, 'Got your things?' meaning my small case and the gas masks.

I nodded.

'Come on, then.' She was rather abrupt and made it quite clear we were a nuisance.

We followed her out of the station, through the town and up a hill named St Leonard's Gate.

43

'Hurry up!' she kept saying, causing me to have to pull Lilly along as her little feet couldn't keep up. As we struggled to keep up with her she asked, 'Have you got your ration books?'

'I don't know,' I said, confused. 'Mam has the ration books.'

'No, no, no, you have the ration books as well; let's have a look in your case.'

We stopped and she opened up the small case and there on the top were our ration books.

'Right, I'll take care of those,' she said, taking them out of the case.

St Leonard's Gate was a terrace of small, dowdy houses; the row was raised up from the road by a sloping pathway with tired old railings along the roadside edge. We followed the lady up the path and stopped outside a small, scruffy house. The door was opened by a very big and very angry looking woman who held a baby in her arms.

'Don't know why we should be saddled with this lot!' she said to the woman who had led us to the house. She was obviously aware we would be arriving.

'Nothing to do with me, they're all yours now; here's the ration books,' said the woman and turning to Lilly she said, 'Stop that snivelling, this is your new home.' Then she walked off.

'Well, come in, then,' said the woman with the baby, glaring at us. 'Sit there,' she instructed, pointing to a tatty couch, which was already occupied by an extremely large, equally tatty dog. I felt Lilly's grip tighten on my hand but then it relaxed and she laughed as the dog licked her.

The woman looked at us and said, 'Scruffy Liverpool bastards. I'm going out now; I've got shopping to do. Sit there and don't move and look after the baby.'

She placed him on the grimy rug in front of the coal fire and went out the front door. Lilly and I sat tentatively stroking the dog and looking at the baby, who suddenly began to talk in his own strange way.

'Cake!' he said, repeating it over and over and over. I decided I'd better look for some cake when the baby began to scream loudly, but there wasn't a cake anywhere in the small house.

For about half an hour the baby screamed louder and louder. I made funny noises and pulled funny faces trying to stop the baby from crying. Then Lilly started to cry and I made funny faces at her as well, hoping the two of them would shut up before that horrible lady came home. Neither did and I wanted to cry myself I was so frightened, but that would have upset Lilly even more.

Eventually, I managed to stop Lilly crying by patting and stroking the dog and enticing Lilly to do the same; as we'd never had a dog before it was a novelty for her and managed to do the trick.

When the baby's mother returned, he was still screaming for cake. She picked him up, reached down and smacked me across the face shouting, 'You little sod, why didn't you give him cake?'

'There wasn't any,' I replied, trying not to cry; after all the smacks from Mam, I was used to it.

'You little swine, what's this?' she asked as she picked up a loaf of bread.

'That's bread,' I said, and she smacked me again as Lilly started to cry once more.

That was when I first realised what life was going to be like as an evacuee, and I didn't like it. Why couldn't we have stayed in Liverpool with Mam?

We lived with Mrs Moss for three weeks. There wasn't a Mr Moss, just Mrs Moss, the baby and the tatty dog. Our ration books, that Mrs Moss kept, didn't do us any good at all; Mrs Moss said that was the only good reason for having us fostered onto her. When Mam had the ration books in Liverpool, we always had something nice to eat, when it was available, and even got sweets on Fridays; now we were always hungry and only got porridge made with water, potatoes and cabbage, or bread and dripping, morning and evening. Mrs Moss and the baby seemed to get all the nice things; we never saw a sweet or a biscuit whilst we were there.

Lilly cried a lot of the time because she was so hungry, but the dog cheered her up. I suppose that's where the fleas came from.

The Wicked Witch, as we called her, made us work.

She would leave all the dishes in the sink whilst we were in school, and then when we had finished the bread and dripping fed to us when we got home, we would have to wash, dry up and put everything away. Lilly and I hated it as we were terrified of breaking something; we knew we would get what Mrs Moss called 'the belt' if anything was broken.

After clearing everything up, Lilly would go upstairs to play on the single bed we shared; she had a rag doll Mam had given her before we left Liverpool. The Wicked Witch would order me to look after the little one whilst she went out.

'Don't you dare touch anything other than the baby,' she would command. 'If he cries, give him his dummy or a cake.'

I'd sit in total fear in case the baby cried whilst she was out; I was certain she went to a local pub as she always smelt of ale when she came home. Sometimes the baby did cry just as The Wicked Witch got home and I would get a belting, depending on how much she'd had to drink. A belt was just a smack across the face, but sometimes it was a real leather belting across the bare legs or trouser-clad bottom; that's where it really hurt.

There was talk that things were going to change; I remembered being sent to see the visiting nurse in the school and she had said to my teacher, 'This boy is filthy! I don't think he's had a bath for weeks, his teeth haven't been cleaned since God only knows when, and he has nits, fleas and what look like bug bites all over him.' She paused and looked at me again, 'I don't think these clothes have ever been washed; the socks have so many holes in them they're not even worth putting on, and his pants need patching. Where does he live?'

'With Mrs Moss in St Leonard's Gate,' answered the teacher. 'Billy's an evacuee. He has a small sister who is in very much the same state, I'm afraid.'

'Well, they will have to be moved,' said the nurse.

A man called at the house to talk to Mrs Moss and said that we were to be relocated.

'Why?' Mrs Moss screeched at the man.

When he didn't respond, she added spitefully, 'I'll be more than happy to see the back of these dirty little buggers!'

The man looked at her and said dryly, 'Indeed, that is exactly why they are being moved, because they are dirty little buggers and the school has complained; let me have their ration books and anything else belonging to them.'

Lilly was almost jumping up and down with delight and went up with me to our pokey bedroom and once again packed the little brown case Mam had given us and rushed back down the stairs. Lilly quickly stopped to say goodbye to the only nice thing in the house, the flea-riddled dog. I think we were terrified that if we weren't quick the man would go without us.

FOUR

With me holding our little case and our gas masks in one hand and Lilly's small hand in the other, I had never been happier. Lilly, however, was very, very tired and the man kept saying to Lilly, 'Not far now,' as we followed after him.

This man was rather tall but he walked as slowly as he could, obviously with Lilly's small steps in mind. 'I would carry you, but you'd have to have a bath first,' he stated looking her over. 'I'm sorry, love, won't be long now.'

Eventually, we arrived at a much nicer looking house with a big field behind it in which there were some swings, a slide and a maypole.

A lady answered the man's knock at the door and I could see a look of disgust on her face when she looked at us.

'Hello, Mrs Bridges,' the man said.

'They don't look very clean,' she commented acidly.

'That's why they're being moved to you,' answered the man. 'Somebody will be around tomorrow with some second-hand clothes from our store; you can burn the ones they've got on.'

'Is anything else wrong with them? They don't look very well. I have my own kids to think of, you know!'

The man then explained that after three weeks with Mrs Moss we'd had very little to eat and had not been well looked after, but that the nurse at Dallas Road had looked us over again and we were, for the time being anyway, free of nits and bugs. He handed her our ration books, at which point her face broke marginally into a smile.

'Thanks,' she said.

He told her he knew it was probably unnecessary but he would be calling round occasionally to see how we had settled in. I liked him.

After beckoning us inside and shutting the front door, she said, 'Don't touch anything and don't sit down. Just stand there until I call you; I'll be in the bathroom, through the door and past the scullery. Come through when I call you,' and she vanished through the door.

The only other person I had ever known to have a bathroom was Uncle Charlie and he was posh! Could this lady be posh?

Mrs Bridges called us through to the bathroom, which also had a toilet. The bath looked really old with brown coloured cracks all over it; but it must have been OK as the water stayed in it.

'Take everything off and get in the bath; put your clothes into that bag,' she said pointing to a bag behind the door. 'Now get cleaned up.'

I was only seven years old, but I wasn't happy at a complete stranger seeing me naked; she must have realised my reluctance as she added, 'There's a towel there to dry yourself with and one for your sister too.' As she left the room she shouted, 'Don't spill any water on the floor!'

She had left a little bit of red Lifebuoy soap on the side on the bath so Lilly and I got in. Lilly had not yet learnt how to wash herself properly, so I had to wash her first before washing myself. One good thing was that the school nurse had washed Lilly's hair before we left the school at Dallas Road, so at least I didn't need to do that. Another good thing was that Lilly hadn't cried yet today.

Mrs Bridges' house had a front and back garden with flower borders. To me it was posh but Mrs Bridges just seemed quite ordinary; however, the house was always very clean and tidy and Lilly and I had a bedroom overlooking the rear garden which allowed us to see the swings and slide. Initially, we would watch kids from our window playing on them and it was a day or two before I plucked up the courage to join them. Mrs Bridges had two children, a boy and a girl like us, but a little older. I don't remember them ever playing on the swings; it is absolutely certain that they never played with me.

Our bedroom was fairly sparse but clean and we would have to tidy it and make our bed, which we shared, every day before breakfast. We were first up every morning as Mrs Bridges' kids would use the bathroom after us because it would have to be cleaned by Mrs Bridges once we'd finished. I suppose she must have been frightened of them catching something.

Our breakfast was usually porridge, sometimes with a dollop of jam in it; it was far better, both in the portion size and the taste, than it ever was at St Leonard's Gate, as was the evening meal.

The school at Dallas Road was probably nearer than when we were at Mrs Moss's horrible house and so looking after Lilly while walking there and back each day was so not difficult.

Dallas Road School was in a pleasant area of Lancaster and because we were evacuees, the school had to accept us. There was another evacuee there from somewhere in Yorkshire; he was older and bigger than me and decided to follow me around.

My first day started badly but ended quite well.

Being new and from a city, I was surrounded in the playground and inundated with questions. Some of the kids had heard from their parents about the war and the bombing of Liverpool; Lancaster had not been touched by the war and not had a bomb dropped anywhere near them, so everyone was intrigued to know what it was like.
I was in my element, the centre of attention, relaying my stories about our house being bombed and Mam still working in Liverpool. When I told them about my shrapnel collection and described the unexploded bombs I had, they lapped it up.

Out of the blue, a big heavy lad who I later learned was from a farm, said,

'You're a liar!' My retaliation was to call him a few names, so he decided he was going to hit me.

Back in Liverpool, I'd only had tussles with other kids the same age and height as me and they were never really fights. This boy was probably half as big as me again so I was definitely worried, but there was no way out of it, I had to fight.

The cry went up from the other kids: 'Fight, fight, fight!' and they all formed a circle around us.

It was probably the shortest fight on record; I ran at the farmer's lad and hit him in the eye. To my surprise his hand went up to his face and he started to cry. Fight over.

The next thing I knew, I was lifted onto the shoulders of some of the bigger lads and was paraded around the playground whilst everyone cheered and shouted, 'Champion! Champion!'

It was a great feeling and I really enjoyed it. I hoped that being a champion, according to these kids, meant that I wouldn't have to have further fights. It was wishful thinking.

Every day at Dallas Road was learning, learning, learning. I seemed to learn quite quickly and became addicted to books on knights, the Wars of the Roses, the Percys of Northumberland and John of Gaunt, the first Duke of Lancaster.

Occasionally, I got into trouble having been in a fight; usually with some lad who had pushed Lilly over or pulled her long hair. She'd always come crying to me and I would have to do my duty and thump the culprit. Sometimes this would be spotted by a teacher who would have to report it to my teacher.

Unlike the other teachers, my teacher didn't use a cane, or a ruler or a belt to punish you. As we boys had to wear shorts to school, she used to roll up one short leg to expose the thigh and wallop you with her hand repeatedly. I'm sure she really enjoyed it as the hand holding up the trouser leg would go higher than was necessary. It certainly worked, as it was very painful indeed. Most of the lads were agreed; we'd much rather have the cane.

On one occasion I did receive the cane from the Headmaster; it was after a chemistry lesson in the school laboratory. We'd been shown an experiment with a chemical that when put in water began to bubble with lots of froth. I hid some of the chemical in my pocket to sneak out of the lab.

Every day during the morning break, small bottles of free milk were brought for all the kids and left in crates in the school yard. The tops of the bottles were made from cardboard where you pressed down on the middle and inserted a straw.

I decided to see if the substance worked with milk. After removing a few bottle tops and dropping the liquid in, the milk went up like Vesuvius. The Headmaster was certainly not pleased and to prove his point he gave me several hefty whacks on my backside with his cane.

'We don't do things like that in this school,' he said afterwards. 'Any more such behaviour and you will be dismissed from here.' I'd learnt to like this school so I heard what he said.

In school I became friends with three lads: Brian Moffat, Peter Peel and Thomas Jones. They lived in nice homes to which they often invited me after school and during holidays. I was very envious of them and, being ashamed of my own background in Liverpool, I would spin yarns about going back when the war ended to my lovely home which was near a wood.

'It's just like the Bluebell Woods here,' I would say, adding that my friends in Liverpool and I would build dens and camp out in them. I talked knowledgably about my imaginary life in Liverpool.

'There's quite a wide river that goes through it,' I would tell the really big rope hung from a very tall tree and we've all learnt to sv

The woods in Lancaster had just such a set up, but with on. from a smaller tree and a narrow stream. My woods in Liverpool were n.

My friends listened to my supposed adventures and inadvertently I bec. gang leader.

I was always reluctant to go back to Mrs Bridges' home with Lilly in tow; I'd much rather go to one of the boys' houses. But, of course, my sister always had to be taken home. I know neither of us liked living with Mrs Bridges; she wasn't cruel in the way the Wicked Witch had been, but she was not nice in other ways.

From our first day staying there, Lilly and I had to sit at a small table in the kitchen, whilst Mrs Bridges and her family of two children ate in the living room. Once again, there was no Mr Bridges; I supposed he must have been away at the war. It was never mentioned as her children were not allowed to talk to or play with us. I'm sure Mrs Bridges considered us well below her status, although it certainly didn't bother me. I had my own friends and kept away from the house most of the time, going back only for food and bed. Sometimes I'd have to take Lilly with me, when ordered to do so by Mrs Bridges.

As it happened, Lilly became quite a favourite with Peter's Mam, Mrs Peel; she only had Peter and he was always with us lads. Lilly, who I suppose was pretty and no longer the scruffy little girl she'd been at the Wicked Witch's house, loved to go there; she'd made friends with a girl in school who lived in the same street as Peter, so she wasn't at all bothered when we Outlaws went off to play without her.

Having read the *Just William* books by Richmal Crompton, whose stories were all about William and his gang, the Outlaws, and with me, the leader of the gang, also called William, the Outlaws seemed the perfect name for us. And Outlaws we certainly became.

chard was safe from our scrumping, even though Peter had a russet apple tree ...en. But although russets were my favourites, I wouldn't have dreamt of stealing ...rs Peel. But we were the bane of the keepers in Williams Park. Life was quite ..

We spent Christmas Day of 1941 at Mrs Bridges' house which was decorated very well, but it was just like any other day to Lilly and me. We didn't get any presents and our Christmas dinner, sitting at our table in the kitchen, was rice pudding. The Bridges family had a real Christmas dinner complete with Christmas pudding, and Lilly and I were aware of them opening their presents; we wondered why Father Christmas hadn't left us ours.

Outside was white with snow and, after finishing our rice pudding, we spent the day making slides and snowballing with other kids and using the sledges of some of the boys who had them, most of whom I knew from school. My gang were having their holiday at home and I couldn't leave Lilly to go and see them; besides which, I was a bit ashamed, as I had no presents to show them.

Lilly and I were moved from Mrs Bridges' house not too long after that particular winter of 1941. I have no idea why we were moved on, though I suppose it was routine for other people to have to take a turn with evacuees. Of course, it could also have been that Mrs Bridges had asked to have us moved.

The same man who'd brought us here called for us. We left without tears or goodbyes and went off, once again, into the unknown. This time, however, the man carried Lilly through the snow.

The next billet wasn't too far away as it was on Dale Street close to Williams Park. The park had been created from a very big and high hill, and was situated next to the Victorian lunatic asylum. Atop the hill was the extremely large Ashton Memorial.

The lady we were to live with was introduced to us as Mrs Breslin. It was obvious she didn't like us from the start. As we stood on the doorstep of her house, she told the man she didn't have the time to look after bloody evacuees, and that she'd been forced to take us in.

'There's a war on,' said the man bluntly. 'Keep them clean and well fed and they'll be as good as gold.'

She did, and we were. We got our food, and our clothes were washed after we'd gone to bed and they were dried on the guard in front of the fire, but she never stopped telling us how much she disliked our being there. I had to stay out of the house as much as possible, so most of the time, when not in school, I did anything I liked. Williams Park was close by and there were woods at the end of the road, but best of all was the river. I'd discovered just how much fun could be had there and the Outlaws, and other kids, would make full use of it.

Mrs Breslin had other people living in the house, which was a pretty big one on three levels. It was an old house with no garden but instead had what was called an 'area' at the front. This consisted of a basement room with a window and was surrounded by railings. It was similar in many ways to our cellar in our house in Liverpool. Lilly and I had what Mrs Breslin called the 'garret'; it was a small room beneath the house's rafters – in the summer it was boiling and in the winter it was freezing. As Lilly and I spent over a year living there, we suffered both seasons.

Mr Walsh was an old man who lodged at the house. Whenever I saw him, he was dressed in a suit and with his grey hair and moustache he always looked very smart. He used to spend most of his time sitting in an old armchair in the parlour, supposedly the best room in the house. He'd either be reading a book or newspaper or listening to the wireless, but he always acknowledged us kids.

Another lodger was a girl, probably in her twenties. Most of the time she was out, probably at work, but occasionally we'd see her all 'dolled up', as my mam would have said, on her way out in the evening. She was pretty and had blonde hair and was always nicely dressed. Although we rarely saw her, she was always pleasant to Lilly and me.

As always, I was constantly hungry; just like in our previous billets, we got only enough food to keep us nourished. I supplemented my diet with apples. In Lancaster there were numerous orchards to keep me well fed.

In Mrs Breslin's kitchen was a big black range, much the same as the one Mam had at Plumpton Street. Like Mam, she kept it well blackened and polished and in the oven, when the fire was lit, she, like Mam, would bake pies. They always smelt delicious but Lilly and I never, ever received a single piece. Her son, who was a year younger than me, would receive a large slice after dinner and she would cover it with thick custard. He would sit grinning at us as he ate, saying things like, 'I really do like your custard, Mam,' and, 'This is your best pie yet, Mam.' How I hated him!

One day I found a large dish of mustard, which had been left on the table in the living room; I had just come in from school and had walked into the room. I knew the son would soon be in so I stayed in the living room sitting at the table. Very shortly, in he came. He looked at me and the dish of mustard in front of me.

'This is nice custard,' I said. 'Want some?'

Of course, he couldn't resist and nodded eagerly. I spooned a large spoonful out of the dish.

'Open your mouth then,' I said. He did as he was told and I fed it to him.

Immediately, he yelled out and desperately tried to spit it all out of his mouth. Mrs Breslin flew in like a hurricane, realised what had happened, rushed her son into the kitchen to clean out his burning mouth and then gave me one heck of a leathering. But I was still pleased I'd done it.

Later, I heard Mr Walsh enquire what all the noise had been about and Mrs Breslin told him what I'd done. The next time I saw Mr Walsh he didn't say a word, but he gave me a little wink as a grin appeared on his face. He sat in his favourite chair by the fireplace; tall, thin and grey haired, I was sure he must have been a soldier in the past, as he was so smartly dressed in his suit, shirt, waistcoat and shining shoes.

He was still chuckling as I left the room.

I spent most of my time when not in school leading my gang; sneaking into the picture house, and playing in Williams Park or the woods at the top of the road. Depending on which film we'd been able to see, I'd be Robin Hood aka Errol Flynn, Tarzan aka Johnny Weissmuller, or one of the Rough Riders – Hopalong Cassidy aka William Boyd. The trick of getting into the picture house without paying was easy at every cinema. There were exit doors that you could only open from the inside. A couple of the boys on the outside would pull one side of the doors when the others would push the other side; a small opening would emerge between the doors up to about 3 foot high. I was so small and thin that with some effort I was able to squeeze through. I'd then lift the bars that secured the doors and the gang would swarm in. We'd be sure to relock the doors as soon as everyone was in, so that no one would learn of our trick.

The rules in those days were that kids weren't allowed into the theatres without an adult, so we'd search for seats alongside an adult and sit down next to them. We were never caught out.

Williams Park was a dream playground; its patches of fully grown trees intermingled with large clumps of bushes were perfect hiding places or locations for making dens. Its large areas of open greens, long sloping hills and its location next to the asylum made it a perfect site for adventure and games. The trees furnished us with branches to turn into swords and bow and arrows, much to the chagrin of the park wardens. We'd become knights, outlaws, Tarzan or perhaps his enemies. The smallest of us, Peter, enjoyed being Cheetah; strange, really, because he was the worst climber.

I learnt to sew, after a fashion, when I cut two flaps of black material I'd found and sewed them on to the front and back of a pair of shorts. I then became Tarzan but had to prove it by climbing trees; again, much to the annoyance of the park keeper! The monument at the top of the hill became a castle; being surrounded by low sculptured walls, it was easily defended against attackers who had to climb the hill. Quite how nobody was injured by the arrows fired from our makeshift bows is still a mystery. The highlight was when we would have to outrun the park keeper who, on occasion, intervened between the warring armies. It really was just like a story by Richmal Crompton about William.

The asylum next door to the park was surrounded by high walls; however, they were naturally very old and were pretty easy for us kids to climb. We had all heard that bats could be found in the rafters above a slaughter house in the asylum. This was something that had to be verified, so armed with our swords and a few glass jam jars, we went in search of them. We found the slaughter house on our first visit but didn't see any so-called 'loonies' walking around, probably because the shed-like building was in a fairly isolated part of the grounds. The building seemed pretty empty, possibly no longer used.

Getting in was no problem and on climbing up into the upper floor, sure enough we found the bats. On the two or three occasions we visited, we took bats with us when we left; they were very small and were easily stuffed into the jam jars. We truly believed we were helping to rescue them.

Knowing they could not be taken home and after comparing each other's for size and wingspan, we would let them go, hoping they would find a new home better than the one they had left.

On another adventure into the asylum whilst looking for apple trees, Peter and I actually met one of the inmates. He was stood watching us from a nearby footpath; he waved to us and asked us what we were doing. Thinking he was one of the people looking after the 'loonies' and suddenly very scared, I answered, 'We were just looking for apples.'

He gave a funny laugh and waved his arms about, possibly trying to point. 'I know where you can find some,' he said. 'Follow me.'

He led us down the path for some way and stopped at a clump of trees; there was still nobody else about.

'There they are,' he said, pointing to one of the trees. We knew immediately that it was a crab apple tree, bearing the sourest apple there is, guaranteed to give you the belly ache and tasting awful.

'Heck!' said Peter. 'He's one of the loonies!' And we ran as fast as we could back to the wall, climbing over like a pair of monkeys. We never visited the asylum again after that.

I came home from school one day to find a van outside and three men in the living room. The fireplace in the living room had a mantel shelf and above that a wooden shelf with a large mirror. It had probably been there since the house was built; it reached all the way to the ceiling and though constantly dusted and polished, it had never been moved.

That is until the men came; they had taken it down off the wall and in its place was the most horrible sight you could imagine. From the fireplace below up to the ceiling, and as I later learned, above the ceiling into the fireplace and chimney in the bedroom above, cockroaches swarmed. Hundreds of them clung to the wall in a red and purple coloured panorama.

The men from the van were scraping them with trowels into glass jars and already half a dozen were laid on the floor stuffed with roaches. Some had managed to escape and were running around the floor; big, awful creatures an inch or more long.

'Hey, boy!' one of the men shouted. 'Stamp on the roaches that fall down for us!'

Well, I wasn't afraid of most creatures, but cockroaches – no way! I disappeared out of the room and out of the house far quicker than I had arrived. I didn't return until the van outside the house finally left and I deduced that all was clear.

Going back into the house, I had no intention of going into the living room, heading instead to the kitchen to have my tea. Some hope. Mrs Breslin was in the kitchen as I entered.

'You might as well go straight up to bed, lad,' she said angrily. 'No tea for you; you should have stayed to help. Now, hop it!'

I didn't dare say I hadn't noticed her son stamping on any stampeding roaches or indeed herself, and of course Lilly, being a girl, could not possibly be asked. The lodgers, if they had been present, would of course be excused, so there was only one person in the world who could be punished for so-called dereliction of duty; me! So, no tea for me; not that there was ever much of it anyway!

For days, possibly weeks after, as I walked into the kitchen I would see the occasional scuttle of a reddish or bluey-purple creature an inch and a half long taking a run from its new hiding place, probably behind the oven. I kept my distance and never mentioned it, hoping that one day it, or its friends, might just scuttle over Mrs Breslin's foot. How I longed to be there when it happened, but unfortunately I never was!

FIVE

It was the summer of 1942; I was about to turn eight years old and Lilly would be seven in the autumn. She now had her own friends to play with and spent most of her time, when not at school, playing with them in their homes. I was more than happy with that as I didn't have to have her trying to follow me around.

I was still happy going to school in Dallas Road and was doing quite well; certainly my reading had developed tremendously and I spent hours of most days reading books and comics. There was *The Beano* with Desperate Dan and Biffo the Bear, and *The Dandy* with Korky the Cat.

Film Fun had fictional adventures of well-known film stars such as Stan Laurel and Oliver Hardy; these were fun but the best were the story articles; no pictures, just adventures.

There was *The Hotspur* regaling us with sports stories like Willie Wallop, the hard-hitting cricketer, and *The Wizard*, which had an eccentric but wonderful athlete known as William Wilson the Wonder Athlete who lived in a cave on the moors. There was also *The Champion* with Rockfist Rogan R.A.F., whom everyone idolised and who made all the boys aspire to be fighter pilots. I was no exception.

My favourite, though, was *The Hotspur*'s main story called Red Circle; it was about a boarding school and the adventures of the main characters Rob Roy McGregor, Numb Ned Newton and Ginger Robertson. They were always solving riddles and having wonderful adventures; how I envied them and wanted so much to be able to go to such a school and be accepted as one of the elite group. Of course, it could never have been, but I was never jealous of these pretend heroes, because in my imagination, when reading about them, I became them.

It was shortly after the cockroach infestation that we got a very big surprise. Mam arrived to see us! Lilly was beside herself with joy. I was quite nonchalant about it, because I'd got so used to her not being there. Mam had been given leave from her work on the docks, got a train ticket and arrived at Green Ayre station that morning.

Mam was in the clothing she wore at the docks; an overall with a bib top and blouse underneath. At the time it didn't seem strange to me, because the last time I had seen her, about a year ago, she was wearing the same type of clothing.

As it transpired, it was only to be a short visit. Mrs Breslin found her a bed for the night and, quite astounding to me, she also gave her some proper food – egg and sausage. Lilly and I had never had that, though I'd seen Mrs Breslin making it for her family and the lodgers. I spent the entire time leaning on the table and watching Mam eat every mouthful. Half-way through the meal, she pushed the plate over to me, saying, 'For God's sake, Billy, stop staring; you can have it!'

I ate it all without a second's thought.

Obviously, she was not to know that Lilly and I never had such food and were hungry all the time.

Later that day, Mam embarrassed me to the point of tears. Ordering me down to the basement, where there was a large table next to the sink, she undressed me and stood me on the table next to a large bowl of water. I was horrified because the girl lodger was there washing something in the sink and she was laughing at me as Mam scrubbed me down whilst I tried to cover myself. Crying with embarrassment and trying desperately to hide myself only made Mam angry.

The following morning, Mam was off back to Liverpool. After giving Lilly a kiss she reached for me, but I was having none of it and backed off. I had still not forgiven her. I don't think it bothered her that much; Lilly had always been her favourite and the receiver of her kisses and cuddles.

It was to be another year before we saw Mam again.

In Lancaster, not too far from the town centre and opposite the infirmary was a slaughter house. The gang and I visited it often because we were allowed to watch the slaughter men do their work. When it was sheep killing day, we would help the farmers herd their sheep into the pens and watch as the slaughter men pulled them out, lifted them sideways onto a canvas trestle arrangement, plunge a knife into their necks and leave them with their blood draining onto the floor. They would then get another terrified animal on to another trestle to do the same again. At any one time, there would be up to thirty or more trestles all being used by about ten slaughter men.

Some days, cattle would be brought to be slaughtered and this would be as bloody as the sheep. They would be held by the head in a sort of vice and then hit in the front of the head by a very big man holding a sledge hammer; thus, as they say, 'poleaxing the animal'. On occasions, a terrified steer would manage to jump over the steel barriers penning them in and attempt to escape; we became very adept at getting out of the way, sometimes getting in the way of the men chasing them instead!

The most brutal, and yet for us kids, the best day, was pig day. These poor animals were herded in and dispensed by slitting open their bellies. One slaughter man would upend the pig, holding apart its front trotters whilst another slaughter man used the knife.

The benefit to our gang was that on the odd occasion we would be given the bladders of some of the pigs. When cleaned and blown up, they made excellent footballs.

One day, whilst walking to the slaughter house on my own, I was amazed to see a gigantic bomber on the lawn in front of the infirmary. I couldn't believe my eyes; it was a Lancaster, the biggest bomber in the Royal Air Force, named after this city.

Amazingly, it was open to the public to go aboard and kids were especially welcome. It was magic, probably one of the happiest moments of my evacuation. The plane had been brought to Lancaster just in time for the school summer holidays and I visited it every single day. It was a great attraction to virtually every other child too, especially in Lancaster and also from surrounding areas, but I don't believe anybody visited it as much as I did.

One of the gang's favourite escapades would be to go swimming in the River Lune and, happily for us, the way to the Lune was past the infirmary, so boarding the bomber en-route with towels under our arms was automatic.

The RAF man in charge would see us climbing up the ladder into the plane and, bemused, enquire, 'Not you lot again?' Or more often than not directly to me, 'Not you again, son?'

There was one occasion when he asked me if I was going to join the Air Force and become a bomber pilot. I think I spoilt his day when I answered, 'Yes, I'll be joining up when I'm old enough, but as a fighter pilot to fly Spitfires.'

Sadly, when I was old enough to do just that, Spits were obsolete. Strangely, I'd never even thought about the war ending; it was all too exciting and I really believed the RAF would require my services before the end!

One of the most terrifying days in Lancaster was on one of our days at the River Lune. The routine was to sneak a towel from home, meet near the infirmary and walk along the canal bank towards the countryside. A couple of us would have empty lemonade bottles, which we would fill up with water obtained by stopping and knocking on somebody's house door bordering the canal banks and asking them to fill the bottle, please.

Alongside the canal on the opposite side to the public footpath was an army assault course used by soldiers in training. At the infirmary end of the canal was a small private footbridge, ideal for the gang to cross over.

The assault course was a big adventure and running, climbing and swinging as well, if not better, than some of the soldiers we'd seen training on it, would set us up nicely for what we called 'running the tide'. From the canal to the banks of the Lune at a place called Aldcliffe, it was a good two to three mile walk, but we never noticed. Arriving at the Lune we would strip naked, stash our clothes above the tidal mark and head for the gullies. The River Lune was, and still is, a very dangerous river, although that never occurred to us until the day Brian went missing.

The river, when the tide is out, consists of many deep gullies which always had a shallow depth of water in them, ideal for us kids to splash about in. Sometimes, if we were lucky, we'd find a little pink octopus to play with.

The real game was to race the tide; the river had a very fast current, causing the tide to race in and fill the gullies in minutes. The game was to wait for the first surge of water and then to race up the gullies before the tide could take us with it, then scramble up the gully bank. I remember doing this many times until that awful day.

As we had done so many times before, off we went to Aldcliffe, Peter, Brian, Thomas and I, plus a couple of fairly recent members of our gang, John and Charlie. It was, as it always seemed to be, a lovely summer's day.

It was obvious that the tide had been out for some considerable time as the water in the gullies was very shallow; without even realising it, we had learnt to gauge the tidal flows. Off we stripped and into the gullies we went, running up and down the sides of the channels and covering ourselves in sandy mud, which we knew would soon wash off in the race with the tide.

Sure enough, as always, the river waters poured in and we raced ahead of it until we were forced to climb the gulley banks before it could engulf us.

This time, something went wrong, and Brian disappeared. He was nowhere to be seen.

It was no longer a lovely day.

As we raced back to where we'd left our clothes, all crying with fear and despair, it was agreed none of us would say anything and prayed we wouldn't be found out.

I went back to Mrs Breslin's as fast as I could and on entering the house went straight up to the garret. I sat beside the small window peeking out, looking for the policemen that would surely come looking for me. As I was the leader of the gang, I'd probably be held responsible for Brian drowning; that would probably make me a murderer. I'd never see Lilly or Mam again.

How I wished I'd never left Liverpool or even the other places in Lancaster where I'd lived that I'd hated so much! Perhaps I would never have met the gang or seen the river, but now it was too late.

Mrs Breslin called up the stairs, 'Hey, your tea's ready; your sister's having hers now.'

I didn't answer.

'You'd better come down here now!' she shouted crossly. 'If I have to come up there to get you, you'll get a belt.'

I went down the stairs extremely reluctantly.

'You've been crying,' Lilly said immediately.

'No, I haven't!' I denied.

'Yes, you have,' said Mrs Breslin. Looking at me, she smirked unpleasantly, 'Someone smack you, did they? Good for them.'

She didn't mention policemen or anything else, so the thought passed my mind that perhaps Brian would never be found and nobody would know anything about today. Still, as I sat eating my jam sandwich, I knew that any moment the police could come knocking at the door. The parents of the gang knew we all played together, and Brian's mam would obviously tell the police that.

Suddenly, Mrs Breslin came into the room. 'You're wanted at the door,' she said. I didn't move but stared at her, my bottom lip beginning to tremble.

'What's the matter with you?' she asked, looking at me like I was mad. 'It's Charlie Cooney.'

Charlie was an outside member of our gang but he hadn't been with us today; if Peter or someone else had told him what had happened, he'd probably give it away, as he was just a little bit nutty. I went to the door.

'Hi Billy,' said Charlie. 'You coming out?'

He doesn't know, I thought. 'No, not today,' I whispered, looking over my shoulder to check Mrs Breslin wasn't behind me.

'Why not? Peter and Brian are waiting up in the woods for us.'

Without thinking I shouted, 'What? How can Brian be up in the woods after what happened?' I could feel myself tremble.

'Eh?' Charlie looked confused, then smiled. 'Oh, he told me he got washed up the river today; he got stopped by the bridge by that big tree that got blown down ages ago. He said he was really angry you didn't wait for him.'

I started laughing and just couldn't stop; sheer relief washed over me like the river's fast tide.

I rushed out of the door and ran as fast as I could up to the woods, still laughing, to meet my friend whom I'd thought I'd never see again.

I would never forget that day.

SIX

The castle, more or less in the centre of Lancaster, was over a thousand years old and famous for its main gatehouse, named after John O'Gaunt; it also became one of my favourite play areas. The G. A. Henty books I read at the time frequently referred to the castle and the part it played in the War of the Roses. These wars went on for many years with both the House of Lancaster and the House of York winning and losing battles against each other until eventually Henry Tudor, with the help of the very powerful Percy family of Northumberland, finally won and became the legal King of England.

How I loved to fantasise about these battles, imagining myself in one, whilst sitting on the top of an ancient gravestone in the cemetery alongside the castle.
On one wonderful day, whilst studying history at Dallas Road, the teacher said that the following week the class was going to tour the castle from the ramparts to the dungeons; and sure enough, we did.

We spent several hours exploring the huge fortress and, unsurprisingly, the dungeons, with all their awful history, were the highlight for most of the class. I never did understand why a few of the other kids wouldn't go down to see them; especially as they must have known that from then on they would be called 'softies'. Some of us, mainly the Outlaws, volunteered to be locked in one of the dungeons, as did, strangely, two of the girls. As the door clanged shut there was utter silence and after an eerie minute or two one of the girls started crying to be let out; it really was silent in there. It turned out the teacher had ordered those outside not to make a sound; we were all glad to be released, although I never told anyone that!

One day, there was an older boy in the class above me who said to me, 'I'm going into town after school, want to come?'

'Dunno,' I replied. 'What's to do in town?'

The truth was, I didn't really like this lad; he had a thin, pointed face like a weasel, with slitty eyes and a long, sharp nose which was always dripping.

'I'm going to play in the castle grounds,' he said. 'And have a look in the toy shop in the castle square.'

'OK,' I agreed reluctantly.

Shortly after getting to the square he turned to me and said, 'Wait for me by the graveyard, I've got to do a message for Mam.'

I wandered over to the graveyard, sat on a gravestone and waited.

A short time later, Weasel Face returned and sat down next to me; I realised he had something under his jacket.

'What have you got there?' I asked, pointing at his jacket.

He pulled the object out from under his jacket and as he placed it on top of the gravestone, I realised it was a collection box.

'Where'd you get that?' I asked, well aware that he must have stolen it.

'The chemist's,' he answered with a smirk on his weaselly face. 'Let's see how much is in it.'

Now, other than apples I'd scrumped, I'd never stolen anything in my life; fear of being caught being the main deterrent. Now I was party to just that.

As he started shaking the box and lots of coins began falling out, I became quite excited. Lilly and I never had any money, except for the odd penny or two given to us by Mr Walsh, so seeing what appeared to me to be enormous amounts of money, I wanted some. Weasel Face counted the coins and he announced that we had three pounds; the average weekly wage was approximately five or six pounds at that time, so three pounds was a big haul indeed. I sat and stared at the spread of coins and when the weasel-faced thief said I could have some, I didn't refuse.

He gave me three shillings; I'd never had so much money, but I knew exactly what I was going to do with it.

On a few occasions I had stared through the window of the toy shop, just a few yards away in the square. I'd seen a cowboy gun belt with two guns in the holsters on either side. I had wanted them so, so much, and now I could have them. Into the shop I went, and out I came looking like one of my heroes – Hopalong Cassidy.

When I got back to the churchyard, Weasel Face had gone, taking all his money with him. The ransacked collection box was thrown to the side and, looking at it, I began to have doubts. I quickly hid the box and for a while played around the graves, rising up from behind the stones to shoot imaginary baddies. However, all the time, at the back of my mind, interrupting my play, the collection box kept appearing. I realised that stealing a collection box was a very bad thing to do. I sat on a gravestone, guns in hand, feeling very unhappy indeed. 'I'm really not a thief,' I told myself. 'It was Weasel Face.' But I knew I wasn't even fooling myself.

'You should take the guns back,' I told myself. But then the 'keep them' side of me answered, 'You can't, the shopkeeper would start asking why.'

I solved the problem by walking around the town square until the chemist closed, and then, when I was sure no-one was near enough to see me, I left them on the doorstep. It was a relief to know that at least I no longer considered myself a thief of collection boxes, but I didn't half miss those guns!

I should have told a teacher or somebody else about Weasel Face but I didn't; not because I was scared of him, but because it wasn't the done thing to snitch on anyone. I wish I had.

The city swimming baths was another important feature of my busy schedule. Throughout my time as an evacuee, being bathed in an actual bath or shower was a very rare occurrence; therefore, racing the Lune and frolicking in the swimming baths was, without realising it, my way of solving the cleanliness problem.

Be that as it may, during the school holidays I would spend the whole of most days in the baths, even though I couldn't swim. Once you had paid the entry fee, you walked immediately to the side of the pool. All around the pool were small cubicles with neck-high doors; one side was for the ladies to use and the other for the men.

One day, Dallas Road School announced we would be going to the swimming baths the following day. On going home that evening and finding Mrs Breslin in the kitchen chatting to a neighbour, I tentatively asked her if she had a swimming costume I could borrow as I had never swum before, which wasn't quite true, and didn't possess one.

As I expected, she wasn't interested in helping me, but luckily her neighbour said, 'I've got one you can have; come to my house with me and I'll find it for you.'

I was over the moon.

She gave me a costume which was made to cover the body totally from the thigh upwards, except for the arms. It was blue and red and had a flash of yellow lightening across the chest. I was absolutely delighted that it looked like a Superman or Flash Gordon costume. Flash Gordon, played by an actor called Buster Crabbe was the world's first astronaut, on film anyway. He was the Saturday morning Bug Hut Picture House hero who, in a series of films, would take off in his rocket complete with his girlfriend Dale Arden, and fly into space to confront his arch enemy, Ming the Merciless. On the front of his rocket uniform was a yellow flash of lightning, and now I had one too.

The next day, off to the baths the class went and I donned my costume; it felt quite heavy but I was pleased as punch. All non-swimmers had to go to the shallow end and down a ladder into the water. That was when my problems started.

Standing in the shallow end and being pretty small, the costume, as it got wet, began to get heavier and heavier. Because of the weight of the water, it also began to stretch so that the lower half, in no time at all, was dangling around my ankles and the top half was just about level with my privates. I then discovered, as we were given instructions on what to do by the teacher, that I couldn't move. Helplessly, I looked around; the rest of my class were laughing hysterically and pointing. Even the teacher, though trying to keep a straight face, laughed out loud.

It was impossible for me to get out of the pool, so I had to be lifted out with the costume now a foot or so beneath my feet. It transpired that my Superman-lookalike apparel had been knitted in heavy wool, which when soaked, stretched and weighed virtually as much as me!

After that, I was lucky enough to be given a pair of trunks which were to be my pride and joy for the next couple of years. Thankfully, I never saw that woollen costume again.

As always, not having access to money, the only way of getting into the baths was to 'bunk in', that is, sneak in for free. It was, in fact, quite simple, to sneak in when other parties were busy paying the girl at the small kiosk, with its limited all-round view. I would crawl under the guardrails beside the entrance gate and quickly lose myself in the pool area. Once inside, I'd find an empty changing cubicle, strip off to my swimming trunks below, and jump straight into the pool.

Being unable to swim was no deterrent; I'd simply jump in at the nearest point and hang onto the bath side. There was only one attendant and his job seemed to be purely to blow his whistle when those in the bath for that particular period had to leave. I would have to come out of the water as well, but I found it very easy to hang onto the clothes hooks on the door of the changing cubicle, and lift my feet off the ground. The attendant would walk around the pool looking at the space under each door, then call to the pay kiosk to let the next batch of swimmers in. With the new arrivals filling the pool again, I went unnoticed, and was able to enjoy hanging onto the side of the baths for most of the day.

I taught myself to swim by watching mothers and fathers teaching their kids what to do and even learnt how to dive off the high board by watching other people. Spending such long periods of time swimming did, of course, make me very hungry, especially as Mrs Breslin's meals, if there were any at all, were very meagre.

On the occasion when some of the gang were with me and had pocket money, or Mr Walsh had given me a penny or two, we headed to the nearby bakery. For a penny they would give us a large piece of freshly baked bread, still warm from the ovens. It was the best bread, in fact, the best meal, ever.

Alongside the bakery was a small shop that sold anything and everything; if the pennies allowed it, we would buy a bag of parched peas; they and the bread were delicious. Parched peas were incredible; ordinary peas roasted so that they were almost black, and at a penny a bag, they were a great treat.

My life as an evacuee was full and fancy free as the various people we were forced upon didn't give a damn what we did, so long as it didn't interfere with their lives in any way, and they would get away without having to care for us at all. It was amazing how self-sufficient I became, though Lilly not so much. My main source of food, to bulk out my meagre diet, came from the myriad of orchards located all over Lancaster and the surrounding districts – apples, pears, plums and damsons. I was proud to be acknowledged by my gang and others as the best scrumper in Lancaster.

I learnt I could climb just about any tree, any wall and was just about able to get past barbed wire. Carrying a small bag, burglar style, or a wearing my windcheater, I'd climb whichever tree in whatever garden and fill either receptacle with the best apples on show.

One such raid was on a very large garden on the outskirts of the city. It was surrounded by moorland and was guarded by a very high wall. The wall itself was about fifteen inches wide, which made a good pathway for me to walk along. Doing so, and spotting trees I hoped would be bearing apples, I made my way towards them. I stopped short when I saw a man with his back to me digging in the ground. Then, wonder of wonders, a very small tree with just four apples on it appeared in my line of sight between the man and me. The fruit were enormous, beautifully coloured and shining brightly in the sunlight. They could only be designed for a garden show somewhere. I had to have them; man or no man.

Dropping as quietly as possible off the wall into the garden and eyeing up the tree, which wasn't much taller than me, I inched forward. As silently as I could, I removed the four apples from their home and placed them inside my zipped up windcheater. I'd taken no more than three steps back towards the wall when a shout of rage galvanised me to run and leap onto that wall faster than even I could have expected. As I raced away, I could hear the spade clang against the wall where I'd jumped up and shouts of fury from the man.

A lucky escape, but well worth it. The three apples eaten whilst reading a comic were wonderful!

This was one of many close calls during my time in Lancaster, but it must be said that nobody else ever threw a shovel at me; a sobering thought, even though he missed.

I decided I would join the Cubs, the junior Boy Scouts. This came about when I became the owner of a soldier's cap, the type known as an Australian. It looked a lot like a cowboy's hat, with one side turned up and held in place by a stud. I'd made friends with a boy who lived a few streets away, atop a steep hill. His dad had been in the army but had been invalided out after being wounded, and it was to him the hat belonged. I fell in love with it as soon as I saw it and especially so when I was allowed to try it on. I must have had quite a big head because it almost fit me; either that, or my friend's dad had a very small one!

Imagine my surprise when, after a few times of playing with my new friend, his dad said, 'As you really like this hat and David can't be bothered with it, you can have it.'

I couldn't believe my luck. I wore it all the time, except in school. I was the proudest boy in Lancaster, if not the world. Mrs Breslin thought I was stupid, and so did Lilly. Not so the Outlaws, who were most impressed; this hat had been to war.

When doing a school play I was picked to sit around an imaginary campfire and sing 'Waltzing Matilda', so I wore the hat then. During the play, a girl older than me sang, 'My old man said follow the van', and I fell in love with her. A couple of older lads had borrowed their brother's scout hats and it became apparent to me that my hat was not dissimilar to the scout's hat.

So there we were, singing away, proclaiming to the Australian swagmen, and at the same time I was thinking about the Boy Scouts and, later, the girl.

Shortly afterwards, I decided that, as the owner of what was almost a Boy Scout's main piece of uniform, I would join the local troop. Happily, their meeting place was at the end of the road I lived on, an old hut situated on the bushy waste ground behind a low wall.

Joining up at the hut where they met once or twice a week, complete with hat firmly entrenched on my head, I found no Scouts, just a number of boys my age who said they were Wolf Cubs and you had to be one before you could be a Scout. A lady, who I was told was called Bagheera and in charge of the Cubs, said I could join, so I happily sat with the rest of the boys listening to Bagheera talk.

From then on things went awry. I'd been allowed to keep my hat on but told I must in future wear a Cub's hat, which I would have to obtain somehow. Well, one of the lads behind me whispered how stupid I looked wearing what was not even a Scout hat and then proceeded to knock it off my head.

Bagheera was completely unaware of this, as she was busy explaining something to another lad on the other side of the circle. She quickly became aware however, when the sound of a smack and the yell of pain from behind her spun her round. Seeing me standing up and about to hit one of her Cubs again for no apparent reason, she leant across the circle, grabbed me by the arm and marched me straight to the hall door, throwing me out, implying I should never return. With no chance to defend myself, I was seen as just another troublesome Liverpool evacuee. So much for the Cubs; sadly there was no chance of me ever being a Boy Scout.

I continued to wear the hat until one day it mysteriously disappeared. I never discovered what happened to it, but I had my suspicions. Mrs Breslin being one of them.

SEVEN

Lilly and I continued living with Mrs Breslin throughout 1942, although her attitude to us never changed for the better. I, in particular, continued to be given menial tasks to do, such as bringing in coal from the yard at the rear of the house, or running errands for her and the lodgers. I suppose that was why I spent so much time out of the house, rain, hail or shine, simply to keep out of the way and avoid being called upon.

During this time, we didn't see or hear from Mam and, once again, Christmas was suddenly around the corner. As on previous Christmas days, Lilly and I didn't get any presents, so we didn't really think about it; but this time, we were to be surprised. Waking up that Christmas morning, I was amazed to find it had snowed quite heavily. I couldn't wait to get out and play in it! However, a further surprise was to come our way. Running down the stairs, I was determined to have my usual piece of bread with perhaps some margarine or, if I was lucky, some jam, and then get outside to meet my friends and play in the snow.

As I ran into the kitchen with Lilly close behind, Mrs Breslin said, 'You're to sit at the table.'

Stunned, Lilly and I did as we were told.

On the table was the usual bread and, with it, the usual cup for water; but this time, instead of it being water or milk inside, it was lemonade! Then, even stranger to behold, Mrs Breslin put two bowls of porridge in front of us with a parcel alongside each plate; we didn't know what to do and just stared at her.

Without a smile on her face, she said, 'Merry Christmas; you'd better open your presents, they're from your mam.' Later, I thought how hard it must have been for her to say those words, 'Merry Christmas' to us.

I couldn't believe it; other kids got presents, not us! We forgot about the porridge and tore at the wrapping paper. As it came away, I saw I had a box which, when I opened it, contained twelve soldiers, red uniformed guardsmen with black busbies on their heads. I was ecstatic! They were made of lead and were quite perfect. It was the best, and first, Christmas present I had ever had since leaving Liverpool.

I heard Lilly squeal with delight; as I looked over I saw she had got a new doll, and she cried with joy. I remember Lilly dressed, undressed and washed the doll's face every minute of every day after that.

'Right, now eat your porridge,' Mrs Breslin instructed brusquely, breaking the magic of it all. 'And when you've finished and washed your plates, Mr Walsh wants to see you in the parlour.'

I liked Mr Walsh, as he always acknowledged Lilly and me, and if I ran an errand for him, he'd say thank you with a smile. Sometimes, he'd even give me one or two pennies. In fact, once, when I returned some books to the library for him, which was quite a way into town, he gave me sixpence. But today, as it was Christmas, the shops and the library wouldn't be open, so what could he want and why would he want to see Lilly as well?

We did as we were told and once we'd finished our porridge and drank our lemonade, we washed our bowls and cups out in the sink. Carrying my twelve soldiers with me and Lilly clutching her doll tightly, we went into the parlour. Mr Walsh sat waiting for us, sitting in his usual chair by the fireplace.

'Come over here,' he said to us, beckoning us in from just inside the parlour doorway.

I led the way, Lilly treading quietly behind me. He held out his hand, indicating I should do the same, and then he shook hands with me.

'Merry Christmas, Billy,' he said.

Again, he held out his hand to Lilly, and she stepped out from behind me and shook it.

'And a Merry Christmas to you, my dear.'

We both whispered 'Merry Christmas' back to him, assuming that was what we were meant to do.

'Come here, Lilly,' he said to my sister. 'And hold out your hand.'

I had to give her a shove but she then stepped forward, holding her hand outstretched.

'Merry Christmas again,' he said and placed in her upturned palm a two shilling and sixpence silver coin. As she looked at it, she gave him a smile as big as the one she'd given to her doll and turned excitedly to show me.

'Now you, Billy; Merry Christmas again,' he said and placed another similar coin in my hand. We couldn't believe it, two shillings and sixpence each; we were rich, or at least richer than we'd ever been before. A half a crown each; unbelievable!

'Thank you very much, Mr Walsh,' we said and turned, running out of the parlour and up to the garret, where we sat looking at two lovely silver coins.

'That was very kind of Mr Walsh,' Lilly whispered to me.

'Yeah, I know,' I replied.

'And I love my dolly from Mam,' she said.

'Yeah, I know,' I said again.

'And Mrs Breslin gave us porridge and lemonade!' she said excitedly.

'Yeah, I *know*!' I said, amazed.

That one day of kindness meant it was my happiest Christmas ever.

Showing my box of guardsmen to the Outlaws was a very proud moment.

'My Mam sent them,' I said. 'She must have known Father Christmas didn't know where we lived.'

After Boxing Day, the snow was still falling and I walked into town to spend my small fortune on more soldiers for my army and toffee apples.

The week following Christmas the school was closed due to all the snow, so I made the most of it and played all day, every day. David, my friend who lived at the top of Aberdeen Road, and his dad had made a sledge, a wooden one big enough for two and his dad had even found some iron bars from somewhere to make runners.

Aberdeen Road was a very long and steep hill, or so it seemed to us. At the bottom was a junction with another road at right angles, and on the opposite side stood a pub. On one side of Aberdeen Road the terraced houses ran from top to bottom, and on the opposite side were streets with the same terraced houses on either side. David's house was in one of the streets right at the top of Aberdeen Road so that was the obvious point to board the sledge. With the two of us on-board we did half a dozen or so runs, sometimes with David in front steering with outstretched legs, sometimes me. We were then joined by a bigger, older boy who David knew; he was probably about twelve.

'Can I 'ave a go?' he asked.

David was a bit reluctant; he was probably thinking the same as me. Two of us on the sledge at the same time meant we had the fun of it all the time, with the added bonus that there were two of us to take it in turns pulling it all the way back up the hill. This lad was so much bigger, he couldn't possibly get on the sledge as well, could he?

Obviously seeing both our faces showing our reluctance and quickly reading our thoughts, he said, 'We can get three on there.'

David shook his head but before he could say no, the boy added, 'I'm bigger than both of you, so I'll lie on the sledge and you two can lie on my back, and I'll steer the sledge easily with my legs. I've done this before and it makes the sledge go even faster.'

That settled it; he was on.

Well, it certainly seemed like a good idea. This way we wouldn't miss any rides and there was an extra person to pull the sledge back up the hill.

'OK,' said David, and the big lad quickly lay on the sledge with his head protruding over the front and his legs splayed out behind.

David was slightly bigger than me so he was next in lying on his friend's back, and I was last, on top of David.

Now, the thing about sledges is that, as the boy said, the heavier the weight they are carrying, the faster they go, especially on a hill as steep as Aberdeen Road. The previous rides with just the two of us had been exciting; now, shooting down the hill at an unheard of speed, it was quite frightening. Hanging on to each other for grim death, we reached the bottom of the hill expecting our driver to do as we had and swivel the sledge round at right angles, thus coming to a stop. It didn't happen. On reaching the crossroads we continued across at the same speed and only stopped when we hit the pub wall. Our new friend, in fact, stopped us with his head.

Being unable to wriggle backwards or sideways because of our combined weight on his back and not having the nous to throw himself and us off before the impact, he suffered the consequences. His anguished yells must have been heard miles away as, being relived of our weight when we stood up, he rolled over in the snow with blood gushing from his forehead. Before we could ask him why he hadn't turned the sledge away from the oncoming wall, he was off running up the hill leaving a trail of blood in the snow and yelling blue murder. I believe it was for his mam, though it was hard to tell.

It rather put us off any more sledging for an hour or so.

Christmas came and went, as did the snow. Mr Walsh still sat in his armchair reading or listening to the radio, I still ran messages for him and on occasion received a penny or two. The girl lodger had gone and nobody as yet had replaced her. Mrs Breslin was just as cold as ever; well, to me, anyway, and Lilly was still playing with her dolly.

I had taken to visiting Green Ayre Station with my friend Peter, having become interested in trains. We discovered if we went into the sidings, we could play on the footplate of the steam engines which were left there when not in use. On the odd occasion, when a fireman or driver found us there, they wouldn't chase us; they'd just let us play or told us tales.

One day, having spent some considerable time talking and asking questions of one of these men, he pointed out the brakes and levers for starting a locomotive, answering all of our eager questions.

Sometime later, when once again playing in the sidings, we climbed onto the footplate of a shunting engine which was still fired up and yet there was nobody around. Peter excitedly asked me if we should put into practice what he had learnt about engines. I believe it was a mutual decision to give it a go, although Peter said later that it was all my fault!

Between us, we let off the brake and moved the levers we had been shown, never for a moment expecting anything to happen. It certainly did, though! The engine started to move down its track. Panic-stricken, we jumped down to the track alongside and legged it towards the station. Halfway there we heard a clanging sound as the engine hit the buffers a hundred yards or so down the track. Luckily, the buffers stopped it, but we didn't hang about.

Unsurprisingly, we never went near Green Ayre Station again.

How or why it happened, I don't know; I certainly can't remember anything being explained to me, but in the late spring of 1943 I found myself living on Aberdeen Road at the top of the hill not far from David's house. Lilly was not with me and I can only assume that the people responsible for us evacuees had decided, possibly with the help of Mrs Breslin, to separate us. I think that as far as she was concerned, I was too much trouble and she'd put up with me long enough. Lilly was much less trouble and, anyway, if Mrs Breslin kept her, she wouldn't lose both ration books.

I was living in a small terraced house with the company of an old couple, two girls and a dog which, for reasons I didn't understand then, spent most of its time wrapping his paws around my leg and humping away. The girls seemed to find this hilarious; I thought the dog was just being friendly.

The girls were probably eighteen or nineteen years old and one of them had a wooden leg. I got on very well with them, as I also did with the elderly couple; whether or not they were the parents of the girls, I don't think I ever found out. What I do know is that they treated me well. I ate the same food as they did, they found time to talk to me, they had a bathroom which they allowed me to use, though as I still spent hours, if not days, when not at school at the swimming baths, it was the norm in those days to use the bath only once a week. I'm pretty sure, though, that the girls washed all over quite frequently, judging from the conversations I heard from time to time.

Somewhere close to Lancaster was an American base, though I didn't know where it was situated, and the girls dated airmen based there. I used to run messages for them and for the old couple and do other jobs such as washing the dishes after tea. On what I called 'Date Night', I used to do one job, which for reasons unknown to me then, I really enjoyed; I suppose, at nearly nine, I was beginning to grow up.

After the girls had dressed up and made up their faces, it was leg-tan time; they made the brown colouring from cocoa mixed with water and whatever else they needed to make it work. As we were at war, nylon or silk stockings were virtually impossible to come by. The girls would hitch their skirts up to their knickers and apply the concoction to each other's legs; I would stand there watching.

I used to spend quite a lot of time in the evenings drawing, just copying pictures out of books or comics. The girls had noticed that I was quite good at drawing straight lines and that became one of my other jobs. After the leg makeup had dried, they would stand with their backs to me, skirts still up around their waists and I would take a black lead pencil and draw as straight a line as I could down the back of each leg, from thigh to heel. It was years before I realised why I enjoyed it so much!

The girl with the wooden leg would use the same tan stuff on that leg as well, obviously in an attempt to disguise it and I would draw on that one in exactly the same way. They were brave, kind and lovely girls trying whatever they could to forget there was a war on.

I shared a room with one of the girls, although my bed was a low camp bed as there just wasn't enough room for two normal-sized beds. One night, I heard them come home giggling and whispering to each other and two other girlfriends they'd brought home with them. Though they tried very hard not to make a noise, I realised they were probably slightly drunk and that they'd been out with some Yanks. Lying there, quiet as a mouse, I heard practically every word.

After leaving the pub, they'd gone off in one of the American's jeeps, taking with them some bottles of beer. They'd stopped in a country lane to drink the beer and Miss Wooden Leg had eventually needed the toilet. From that night to today I cannot understand why she did what she did; after all, they were out in the countryside surrounded by fields, hedgerows and trees. She decided to take an empty beer bottle with her, away from the jeep, and tried to wee into it, and this is what all the hilarity was about. Now, young as I was, I knew that for a boy it would have been a pretty simple task, but for a girl, who I knew from seeing my sister and other girls in school had to sit down to achieve relief, it was going to be a much harder job.

It eventually became clear that the only thing she did achieve was to wet her knickers, but for this, through gales of laughter, she blamed her wooden leg.

I stayed at this billet for some weeks and during that period I lost touch with the boys in my gang. One reason was that I'd been moved some distance from their homes and spent a great deal more time with David and some of his friends, who lived much closer to my new home. I did still see them in school though.

We played all the same kind of games together that I'd done since coming to Lancaster, but I found I quite enjoyed sitting in the house with the girls and even with the randy dog, listening to the radio, talking about Liverpool and reading.

The radio was king. Every house had one, or more than one if they were rich. We would virtually cry with laughter at Tommy Handley's ITMA (It's That Man Again) Show, with its catchphrase by a supposed office cleaner, 'Can I do you now, sir?' or its resident Deep Sea Diver saying, 'Don't forget the Diver!' I was quite proud when I discovered that Tommy Handley was a Scouser like myself.

The other wonderful radio show we listened to was called Happidrome, with the extremely funny stars called Ramsbottom, Enoch and Me, who sang, 'We three at Happidrome, working for the BBC, Ramsbottom, Enoch and Me.' They were like three circus clowns with broad Lancashire accents, and for kids like me, their jokes and acts were fantastic, never to be missed!

In the evening, as it got dark, we would listen to Valentine Dyall, also known as The Man in Black, tell us a half-hour-long spooky story. The girls, the old couple and I would listen, frightened to death by his deep silvery voice telling us his sinister tales. Afterwards, we would talk about it and then have to wait impatiently for his next episode the following night.

Being a little bit older now, I could appreciate that things were getting better for our servicemen. Some of the news on the radio involved programmes about battles won and U-boats sank and how Uncle Joe Stalin was to help us out. Unsurprisingly, I believed every word and would talk with David and others about it, though they never seemed as interested as me; possibly because they hadn't gone through the Blitz.

We learnt all the rude songs that were versions of well-known songs of those times and we'd sing them loudly when not within earshot of any adults. I still remember all the words to songs like, 'In the shade of the old apple tree, a pair of fine legs I did see.' Then there was 'Coming Round the Mountain', where our version was, 'She'll be wearing Woolworths' knickers when she comes!' Of course, everyone knew and would always sing the Old Colonel Bogey song, 'Hitler Has Only Got One Ball'. Half the time we didn't know what we were singing about, but we loved to do it anyway.

I was very happy living in Aberdeen Road, but then came the time when I messed it all up.

At school, I had discovered that I quite liked writing what was then called compositions; these were short stories we invented and liked to put down on paper. Outside school, paper was in short supply, certainly so far as I was concerned. Added to this, I didn't have any pens or pencils. Sometimes, when the girls were out and I was at home, I would, if I could find a pen and some paper in their room, write a story - always an adventure.

One day, having nothing to write on or with, I decided how to solve my problem. Nearby was a junior school which, when closed, had an easy-to-climb gate with a playground on the other side. David and I, along with his dad, had made a soapbox cart using wooden planks we had found and some old pram wheels. David's dad said that on no account were we to use it on the road so the obvious place to play with it was the school yard. This we did, pushing and pulling it over the gate and then pushing each other around on the concrete playground.

After some time, we decided to look for something else to do. Walking over to the school building, we peered through the windows of different classrooms; lo and behold, to my fascination I saw books, exercise books, pens, pencils, rubbers and rulers all stacked on shelves. The die was cast.

We found a window slightly open and decided to explore inside. Like myself, David enjoyed reading so we helped ourselves to some books and, in David's case, a slate board and some chalk. For myself, as well as two books, I took drawing paper, lined writing books and pencils. We quickly climbed back out of the window, shutting it behind us.

We knew we'd done wrong, but we convinced ourselves that no-one would know; we hadn't taken much and, anyway, we really needed it.

The same evening, as I sat with the girls listening to the radio, there was a knock on the front door. I ran to open it and got the shock of my life to see a policeman standing there.

'You must be William Mansfield,' he said sternly. I nodded slowly and felt my stomach tighten into knots. He stepped aside and I saw David and his dad standing there behind him.

'May we come in?' he asked; I could hear the old couple behind me, obviously coming to see what was going on.

As they all walked past me into the parlour, I could see David had been crying; his dad just looked at me and shook his head. The old lady bade them to sit down, whilst I stood in the parlour doorway absolutely terrified and wishing I could just disappear.

Everyone stared at me for what felt like an eternity until one of the girls said, looking at me but talking to the policeman, 'Well, what's he been up to then?'

The policeman told them about us sneaking into the school and taking our loot, and it transpired that David's dad had become very curious about David's new slate board and chalk. David had been forced to tell him where he got it. David also managed to tell his dad that it was all my idea, which was most certainly not the case, but of course being just an evacuee from that awful place Liverpool, it was obvious that I was guilty as sin.

'Are they going to the Police Station?' asked one of the girls. 'You'll be going to jail, Billy, if you are.' I'm sure she was grinning as she said it; she probably thought it was all a joke.

By then I had joined David, who I no longer liked, and was crying my eyes out.

When the policeman eventually answered, having let us suffer for a moment or two, he said, 'No, but someone will have to bring them down to the Magistrate's Office tomorrow and they'll decide what's going to happen. I'll be in touch with the people responsible for evacuees; they'll probably come for him.'

I ran out of the room and up to my bedroom where I lay crying on my camp bed.

Nobody from the house came up to see me, and the following morning nobody had anything to say even then, though I did get breakfast, which went uneaten.

The man sent to fetch me arrived and had a short conversation with the old couple; the girls had left for work without saying a word. There had been no, 'Bye bye, Billy' for me.

'Have you got your belongings packed?' he asked me. Now I knew I must be going to jail.

'No,' I replied, my voice shaking.

'Well, go and get them,' he said sternly. 'You won't be coming back here.'

Crying yet again, I put my few things into my small case and went down the stairs. I looked to the old couple for a goodbye, but no words were uttered and no looks were exchanged.

It was obvious I didn't have a friend in the world.

When we arrived at the Magistrate's Office, I was led into a small waiting room where David and his dad were sat. Neither of them said a word or even looked at me. I knew David had convinced his dad that it really was all my fault and therefore I'd get the severest of whatever punishment was to be handed out. I wondered what jail was like; I'd read in my history books about places like the Tower of London, and knew that most people sent there didn't ever come out, at least not alive.

David and I were both marched in to face a man and a woman who were sitting behind a large desk. They questioned us intently and told us just how naughty we had been, but as neither of us had been in trouble before - at least they didn't have any records about us - we wouldn't go to jail this time, but from now on we were to be as good as gold.

'Say thank you very much,' said the evacuee man to me.

I immediately did as I was told and followed him outside. David and his dad followed; they didn't say a word or even turn to look at me, just continued to walk away as if they'd never known me.

I had thought, in my moments of contemplating jail, that he might ask for his Australian hat back, but he didn't.

'Come along,' said the man, and we set off walking.

'Can I go home now?' I asked him.

'Oh no, you don't live there anymore,' he said, continuing to walk at a brisk pace. 'Those people weren't happy that you were a thief. You're going to Morecombe.'

EIGHT

Morecombe was, I knew, by the sea; I'd been told it was close to Lancaster but I'd never been. The thought of once again being by the sea was quite exciting, though leaving my friends in this city, leaving my very nice home in Aberdeen Road, and even thinking that I'd be much further away from Lilly, made me quite sad.

What was just as important was the fact that racing the Lune, having all those orchards to raid, Williams Park, the picture houses and even Dallas Road School would all be left behind, plus of course my beloved swimming baths. How stupid I had been to give it all away for a few books, which I no longer had anyway.

Then again, being sent to a seaside resort was not so much a punishment for my misdeeds as a prize for committing them; such thoughts made the short journey pleasant.

The evacuee man and I crossed Skerton Bridge in a car on the road to Morecombe. As we drove along the man said very little to me, except to say I'd have a surprise when I got to my new billet.

Arriving in Morecombe, we drove along the promenade with the sea stretching out to my right-hand side; this was the surprise he'd mentioned, I thought. It was so good to see the sea again, but it wasn't that at all. We turned off the promenade into a side road with very tall houses all the way along. I later learned these were known as Victorian terraces and were three or four stories high.

The one we stopped at looked very drab and not at all inviting but when a lady opened the door to us there was the surprise. Lilly was standing next to the lady, smiling at me; she'd been brought from Mrs Breslin's house to join me. I was amazed to find I was glad to see her. It was fairly obvious that she was equally pleased to see me and, happily, nobody there appeared to have been told of my crime.

She'd grown up quite a bit since I'd been sent to Aberdeen Road but she told me she was glad to have left Mrs Breslin's, where she'd had to do the same chores I used to do. Mr Walsh had been very kind to her whilst I was away, and on leaving had given her two half crowns, one of which was for me.

We were shown to a room where we'd have to share a bed again and, once more, it was right at the top of the house. Big as it was, the house didn't have a bathroom and the only washing place for everybody was a very big sink in the kitchen. I hoped that there would be swimming baths in Morecambe where I could bunk in, but later I realised that wouldn't be necessary as I would spend much of my time in the sea.

We had porridge for breakfast every morning and stew or something like it in the evening and, because it was a fishing town as well as a resort, we occasionally had fish. The school we both had to join was a very grim place, a true relic of Victorian times. Dark and dismal, it felt a bit like the loony bin in Lancaster and not at all like Dallas Road. The only good thing about this school was that we were entitled to a dinner, of sorts, at lunchtime. This was amazing for us; we were both getting more food than we'd ever had, even in Liverpool.

Lilly, because she'd left her friends behind in Lancaster, took to following me around everywhere; in school there was no segregation between boys and girls, or in the playground. It was embarrassing and made it very difficult for me to make new friends; the boys, like me, didn't want a small girl in tow.

Eventually, she did become friendly with girls in her own class so I then had the time to do the same with the boys, though I had grown so used to not having my gang around that I became quite a loner.

Out of school hours I had plenty to do. Morecambe did indeed have a swimming pool, an open air one with no roof. It also had a very high diving board and, best of all, it was easier than Lancaster to bunk in. Knowing it had not been long ago since I nearly (as I thought) went to jail, I perfected the best way not to get caught.

The baths had an entrance with a pay kiosk and a turnstile. Still being very small, I was able to insert myself behind a grown up in the same space inside the turnstile; when they paid and the turnstile revolved, I would exit it at the same time as the adult. I couldn't be seen as my height, and crouching ever so slightly, kept me below the height of the pay desk. I used to see lots of kids doing the same thing and even if the adults saw us behind them, they never said anything.

I was pleasantly surprised that Morecambe also had a fairground; I'd never seen one before and had lots of fun jumping on the roundabouts as they started up and jumping off again when chased by the angry man running the roundabout. He had his work cut out as every kid in Morecombe, or so it seemed, did the same!

Best of all were the slot machines. They were penny or halfpenny ones where a steel ball was propelled around by a lever pressed on the outside. The ball would have to enter one of a row of holes when you would win and receive more coins out of it. If it didn't go down one of the rows, and frequently it didn't, it would disappear through a much bigger hole and your money stayed in the machine.

On one very lucky day, I remember finding one of these machines where the ball was returned to its firing position every time without having to put your penny in. It paid out coins all the time and I left it only when some bigger lads turned up. I had pockets full of pennies which were put to good use on ice cream and the swing boats, where you hauled mightily on a rope with somebody sat opposite you hauling on an opposite rope thus swinging the boat higher. Of course, you didn't sit, but stood going higher and higher until the swing man would order us off. Other pennies were spent on shooting targets and the 'What the Butler Saw' film machine.

When I had lived in Aberdeen Road and had shared a room with one of the girls, other than when I'd done their stocking seams, I'd never seen a grown up girl in any form of undress. At our billet in Morecambe, a girl of about sixteen also lived there. Whether she was family or just lodged there, I had no idea; I only saw her occasionally, so I expect she worked most of the time. Having finished my breakfast one morning and taking my plate out into the kitchen, I saw the girl standing stripped down to her knickers, washing herself in the sink. I just stood there looking, not really giving it a second thought until I said, 'Hello.'

She spun round looking at me, startled.

'What are they?' I asked, pointing to her breasts.

Her hands flew up to cover them as she let out a gasp and hurriedly ran out the kitchen. I had no idea what I'd said or done wrong and it was many moons later that I remembered how pretty she was. I'm certain she was laughing as she ran off.

Bizarrely, I cannot remember any other person other than Lilly in that house, though there must have been half a dozen or more.

As in Lancaster, Lilly now had her own friends and, other than having to share a bed with my sister at night, I didn't see a great deal of her. Occasionally, she'd ask me to let her go with me to the beach and I'd take her and help her build a sandcastle, then I'd go for a swim. It never entered my head that I shouldn't leave her by herself.

One day, as I returned from my swim in the sea, I heard Lilly scream my name. Racing out of the water I looked all around me but couldn't see her. I panicked, frantically looking around me until I heard her again and the top of her head popped up. Somebody had dug quite a deep hole in the sand which had filled with water when the tide came in. Lilly had decided to go for a paddle, though she knew she shouldn't as I'd told her on a number of occasions not to go into the sea. She had fallen into the hole and, being very small, the water came up over her head.

I rushed to her and reached down to get my hands under her arms. With all my strength I tried to pull her out, but I couldn't; luckily, a man and a lady walking along the beach heard my yells for help and ran over to help pull Lilly out of the hole. They sat her down on the beach and checked she was alright but Lilly was busy crying for all she was worth. I thanked them for their help and then turned to her, blasting her for what she had done.

The good thing was she never asked to come to the beach with me again!

Morecambe was a holiday town, though nothing like its neighbour, Blackpool. Most of the Victorian homes were run as Bed and Breakfasts; though the one we lived in could never have operated as one due to its lack of bathroom facilities. I found Morecambe to be a rather dull place; even the sea seemed to be of the same mind as when the tide went out, the sea seemed to disappear altogether, leaving miles and miles of sand.

Naturally, in a holiday destination with long stretches of beach, one attraction you would always find was the donkey rides. Morecambe was no exception and up to twenty or more donkeys would be employed to give kids rides from morning to evening, every day. I used to sit and watch them for hours wishing I had a few pennies to pay for a ride. On the occasion when I had won lots of them on the slot machine, I'd got carried away spending them on ice creams and cakes for me and Lilly, and so I had none left to pay for a donkey ride.

In the evenings, the donkeys would be taken back to their stables. They would be ridden usually by boys a lot older than me, up the slope from the beach and along the promenade road to the stables not far from my billet. It was some time before I discovered that the boys weren't employed by the donkey man to do that, they would just come down to the shore when the rides were about to finish and volunteer to ride the donkeys home. Some of the lads would have spent a good part of the day just walking up and down with the donkeys whilst they were giving other kids rides; doing this entitled them to ride them home when they had finished.

One day, I decided to offer my services as a donkey walker and approached the donkey man as he was taking money off a young family; he looked me up and down and said, 'Sorry son, you're too little and too young, I need bigger lads for this job.'

Nonetheless, I still liked to sit and watch.

A few days later, as they were packing up, I realised that one of the donkeys didn't have a boy on it when all the others had and were ready to go. I was up and running in a flash to the donkey man, eagerly asking him to let me ride the animal.

'Please, sir, please can I ride that one back to the stables?' He was a bit uncertain and I could see him pondering, but then he asked me if I'd ever ridden a horse or donkey before.

I hadn't, but there was no way I was going to tell him that. 'Yes, course I have,' I said earnestly.

'OK, up you get,' he said, hoisting me up onto the saddle.

I was so happy; there I was, in charge of my steed. I was Roy Rogers, Errol Flynn in Robin Hood, and all my other heroes rolled into one!

Having watched so many times all the other kids handle their donkeys, I knew exactly what to do. Pulling up the reins, I turned his head towards the slope which ran from the beach to the promenade where all the others were trotting.

'Giddy up!' I said and bounced up and down on the saddle; at my orders the donkey set off, but there was something wrong. He was going the wrong way! Panic immediately set in.

Heaving as hard as I could on the reins, attempting to turn him back to the slope, was to no avail. Resolutely he headed for a set of steps further along the beach. On the steps sat families with small children, enjoying their ice creams. My donkey wasn't remotely bothered! He'd decided the steps were a shortcut back to his stable and food, so that's the way he was going to go. A couple of men stood up, attempting to shoo him away and started shouting at me to go up the slope and away from them. Wishful thinking! There was as much chance of me doing that as attempting to make him fly.

Fortunately, or unfortunately, the donkey man had gone off up the slope after putting me aboard, obviously secure in the knowledge that I could ride. Now he was running along the prom in an effort to cut us off, but it was too late. The people on the steps disappeared in all directions as my steed started up the steep steps with me clinging on for grim death. Reaching the top, he raced off like the winner of the Grand National down the promenade with the donkey man in hot pursuit behind us and me trying not to fall off. I didn't have the faintest idea where we were going, but fortunately he did. We were the first back to his stables! I climbed off, tethered him up and scarpered before the donkey man arrived.

From that point on, I kept well away from the donkey rides and the donkey man; although often watched from a distance and longed to ride again like my heroes. It would be many years and heroes long forgotten before I rode such an animal again.

NINE

I began to really miss my friends in Lancaster and I definitely missed the orchards that abounded there; I'm sure I had apple withdrawal symptoms! Morecambe appeared to be devoid of my favourite source of food and I was sad at not being able to scrump the orchards. However, Lilly and I weren't billeted in Morecambe for long when a massive change to our fortunes took place. Mam arrived.

She was no longer required on the docks in Bootle, so she was able to leave Liverpool. Having had plenty of experience, she applied and got a similar kind of job in Green Ayre Station in Lancaster. She'd arrived to tell us we were going with her to a new billet in Lancaster.

Lilly and I were over the moon to see her, although I did act rather blasé about it at the time. Of course, I was ecstatic about going back to Lancaster, but we had been so long without Mam that I had become completely independent of her. I'm sure she must have been hurt by my casual acceptance that she was going to live with us again, but then Lilly had always been her favourite and now she had her back for good.

It transpired that Mam had been put in touch, by the powers that be, with a Liverpool family who had also been evacuated to Lancaster, but unlike us they had come as a complete family.

There was the father and mother and three girls, Olive who was eighteen and serving as a Land Girl, Brenda, who was twelve, and Loretta, known as Lottie, who was the same age as me. There was also a boy, Reginald, or Reggie as he was called, who was fifteen. They were the Johnson family, and for the first time in those years of being an evacuee, I learned to love them.

They lived in a simple two up, two down railway cottage with a small kitchen served by a well; they also had a toilet with a wooden seat which fitted from one side of the closet to the other. There was no flush, so buckets of water would be poured down into it after each visit. One of my jobs was to cut old newspaper, and any other paper available, into small squares and hang them up on a nail in the toilet wall. The toilet stood at the far end of a rather large garden which could be quite difficult to negotiate in the dark of night, with no lights available, so each bed had under it a gazunder bedpan.

Happily, it was never my duty to empty them, as being small and, I believe, undernourished, I wasn't trusted to carry them down the stairs without spills.

The single cold water tap in the kitchen was fed by a well, though how it was pumped up I never knew. It had to be run for some time to clear away any dirt and, more frequently than not, worms. Then it would have to be boiled and kept in large jugs until it was used up.

None of this bothered me in the least; at nine years old it seemed quite normal and, more than anything, it was finally nice to live with people who really seemed to like us living with them and shared everything with us. They had been late evacuees, leaving Liverpool more than a year after Lilly and I did; they had asked to leave Liverpool as evacuees because, although the bombing by then was infrequent, it was still not a pleasant place to live.

After arriving in Lancaster, and being a whole family, they had been offered the cottage which belonged to L.M.S. (London, Midland and Scottish Railways) rent-free. Alongside the cottage ran a single track railway line, along which, once a day, a shunting engine with a couple of trucks in tow would pass on its way to Heysham a few miles away.

The cottage stood at the junction of a country lane which led back to Lancaster, so at this point the track and line formed a level crossing. As at all crossings of this sort, a crossing gate formed a barrier across the line and the cottage occupiers would have to open the gate when the engine arrived and once again when it returned. To us kids, the train arriving and returning each day was a pleasure. Lilly, Lottie and I, and sometimes even Brenda, would stand on the wooden gate and, as it swung wildly across the lane coming to a halt with a shudder against an upright on the other side, we'd fall off clapping and cheering. The engine driver would blow his whistle and wave to us as he went past. Sometimes, he would stop very briefly and hand over to Mr Johnson some bags of coal for free and would be handed back an apple pie Mrs Johnson or Mam had baked or, occasionally, a fish.

The cottage was in Aldcliffe, right beside the Lune, my old stomping ground. When my old gang, Peter, Brian and the others used to come down to race the tide, we never noticed whether anybody lived there. Now I lived right alongside my beloved river, but I couldn't play in it any more. Mam and Mrs Johnson made sure of that; however, there were lots of other compensations.

One of these was to be roused out of bed early in the morning by Reggie. The previous evening, at low tide, he would have erected some old lengths of fishing net he had found, about twenty or thirty feet of it. It was strung about three foot high between uprights he'd sunk into the river sand. He'd put them up as late in the evening as possible and would get up early the next morning to retrieve them. The reason for this was that it was illegal, as the Lune was a salmon river, but that didn't stop Reggie!

He'd wake me up, we'd dress and he'd put on a long pair of waders; we'd climb over the stile between the house and the riverside, he'd hoist me up onto his shoulders and we'd go looking to see if we'd caught anything. It was such an adventure to me; it was a bit like being an Outlaw again.

Sometimes we'd find nothing, especially if it had been a low tide; other times we'd find small fish, and occasionally we'd find a salmon, or even two, if we'd been really lucky. That was definitely the best, as the whole house would feed on fresh fish and it also kept the engine driver happy.

It was shortly after arriving at Aldcliffe that I started to learn a little about girls; though without really understanding what it was all about. I'd had very little contact with girls of my age up to this point, though of course I'd had plenty of association with much older girls. I just happened to be there, in the same house, in my different billets; I was the small boy who could run errands and do small jobs for them. I never really thought about them as girls, just as different to me; though I was certain the Lillys of this world were a damned nuisance!

Now, living with the Johnsons, I was to learn things about girls that I quite liked.

With so many of us living in this little cottage the sleeping arrangements were, to say the least, a bit crowded. Mr and Mrs Johnson had one bedroom, Mam, when she was there, slept on the settee in the front room, and we children, including Olive who was eighteen, all slept in two beds in the other bedroom. In one bed, against one wall, slept Olive, Lottie and Lilly; in the other bed on the opposite side of the room slept Reggie on the outside, Brenda in the middle and me against the wall.

Once a week, the grey tin bath would be hauled in from the outside shed, placed in front of the fire and filled with numerous pans and kettles of hot water. We younger kids would have to undress and take our turn being scrubbed down, usually by Mrs Johnson. Lilly and Lottie would be bathed first whilst the water was nice and warm; I would be next and Brenda would be last. Reggie and Olive would make their own arrangements, as would Mam and Mr and Mrs Johnson.

One night, after I had been hauled out of the bath and dried in front of the fire, I was lying on my back on the old rug made from old pieces of clothing when Brenda stepped out of the bath and straddled her legs across me whilst her mother dried her. I couldn't help but see her naked and I couldn't understand why I couldn't stop looking. When I did avert my eyes and looked up past her legs, there was Brenda looking down at me with a grin on her face. I quickly rolled away feeling guilty, though I didn't know why and wondered why Brenda had been grinning. That night, after the four of us had been chased up to bed, I was lying on my side when Brenda whispered, 'Did you like my fanny?'

I was so startled I didn't know what to say, but she was grinning at me, so I nodded my head affirmatively.

'Would you like to feel it?' she asked and without further ado she pulled my arm down and pushed it between her legs. I immediately tried to pull away but, being twelve, and bigger and stronger than me, she held it in place saying, 'Go on, feel it.'

I did and slowly realised I liked doing it though I hadn't the faintest idea why.

That was to become a nightly happening, even when Reggie was snoring alongside us; Brenda would wake me up and say, 'Go on!' to be followed by, 'You can look at my bum if you like.' I did, but it was some years before I understood why I had enjoyed it.

Olive, being a Land Army Girl, would always be up very early, certainly a long time before we rose. Sometimes she would wake me up by making a noise, though she tried not to; she would slide out of bed completely naked and quietly creep downstairs carrying her clothes. To this day, I can still see her quite large bottom in the dawn light.

At this time, Mam wasn't home a lot; she continued to work at Green Ayre and she would tell us that she'd be working late and would probably not be home. On these nights, she'd be sleeping in one of the train carriages in one of the sidings, she would claim. I used to think, I wouldn't mind that, it'd be much more comfortable than sleeping on the settee or, like me, three in a bed. Sometimes Mam would be away for two or three days. I didn't really mind because, after all, she'd been separated from us for so long; Lilly missed her terribly, though.

As we were back in Lancaster, we had been reinstated at Dallas Road School and I was back with my old gang. But it wasn't quite the same. Living in Aldcliffe was quite a distance from my old stomping grounds, which had always been somewhere in the city. I'd still see Peter, Brian and Thomas and other lads who were in our gang, but it just wasn't the same.

Each morning, after whatever was available for breakfast, Reggie, Lottie, Brenda, Lilly and I would have to go to school by bus. The long walk up the lane from the cottage would end at a farm, which happened to be the home of the big lad I had won the fight against on my very first day at Dallas Road. We still completely ignored each other, even when boarding the same bus.

Halfway up the lane, prior to the farm, was a very old house with a large garden which had an orchard in it. An old lady lived there and every morning she would leave five apples on the surrounding wall for us to pick up on the way to the bus. I thought this was very kind of her, but wished she didn't do it, as it stopped me from performing my favourite skill - scrumping apples. In all good conscience, I couldn't bring myself to rob the orchard of this kind old lady; it was highly frustrating, but I never did!

Being back in school at Dallas Road, but now under a different teacher, I found life quite pleasant. My previous teacher was still up to her old tricks of leg smacking, I heard, whereas now I had a man teaching my class and he'd give you a clip around the ear when you weren't listening. He also had the unfortunate habit of throwing his blackboard wiper at you when you weren't paying attention; as it was solid wood on one side, it could be quite painful if the wrong side hit you. However, it achieved what it was meant to do; certainly in my case, anyway! I listened to him more than I'd ever listened to anyone before.

He taught English and Maths and made everything he did interesting. I learned from him how to make up stories and loved to write compositions. The whole class loved it when, if he'd had a good day with us and not had to clip anyone round the ear or throw his chalkboard wiper at anyone, he'd read us a story. Happily, one of his favourite authors was W.E. Johns, who wrote the Biggles books, and I was already an avid reader of the adventure novels. I do believe, because of this, I became one of his favourites. Anyway, he certainly put me on the path of enjoying learning; I even enjoyed Maths which, thinking back, was a minor miracle!

After school, we would board the bus again to be driven back to the farm at Aldcliffe. Lilly would, as often as not, try and sit by me - try as I might to avoid her - and tell me what boy or even girl had been pulling her hair that day. It really was all Mam's fault, because now that she was back living with us, Shirley Temple and her long curls had come back into the picture. I could well understand what an attraction the long curls with ribbons were to young lads; nevertheless, I would be ordered by Mam to make sure it didn't happen again.

Of course, it always did!

It was about this time that we discovered Mam was courting, or at least she was seeing somebody. Although we didn't realise it at the time, it explained why Mam was away so much.

It was now 1944 and that was the year Lilly and I were introduced to Fred, or, as Mam told us to call him, Uncle Fred. This puzzled me somewhat, because I knew I had a lot of uncles with Mam and Dad having such large families, but they were all in Liverpool or the army and, as far as I knew, not one of them was called Fred.

Mam said Uncle Fred lived in Morecambe (I thought, 'Oh no, not Morecambe again!'), and that he was a fisherman who had his own boat which he also used for cockling, whatever that was. I suppose had Lilly and I been older, we would have understood that Mam, who was still only 36, and as I remember from early photographs rather attractive, would be fancied by other men. After all, Dad had died some time ago. Most of the available men at that time were either medically unfit to be called up for the services or were in employment necessary to keep the home fires burning. Fred, being a fisherman, was one of the latter.

One day, Mam said she was taking us to meet Uncle Fred and we'd be going on a bus to Morecambe. I wasn't enthralled with the idea, as I didn't need another man in my life, but Lilly was babbling with excitement.

We arrived at Morecambe bus station and met this quite tall, slightly tubby man with a red, jolly face. He picked Lilly up and told her how pretty she was and then shaking my hand, he said, 'So, you're Billy. How would you like to go to the fair?'

I just nodded to him.

'Good, but let's have something to eat first.'

He held Lilly's hand, linked arms with Mam, and with me trailing behind, led the way into town.

We stopped at a café and sat outside on the seats provided. Fred went inside and eventually came back out with plates of fish and chips. I'd never had fish and chips before, but boy oh boy did I enjoy them! It was the biggest and best meal I'd had since being evacuated, possibly the best ever.

Suddenly, I liked Fred; even more so when, having finished the fish and chips, he disappeared back into the café and returned with large cones of ice cream.

Eventually, we finished a long day, most of it spent at the fair. Neither Mam nor Fred could understand why I didn't enjoy it as much as Lilly; I couldn't tell them I'd been there on any number of occasions and found it much more enjoyable bunking onto the rides!

On the way home, Mam quizzed us on how much we liked Uncle Fred. Lilly thought he was wonderful; I said I thought he was alright and I quite liked him.

The quizzing started all over again when we got back to the Johnsons and Brenda and the others were quite impressed, as well as jealous, that we'd had fish and chips in a café. We saw Fred two or three times again, and he showed me his boat, just a small craft with a sail. He said that one day he'd take me out with him, but he never did because I never saw him again. As it transpired, Mam had found somebody else.

TEN

At this time, the war was at last going in favour of the Allies, though in Lancaster we kids were cushioned from it. It seemed to be going on in another world totally alien to ours in this city. This didn't stop our war games when everyone wanted to be on the British side and some lad, usually one we didn't like much, would have to be Adolph. Part of his role would be to goosestep in front of his troops with a finger under his nose and one arm stretched out straight, signalling his salute. Sometimes, we'd even have somebody on our side representing the Russians. We really thought Uncle Joe Stalin was a very nice man – so much for propaganda. Of course, the British side always won!

One night at the cottage, a storm blew up; a very high tide came racing up the Lune and everyone was glad to be safe in doors in front of a lovely roaring fire. The Lune was known as an extremely dangerous river and on this night it continued to prove to be the case. We suddenly heard a heavy banging on the front door, and on opening it Mr Johnson was confronted by a soldier. They stood talking for a short time and then the soldier came into the cottage.

'Hello, sorry to trouble you all,' he said.

Then Mr Johnson came in herding some half a dozen other soldiers into the room, one of whom was on a stretcher. They were all soaking wet. Mam cleared all us kids away from the fire and ushered the soldiers to get up close to it.

The soldier in charge told us they were from a group who had been putting a bridge across the river further upstream when this storm had come in, demolishing the bridge and washing some of the soldiers away. This party had been one of the search parties sent out to find the missing soldiers. The one who was injured was the only one they had found and, as the cottage was the only habitable place in their area of search, they'd come straight to us.

Making everybody comfortable in such a small space was practically impossible, but for us kids the discomfort didn't matter we were all so excited. Real soldiers, here in our home – it was a dream come true for me! What stories I could tell the gang; they would never have something as exciting as this happen to them!

One of the soldiers had brought in a large box with him, and in it were the rations they'd been supplied with for the duration of their search; they had tea, sugar and milk for their Billy Cans, plus biscuits – and, lo and behold, sandwiches - banana sandwiches. We'd never seen a banana, never mind eaten one! We kids stuffed ourselves with the wonderful sandwiches until we were fit to burst.

Mam and Mrs Johnson made pots of tea into which they could actually have sugar, something virtually unheard of; the water from the kitchen tap which had to be boiled was continuously on the go, the kettle being refilled again and again. The soldier on the stretcher was more exhausted than was first thought, and he had a damaged arm which the Sergeant attended to.

All in all, that stormy night was a wonderful adventure for me and in the morning, when a military vehicle arrived to take the soldiers away, we were all really sad.

However, it wasn't long before some other soldiers arrived.

These soldiers arrived in trucks and had been sent along with a load of wood and lots of materials required to re-build the bridge. Army trucks were quickly emptied and their contents put into the field opposite the cottage. None of the soldiers were our friends from the storm so we weren't able to talk to them, and as we went off to school, we were all puzzled as to what they intended to do.

Rushing home from school, we found they had dug a number of deep holes in the field forming a rectangular shape, and into the holes they'd poured cement and then stuck wooden uprights into them.

The following morning, the same soldiers returned but this time in a smaller truck. Once again, returning from school we discovered what the poles were for; they supported long wooden planks which had been hauled up on top, then they'd laid other planks across from one side to the other to form a floor. Still not sure what was going on, once the soldiers had left for the day, we later used this part of the building to play on.

This went on for almost a week; we'd go off to school and return to find more work completed until there, in what had been an empty field, stood a large wooden hut complete with windows, steps up to an entrance door at one end, and a roof. Internal walls had been fitted and formed three different rooms.

We then discovered it was to be used by the army for emergencies, but for as long as Mam, Lilly and I lived there it was never used, except for cattle. Up until the time the hut was erected we'd never had cattle in that particular field, though the fields around were always in use. But a short time after the hut was finished, we returned from school to find a dozen or so cows munching the high grass all round the hut.

We kids had always used the field to play in, and now we had to share it with a herd of cows. For us active children, the cows presented a wonderful opportunity to play new and more exciting games, like playing cowboys.

We all knew what cowboys did from the various films we'd seen over the years, though we didn't have horses or lassoes. The odd pop-gun or two that had lain around the cottage since Reggie was little now came into good use, and our wellies became riding boots.

Finishing school on a Friday, it was decided 'Roundup Day' would be Saturday; we cowboys - who were actually predominantly cowgirls as I was the only boy! -

couldn't wait to finish our breakfast and head outside. Being the only cowboy who knew everything about roundups, I pronounced myself as the leader or, as I liked to call it, the Roundup Chief. As it happened, it wasn't unanimous that I should be the Roundup Chief because Brenda, being the oldest, thought that she should be the Roundup Chief.

Standing in the field with cows chewing the grass around us, it was decided we'd have to wrestle each other to decide who the best leader was. Now, Brenda was not only three years older than me, she was also bigger, and, as I suddenly realised, by quite a large margin. I deliberated over what I should do. I couldn't hit her; she was only a girl.

We squared up and Lilly, nominated to start the contest, shouted, 'Go!'

Immediately, Brenda jumped on me and wrestled me down onto the grass. Thinking she had won, she released her grip on my neck and went to stand up; I pulled one of her legs and as she fell she let out a very loud scream that started the stampede.

Until that moment, the cows around us had totally ignored us, contentedly feeding themselves. Now, mooing in panic, they went racing down the field away from us. I realised that, as the yet uninitiated Roundup Chief, it was up to me to get the herd back to where they'd been.

So, yodelling loudly, which I'd learnt to do in my previous games as Tarzan, I started off after the cows with the cowgirls trundling behind me, all yelling what they thought was cowboy talk like, 'Giddy up!' and 'Yippee!'

The cows, now at the far end of the field, seeing us approaching and smacking our behinds, which served as horses, decided they were better off where they'd just come from and commenced a mad gallop with us in hot pursuit. Unfortunately, the area of field they were escaping to was now somewhat limited by the large hut occupying a substantial part of it. The pair of cows leading the stampede, who had the hut directly in front of them, in their panic from the awful creatures screaming and yelling behind them, didn't slow their pace at all; they simply went up the two steps, smashed through the door and part of the wall, and galloped into the hut.

Shocked, but still full of excitement, we followed up what was left of the steps and into the hut; one cow had stopped at the first dividing wall, the other had gone through the open door. Seeing and hearing us, the first cow went through the doorway joining the other cow. The next dividing wall had its door shut so they simply charged through it. Panicked even more, they broke the outer wall completely as they fell through onto the grass.

It was at this point that we stopped being cowboys; in fact, we stopped being anything other than very frightened children. It had taken only three or four minutes of playing our game to utterly destroy the army's lovely hut.

Out of the house ran Mr and Mrs Johnson; they stood staring, with horrified looks written all over their faces, at us standing in the newly formed opening in the hut.

'Get out of there!' screamed Mrs Johnson. 'Get into the house right now!'

Crying loudly in obvious terror, we all jumped down and trooped into the house to await our punishment.

Lined up in the living room around the table, we were not allowed to sit down as Mr Johnson sat at the head, staring at us one after the other. Looking at me, I suppose because I was still holding the pop-gun, his eyes bore into mine.

'What were you doing with that?' his stern voice asked as he nodded to the gun.

I looked around at the girls and realised Brenda had obviously dropped her gun whilst Lilly and Lottie looked on innocently; sneaky girls, I thought bitterly.

'I'm waiting,' said Mr Johnson grimly.

'Playing cowboys,' I answered.

'So you were chasing the cows,' he accused.

'No, Brenda screamed.'

'He pulled me over!' Brenda shouted, defending herself.

'Yes, but she pulled me over first,' I said in return.

'It was his fault,' said Lottie. 'He was the Roundup Chief.'

'No it wasn't,' piped up Lilly in her little voice. 'Brenda said she was the Roundup Chief.'

For the first time in my life, I was proud of my little sister; she was actually sticking up for me. Mr Johnson took Mrs Johnson into the kitchen and we could hear them talking very quietly. A few minutes later they came back in.

'You know we'll be in big trouble with the army,' he said. 'We'll also be in trouble with the farmer if he finds out; we could even be thrown out of this cottage.' Looking at me and then Lilly, he added, 'I'll be telling your Mam about you two; she'll decide what to do with you both.'

Turning to Brenda and Lottie, he continued in his stern voice, 'You two will stay in your room; you won't play outside. You will still go to school but will spend the rest of your time in your room. Now all of you, you are to forget all about this and don't tell anyone. I'll tell the farmer something must have frightened his cows, and he can tell the army.'

When Mam arrived home, we didn't just get the same punishment. Lilly got a smack and I got a heck of a beating.

Whether it was due to this escapade or whether, as Mam said, she needed to be nearer her work, it wasn't long before we moved back into Lancaster proper, into No 2, Alfred Street.

Our new abode on Alfred Street was a small terraced house, in which we had one room. It was the biggest room in the house, but small nevertheless. An elderly lady was our landlady and a girl of about eighteen called Frances lived with her. In our room we had a large double bed, in which Mam and Lilly slept, whilst I slept on a settee. A table with chairs and a small sideboard completed the furniture. We shared a bathroom, complete with toilet, with the landlady and Frances. The house was, as Mam said, much closer to her work at the Railway Station and also, as I later found out, much nearer her new man friend. We had been tightly packed together in the house in Aldcliffe, but eating, sleeping and just living in one room made me miss the cottage and the Johnsons.

After a week or two of becoming accustomed to our new billet, I just accepted it and got back into the old routine with my previous pals, plus some new ones who lived around Alfred Street. Once again, Williams Park was close by as was the town itself, then there was the castle, whose grounds were the perfect play area for being knights or just playing hide and seek amongst the gravestones of long dead warriors. Best of all, the source of my favourite food, apples, was now back within easy reach. It wasn't long before I soon forgot all about Aldcliffe.

Lilly and I were still at Dallas Road and it was there I became friends with a boy who had only recently joined the school. James lived with his dad on the other side of the Lune over the Skerton Bridge. Like me, he had a love of comics, not so much the funny ones like *The Beano*, but *The Champion*, *Adventure* and *Hotspur*, which contained no pictures other than an artist's impression of the hero or, on the very odd occasion, the heroine. During the war years there was plenty of scope for writing about heroes, but space was very limited as there was a great shortage of paper; most comics consisted of no more than four or five double-sided pages. Swapping comics with James was a weekly routine; we carried them around everywhere we went, looking for further swaps.

One day James said, 'My dad's got a collection of *Beanos* and *Dandys* from before the war; he said we can go and look at them if we want to.'

Did I want to? I couldn't wait to get to his house! James lived in an old Victorian building with a park opposite, just grass and trees and walkways. The house was, in fact, just two or three rooms of the building, but as far as we were concerned it was his house.

Meeting his dad, I liked him from start; he gave us both a glass of Dandelion and Burdock, also known as pop, then he brought out the comics, at least twenty or so and amazingly thick. Each comic must have had more than twenty pages filled with characters on both sides of the page; it was fantastic! What a day we had reading them all, laughing uncontrollably for hours.

Later on, when it was time for me to make my way home, James said, 'Want to go eeling tomorrow?'

'What's eeling?' I asked curiously.

'We go in the river and catch eels.'

Remembering how I used to go looking for fish with Reggie, I assumed we must use some kind of nets. 'But how do we put the nets out?' I asked.

He looked puzzled. 'We don't use nets, we use spears.'

His dad, who had been listening, laughed. 'You put a fork on the end of a brush handle,' he said and, leaving the room, came back with the spears. As he said, they were just two brush poles with forks pushed into them.

'Tide's out about 3 o'clock tomorrow afternoon,' his dad said. 'Come over and you and James can go and catch our dinner.'

From my previous espionages at Aldcliffe, I knew that when the tide was out the river was very low indeed; hence being able to get into the gullies and walk down to check the nets with Reggie, but I hadn't even thought about it here at Skerton.

The next day, meeting James at the bridge and looking down into the river, the water was very shallow and as clear as crystal. I could see the numerous boulders sitting on the bottom. James had brought a deep bucket with him for our catch. He explained the game, which is how I saw it.

'We go down those steps,' he said, pointing to nine or ten steps leading down into the river near where we were standing. 'Course, we leave our shoes half-way down,' he continued. 'When we get into the water, we walk out towards the middle and start turning some of those big stones over.'

I'd been wondering how we were going to spear the eels, as I knew they were very fast creatures and we'd have a heck of a job to catch one, let alone spear one with just a fork in the end of a pole.

James explained, 'On sunny days like this, the eels find a big stone and get under it and go to sleep; that's when we stick 'em.'

I couldn't wait to start! Holding my spear like a Zulu warrior and feeling very excited as well as a bit scared, we headed towards the steps.

We had both turned over two or three big rocks when quite a big eel shot out from under the next one I turned over. The fearless Zulu warrior staggered back in shock and fell down into the river. Soaked, I stood up, retrieving my spear to find James almost falling over himself with laughter. Fortunately, in those days, boys up to the age of fourteen or fifteen always wore short pants, so it wasn't so bad.

We continued our search and after turning over another half a dozen rocks, James stabbed down quickly and lifted his spear with an eel wriggling on the end of it; it was about 18 inches long and looked like a big snake. He quickly held it on the fork with his other hand and waded back to the steps where we'd left the bucket and dropped the eel in.

About five minutes later, he caught another one. I was getting a bit frustrated at my lack of success - and then it happened.

Turning over a rather large rock, there was an eel lying there; it must have been very sleepy because I managed to spear it before it shot off.

'Yes! Yes! I've got one!' I cried, as I copied what James had done and waded to the steps to drop the eel into the bucket.

It was one of the most exciting moments of my life up to then, made even better because my eel was at least a foot longer than either of James's. Having now broken my duck, between us we caught another three and returned triumphantly to James's house.

His dad was very pleased. 'Well done!' he said. 'You boys have had a good day's catch. Billy, how did you enjoy it?'

'It was great, thank you.'

'James, go and find a pair of your pants for Billy, whilst I dry his; they're soaking.'

I'd been so exhilarated I'd forgotten all about my wet pants, which had barely dried on the walk home.

James and I watched as his dad prepared the eels with a sharp knife; he cut off the heads of the still live eels, then running the knife from where the head used to be along the whole length of the body, he slit the skin down to the tail and peeled the skin off, leaving a pink-coloured body. I was fascinated; it was gruesome, but after the abattoir scenes I'd seen, it didn't bother me at all.

He then cut it up into chunks, put them all in a pan with some kind of oil, fat and salt, and fried them. When we were used to getting so little food, I wouldn't have cared what they tasted like, but the plateful he gave me was absolutely delicious.

ELEVEN

Mam still used to spend a lot of time away from our new billet in Alfred Street, still working day and night at the station, she would tell us. It never bothered me in the least; I was free to do whatever I wanted, just so long as she fed me and Lilly.

As we never got much anyway, due to the rationing, I was back to scrumping; there was nothing I liked better after school than to raid somebody's orchard. I'd now begun to take a bag with me and I'd fill it full with apples or pears, sometimes plums, and then return to Alfred Street, lie stretched out on my settee bed, pile my comics alongside me and read for hours whilst munching apples. Sometimes, when Mam wasn't home, I'd carry on reading by the light of a candle until I fell asleep. How I didn't set the house on fire, I'll never know!

I continued to spend a lot of time, when not in school, bunking into the swimming baths. Living in Alfred Street, I was much nearer to them now, and some of my new friends who lived nearby used to come with me. On the odd occasion, Mam would actually give me the sixpence entrance fee, but I never paid; I put the money to better use at the bakery. Even after spending some of it there, I still had pennies left over; brilliant!

Another new friend, George, wasn't an evacuee, but a true Lancastrian; he always got the fee for the baths from his parents but was always too scared to bunk in, even though I showed him how it was done. George was the leader of his little gang when I arrived in Alfred Street, probably because he was the biggest and most of his gang were younger and smaller and didn't really know about fighting. I was about the same size as him and therefore felt I couldn't possibly take orders from anyone or join in some of the childish games like tag and hide and seek; there were far better things to do. So I challenged him to a wrestling match with the winner becoming the gang leader. Urged on by the rest of the gang, he reluctantly agreed; I won. I happily became leader of the gang and, though disappointed, George accepted it and we remained friends.

Once again, Williams Park was put back in use, to the annoyance and complete frustration of the park keeper. The younger members were also introduced to the joys of raiding orchards or back gardens and tying long lengths of string across the narrow streets in the area to two opposing door knobs, knocking on both doors at the same time and then hiding, watching the result whilst stifling laughter.

Although Mam was out a lot, Frances, the girl who lived with us, was very kind to us; she was a very pretty, dark-haired girl who worked as an usherette in a local cinema named the Cozy, situated in William Square.

The Square was located right in the middle of Lancaster with houses on two sides; the Town Hall at one end and the cinema facing the Town Hall at the other end. The whole middle of the Square was given over to lawns and flower gardens, with gravelled paths and bench seating; a Victorian pillared wall surrounded it and it was another ideal play area.

Once a week, when she was on duty, Frances would take Lilly and me to the Cozy; she would sneak us in and put us in seats in the dark, where we wouldn't be noticed. During the film, she would slip us a choc ice, the best treat you could possibly have. Sometimes, when she came back on nights she hadn't taken us with her, she would bring choc ices home. It was at the Cozy that I saw *The Wizard of Oz, Robin Hood, Pinocchio, Snow White* and others. I also saw *Pathé News*; it was always about the on-going war and, though a lot of it was beyond me, I learnt a great deal about battles won and lost. I can still hear the perfect Oxford English tones of the news commentator to this very day.

Mam was still working and courting; we overheard Mam's conversation with the lady who owned the house that she'd met somebody from the Railway named Billy Bell. Unlike 'Uncle' Fred, she never took us to meet him; it didn't concern us at all. On the contrary, it was fine with us as it kept her busy and she was never there to stop me doing the things I loved, and which she would most certainly frown upon.

With the Alfred Street Gang, we had taken to playing up at the Lancaster Canal; fortunately, most of us could swim by now. We had discovered a pile of railway sleepers stored on the canal banks, which we turned into rafts, which would then become pirate ships or Indian canoes. They were extremely heavy, but with a lot of pushing and pulling we would manage to launch them off the bank and into the water.

Having taken off shoes and clothes, except short pants, we would climb aboard and, using lumps of wood as makeshift paddles, we would paddle around.

As often as not, some of us would fall in and trying to get back aboard would tip the sleeper over, so that anyone left on board would fall in and have to swim to the bank. It was then a mad scramble out of the water to launch another sleeper to be able to continue with our game. The games only finished when an adult or a barge came into sight. With clothes under an arm and wet pants dripping, we would run as fast as we could away from the canal banks.

My discovery that very large barges used the waterway to transport coal and all other kinds of things up and down the whole country mesmerised me, although I really couldn't understand how the locks worked. I was lucky to make friends with some of the barge men who would let me climb aboard and give me a ride for a mile or so along the canal. Imagine my delight when, on one occasion, one of the men asked me if I wanted to lead one of the great shire horses which pulled the barges along. I had a few spare apples in my windcheater pocket from scrumping the day before, so offered one to the towering horse. He duly ate it and then happily let me hold the harness, leading him along the bank for about half a mile.

Next door to the house we lived in on Alfred Street, lived a teenage lad called Jack. One day he asked me if I wanted to go to a fishing tournament with him. I thought he meant on the Lune, but it was actually on a stretch of canal some miles along from where the gang and I played. We had to get the bus, but Jack paid my fare so I didn't mind. All I had to do was carry his fishing bucket, which was really heavy, Jack carried bottles of water and some sandwiches for both of us.

When we arrived at the finishing spot, Jack introduced us to some men. 'This is Billy; he's here to make sure I win!'

Everybody laughed and one man ruffled my hair. 'Good luck!' he laughed.

I had no idea what they were laughing at or what this was all about.

Jack was allocated a section of the canal, where he sat on a small folding stool he'd brought with him; I had to stand. Jack explained my job was to delve into the bucket and hand him the bait. On the bank of the canal were rings used to tie up the barges; Jack attached his rod to the ring and then dangled it in the water. All the rest of the group did the same and then a man gave the order to start fishing.

For the first few minutes nothing happened and I was starting to get bored, thinking fishing really wasn't much fun. It was also cold, especially as it was an autumn day and I just had short pants, ankle socks, a shirt and my good old windcheater on. I just kept eyeing up the sandwiches and couldn't wait to eat one.

Suddenly, movement from further along the bank caught everyone's attention and one the competitors reeled in a big, wriggling fish. I was suddenly very interested and it wasn't long before Jack and the others were shouting out that they had 'bites', and in no time things got really busy. Jack yelled at me to open up the big net whilst he unhooked the fish from his rod and dropped it in.

Having decided he'd found the right bait to use, Jack kept hauling fish in; some tiny, others rather large. Stopping only for lunch and to finally devour the egg sandwich I'd stared at all morning, we quickly resumed at the sound of the whistle from the man in charge. Jack's bucket was filling up and I was certain we were going to win the contest and, boy, would we have a big feast with all the fish we had to eat!

At the final whistle, all the men stopped and reeled in their lines. One by one they had their buckets weighed, but then I watched in horror as they began to throw their catch back into the canal.

'What are they doing?' I whispered to Jack.

'Putting it back.' He saw my confused face. 'We can't keep the fish, they've all gotta go back in the canal; it's the rules.'

At that moment, I decided I had far better things to do than help Jack in a fishing contest, especially if I wouldn't even get one fish to eat at the end of it!

Woolworths, in Lancaster town centre, with its long aisles full of toys, books, comics and, in one area, sweets, was like a magnet to me and my gang. Of course, we never had any money, and even if we had, you needed coupons out of the ration books to buy any sweets or chocolate, but one of the gang was an expert at removing sweets from the open counter. My job, together with other gang members, was to keep the girl behind the counter busy by asking her questions, some of them cheeky and even rude. In no time, our thief would have pocketed a couple of handfuls and abruptly depart, at which point we followed and met at a suitable hidden spot to share out our spoils.

On only one occasion did I steal anything from Woollies; it was a comic, but no ordinary one. It was an American one, nothing at all like our *Beano*. The Marvel comic was much thicker and its hero was Captain Marvel. His arch enemy was Doctor Sivana, an evil scientist who wanted to rule the universe. A lad at school had said it was fantastic, the best he'd ever read, so I just had to have one. We knew of other American comics, one of whose heroes was Superman, but they were DC Comics and virtually unobtainable; they certainly weren't displayed and sold in Woollies.

One day, on a lone trip to the great store, there they were; a whole pile of Marvel comics on the main counter. Usually, it was the job of the paper shop to sell comics; I'd never, ever seen them before in Woollies. When a customer on the other side of the counter distracted the girl's attention, one of the Marvel comics disappeared into my windcheater; I just couldn't resist it. Once back outside, I quickly sped up my pace and headed for home.

My only other crime, apart from scrumping and thieving from the school, was to take a small pocket book from a model shop on the outskirts of the town. I'd been introduced to train spotting by a lad from school and told I could buy a book with all the numbers of trains, and all the names of the world famous engines which ran up and down the country in it. Buying the book was out of the question, so I stole it, then spent my time writing the numbers down into my small pocket book, then all I had to do was cross them out as I saw them again.

My purloined book gave me hours of pleasure as I would sit by myself on the side of the main LMS line on the outskirts of Lancaster, waving to the drivers of the many trains passing by and hurriedly crossing off the names and numbers.

Mam was now working at Heysham Port, not far from Morecambe where Lily and I had been billeted. She now spent even less time at Alfred Street; she explained that this was to make it easier for her to do her new job as she didn't have to travel back and forth every day. I'd gotten used to her not being around very much and, as far as Lilly was concerned, Frances had become like a sister to her and liked nothing better than to play with her. As for me, it was the same as it had always been in Lancaster: school, swimming at the baths, scrumping, my gang and adventures.

1945, for a myriad of reasons, was so, so different. I was still bunking into one of the cinemas in town and being taken to another one by Frances, and, on a weekend when Mam was home, I was taken to yet another picture house. When Lilly and I went with Mam, it was so much better because Mam now had our ration books, so she was able to buy our quarter of sweets for the week and we would sit watching films, sucking happily on pear drops on or the occasional piece of chocolate. Pathé News was always shown before the start of the main film.

The war was going very well for us and I was now fully aware of it and able to appreciate just what we were achieving. The downside was the reporting of the Nazi death camps and the horrors of Belsen; we were to learn later of even worse camps and atrocities committed. I was now at the age of realising what had been done to so many people, but at the same time not completely comprehending why.

For some time, even though we saw each other in school, most days Peter, Brian and Thomas had lost touch with me. I suppose it happened because of my friendship with my new gang when I moved to Alfred Street; now, for no particular reason we got together again. Peter told me during playtime that Brian and he had decided to build a go-cart and Thomas would be helping; was I interested too? I certainly was, as they were being allowed to build it at Brian's house and Brian's mam had always been very generous with cakes and biscuits, even the odd sweet!

They'd decided to start the build on the coming weekend. Each of the boys had arranged to find suitable wood, nails and rope, and I was set the task to find some wheels. The wheels we needed were the same as those on baby prams and I would look at every pram I saw, wondering if it would be possible to borrow one. Fortunately, that wasn't necessary, as not too far from Williams Park was a council dumping ground; when I went there to search for wheels, lo and behold, there was a battered old pram. It was like finding a pot of gold.

I could feel everyone staring at me as I pushed the wreck of a pram, squeaking and grinding, up to Brian's house. His mam wasn't best pleased, her house being in a well-to-do neighbourhood, and for the neighbours to see the ramshackle pram parked on her pathway just would not do. We had no option but to get the tatty wheels off there and then. It certainly wasn't an easy job as some of the screws holding the two bars secured to the bottom of the pram were rusty; try as we might, we kids just couldn't budge them.

'We'll have to wait until Dad gets home,' Brian said, and went in to tell his Mam, but that pleased her even less.

Coming out of the house she said, 'OK, here's what you boys do, you wheel your future chariot down the road and round the block and you keep going round the block until your dad comes home. I don't want to see that thing back outside my house.'

It was going to be hours before he came home, so we wheeled it down the road and sat on the kerbside guarding our precious carriage until he walked past on his way from work.

'Dad! Dad!' Brian leapt up as he saw him. 'We need to get the wheels off this to make our go-cart.' Brian explained everything and his dad laughed.

'Come on then, boys, let's get to it,' he said. He had the wheels off in no time and then asked, 'So then, what's the plan?'

'We've now got to make the cart itself,' Brian said. The others had got an old wooden crate and some small planks of wood, which Thomas and Peter held up.

'So, who's doing the sawing?' his dad asked. We all looked at each other in consternation; none of us had ever sawed anything before.

His dad was grinning now. 'Well, the three of you have got another job anyway; you've to get rid of the wheel-less pram now or there'll be no cart. That's your mam's orders!' he said, looking at Brian.

'Where do we take it?' I asked innocently.

'Back where you got it.'

'But it's got no wheels so we can't push it,' pointed out Peter.

'Well, I never. Looks like you four will have to carry it then.'

It was a long way to the dump; easy enough when I had pushed it, but now we had to stop every few yards to rest it took ages, and the remarks from other kids we met on the way didn't help. Four very tired, small boys returned hours later to Brian's house, by which time it was time to go home.

After school the next day we all met up again at Brian's house and were surprised to find Brian's dad had cut the wood to the right lengths for us. He had even cut out the side of the box which was to be our seat. Brian's mam said he'd done it all the night before for us, as he didn't want the job of carting us all off to the infirmary when we'd cut off an arm or a leg with a saw.

A pile of nails and a couple of hammers that he'd left for us were rigorously put to use and the only resulting injuries were hammered thumbs and fingers and the odd scratch of a rusty nail. Nailing the crate to the largest length of wood was so easy we thought we were master builders, but when it came to fixing the frail set of wheels to the plank so that they could be steered, our engineering skills were sadly lacking. After a resounding number of arguments as to how to do it, Brian's mother came out and solved the problem for us.

'Wait for Brian's dad to come home,' she ordered. 'And stop that shouting!'

Sure enough, his dad solved the problem in an instant. Taking the half-made cart, he picked up a length of wood, which we had been wondering about, and fixed it between the two wheels by hammering nails alongside the wheels and then bending them over, making them a tight fit. Then, turning the cart over again, he hammered a very big nail through the centre of the main plank into the wood below, before bending that nail where it fitted between the front wheels; they would now swivel.

Brian stood there, proud as punch; we had to admit that his dad was a genius, but when he had gone the other two said that of course their dads would have done just the same.

Two ends of rope tied round the wood holding the wheels on each side of the plank allowed us to steer quite well, but another piece of wood nailed to the outside of the crate was a total disaster. It was supposed to be the brake and break it did, on the first hill we went down.

Brian, having claimed his rights to the first drive, went down at a good rate of knots, feet up on the plank. Upon reaching the bottom he applied the brake, which immediately broke in half. Luckily, he had on a good pair of boots which he dug hard into the ground as he screamed and skidded to a halt. I was very glad it wasn't me on the first ride because my pumps were already pretty ruined.

Thereafter, I didn't take my rides on such steep hills as my pumps wouldn't have stood the strain. I never explained to the gang that they were the only shoes I had; I was too embarrassed.

Our chariot lasted about a week, surprising really, as our joinery skills left quite a lot to be desired. We had carried out remedial repairs on at least three different occasions over the six or seven days, but eventually the cart gave up the ghost after Peter collided with a lamppost which, as well as breaking the main plank, also buckled the front wheels.

We went back to the tip where we spent hours looking for replacements but, finding none, we gave up. The novelty was over.

As it happened, a week or so later I was wishing I still had it, as Mam was given a pair of clogs for me. They were wonderful; slip on, all leather, with a steel strip round the front. Best of all, on the soles they had two strips of steel on either side like a pair of railway lines. They would have been wonderful riding on the chariot, bringing it to a halt on the steepest hill with a shower of sparks bursting from my clogs.

Brian and the rest of the gang played football a lot; they had football boots bought by their mams and dads. I would have given my right arm for a pair as I loved to play football. When I had only a pair of pumps to wear, I'd been able to play all the time, usually with a friend's ball in the street or in the park. Not so with steel toe-capped train-track clogs; wonderful as they were for sliding, making a lot noise and kicking stones, as football footwear they were useless. If you ran too fast, one or the other would fall off, and if you managed to kick the ball, the clog would usually fly away with it. Probably worst of all, if, by some misfortune, you missed the ball and kicked a lad instead, he'd probably be a hospital case. Needless to say, I rarely had a game.

Cricket was a different game altogether. Played on a grass playing-field, which the school had access to, I was able to play in my bare feet to field, bowl and bat. Our master, who would take us to play, wasn't at all sure that this was in the true spirit of the game and suggested I should wear some suitable footwear; clogs, naturally, weren't deemed suitable. Once again, being too embarrassed to tell him I had nothing else to wear, I said I much preferred to play in bare feet. I'm sure he didn't believe me, but allowed me to play anyway. I became good at bowling, average at batting and useless at fielding; so much so that after one of the lads 'skied' the ball, it began its drop right above me. I stood with my arms stretched upwards as the corky dropped rapidly towards me.

'Catch it, Billy!' I heard my team mates shout, and I did. Right in my eye! I'd forgotten to cup my hands together. For some time after, I had the most beautifully colossal shiner; it put me off ever playing cricket again.

Young as we were, us lads suddenly began to take an interest in girls and, surprisingly, the girls, or at least some of them, seemed to be interested in us too. Lilly didn't seem to understand that though we had started to talk to girls in school, none of us boys ever had much to say to her. She always told Mam and Mam told me I had to play with her more.

'No way!' I said, outraged at the thought. 'She's annoying.'

'Billy, the odd chat now and again with your sister won't hurt you,' she insisted. I made sure they were very odd chats indeed.

It all began when Paul, an older boy of thirteen or fourteen, befriended me after finding out that I went fishing with Jack; he was a keen fisherman and always wanted to talk to me about fishing. Then, one day after school, Paul said he was taking his new girlfriend to get her bus from the main bus station as she lived out of town.

'Do you wanna come too?' Paul asked me.

'Yeah, why not,' I said, and I believe I fell in love.

She was thirteen, she wore glasses and she was beautiful; to top it all, she was really nice to this scruffy little boy that her new boyfriend had brought along. We waited for her bus and they talked and even let me join in. We made the trip to the bus station most days and it got to the point where I couldn't wait for school to finish, just to see her. It lasted a couple of weeks and then it was gone.

From this point on, my thoughts towards girls took a completely new tack. When one of the gang suggested that we let a couple of girls, who'd been watching us play Reallio on a few occasions, I readily agreed. Reallio was a game of hide and seek, where we always used a lamppost as the base. One lad was always in charge of the base and all the rest would have to find somewhere to hide. The lamppost guardian would then set out to find everyone's hiding place, and when he found one he'd then shout 'Reallio!', and both would race back to the lamppost. The one found would have to reach the lamppost first, else they would have to become the guardian.

We decided to alter the rules, as boys could always outrun the girls, so this advantage resulted in a cunning plan. The rules stayed the same for the boys, but if the guardian was a boy and he found one of the girls and they raced back together, as he was sure to win, the girl had to allow him to kiss her. She would then have to wait at the post until everyone else was found; if she'd been the first to be found, she would be allowed to be the guardian. Whenever she found one of the lads' hiding places, she would always be beaten back to the post, therefore all the lads would be allowed to kiss her. If the second girl beat the first girl back to the lamppost and shouted 'Reallio', she would then become the guardian.

The result of this wonderful game was that for most of the time the two girls were guardians and were always being beaten by the lads in the race, resulting in us boys always getting kisses. Bizarrely, it appeared to me that the girls enjoyed it even more than we did; in fact, I'm sure they made sure they were always beaten!

TWELVE

By now, our army, together with the allies, were well on the way to winning the war and us kids worshipped the British Tommy, the Royal Navy and our Spitfire and Hurricane heroes. We were beating Herr Hitler and saving the world.

In school, the older boys and girls seemed to spend all their time talking about it, saying what they had heard on the news or read in their dads' newspapers. We younger ones would catch a few snippets of their conversations and then become the victorious Tommies, knocking the stuffing out of the Jerries. There was always the odd fight amongst ourselves from those who had to be the Jerries, but we made sure the British always won.

Now I was ten years old, nearly eleven, I was allowed by the school to take part in other sports. My favourite was cross country running, and I became good at it. At Dallas Road, fortunately for me, they supplied us with the gym kit to do the cross country, as I would never have been able to take part otherwise. I loved running through fields of mud, wading through slimy ditches and streams, climbing hills and arriving back at school so filthy nobody recognised each other. Then, under the supervision of the school nurse or matron, we would have to strip and wash ourselves clean in the bathroom whilst trying to hide our privates; the elderly matrons always seemed amused at our shyness.

Mam was still staying away more and more, and Lilly and I assumed she was doing lots of night shifts. Mam was away again one night when we were woken in the morning by loud shouting and cheering.

Lily looked nervously at me just as the old lady who owned the house banged on our door and shouted, 'It's over!' She saw our confused faces and, with a grin spreading on her face, shouted again, 'The war! It's over! We've beaten those bloody Jerries!'

The war was finally over, not that you would have noticed any change here in Alfred Street. As far as us kids were concerned, everything stayed the same. When we went to the cinema with Mam or Frances, we saw on Pathé News that the world was celebrating with towns and cities throughout Britain decked out with flags and bunting, and streets were lined with tables covered with all kinds of goodies. Not in Lancaster. Alfred Street stayed just as it had always been, dull and unexciting, and, as far as I was concerned, so did the rest of the city.

It was several months later, after victory over Japan was declared, that Lancaster finally arranged celebrations with a bonfire and fireworks display in a field on the far side of Skerton bridge, opposite the houses where my old friend James and his dad lived.

Mam said neither Lilly nor I could go on our own as it wouldn't be on until late, and she wouldn't be going as she would be out anyway. Frances said she would have taken us, but she had to work. I had to find another way to go.

James, who I hadn't seem for some time, mainly because I preferred playing with my gang, especially the girls, was quite surprised when I suggested I had some comics and would he like to do some swaps? A couple of days later, I took my comics with me to school and suggested I take them over to his house; I pretended to be surprised that there was to be a fireworks display right outside his home.

'Would I be able to stay and watch?' I asked him, casually.

'It'll be late before it's finished; if your mam lets you, you could stay at my house,' James suggested.

Yes! It was working out exactly as I had expected but I knew Mam wouldn't believe me. I told him what a great idea it was and could he come to my house after school and tell my mam? He did, and Mam reluctantly agreed. Luckily, she didn't insist Lilly came with us, as neither she nor Frances would be at home to look after her, but that wasn't my problem.

James's dad seemed pleased that we were friends again and even let me eat tea with them; I couldn't believe I was sitting at the dinner table eating food with my friend and his mam and dad. After tea, we spent a long time swapping our comics.

'Look!' James said looking out of his window, 'I think they're about to light the bonfire!'

People had been taking stuff to build up the bonfire for days and you could see pieces of old furniture and clothing amongst the huge pile. Some people had made models of Hitler and Tojo out of the clothes and they were piled as near as possible to the top. We couldn't see where the fireworks were going to be, but his dad said they were definitely there.

'I know we can all see the fireworks from here, but why don't we go and join the crowds, it'll be much more exciting,' James's dad suggested to my delight.

James and I hurriedly left the house and joined the growing crowd. We spotted some of the lads from school and joined them, trying to get as near to the bonfire as we could. We squeezed our way right to the front and found ourselves in amongst a large group of Land Army Girls; they were all still wearing their uniforms of baggy pants tucked into long socks and boots and a green shirt. I looked around for Olive Johnson, but she wasn't with them.

With a loud 'Whoosh' the bonfire roared to life and fireworks exploded in the warm night sky; everyone began to cheer and clap, and there was excitement and happiness on every face that I could see.

Someone had brought along an old squeeze box and another had a drum, and people began to sing the good old war songs, 'It's a long way to Tipperary' and 'Pack up your Troubles'. The Land Girls formed a circle, holding hands by the fire, and began to dance to the music. Everyone cheered and then began cheering even louder as the girls dropped their hands and began to take off their clothes, still dancing and singing. Loud whistling and cheering from men in the crowd really urged them on. I was astounded. I couldn't take my eyes off them as they danced in their underwear. James looked aghast at me, then looked up at his dad, who seemed to be having a fine old time.

Never having seen so many undressed grown-up girls before, it all came as quite a surprise to me; they were all the same but all rather different too, and as I watched them, I realised I was enjoying it. That was when I started to grow up.

Early on, a farmer had turned up on a tractor with several sacks of newly picked potatoes which they piled round the perimeter of the fire. Now cooked, everyone was told to help themselves to the spuds; James's dad made sure he got us the best he could get and, although they were delicious, not having a spoon or fork, they were a bit hot on our fingers.

As the Land Girls finally broke their circle and began to disperse into the crowds, mothers started to move their children away.

'That's enough now, boys,' James's mother said. 'Come now, back into the house.'

As we lay tucked up in bed that night, James and I talked for hours about the bonfire and the fireworks and, upon hearing his dad snoring loudly next door, we then whispered our thoughts on the Land Girls. We each had chosen the ones we thought were the prettiest and pointed out some of the various features of their bodies. We were hard pressed to suppress our laughter; young as we were, we both decided we preferred big girls to little girls, though neither of us actually knew why.

Even though the war was now over, I never gave a single thought that we would eventually go back to Liverpool, so it was quite a surprise when Mam said she was going there to see some of my aunts and uncles.

'But why?' I asked her, perplexed.

'To see where we're going to live again, Billy,' she replied.

I wasn't sure I liked the idea, but it was soon dismissed from my mind as it was getting close to Guy Fawkes' night.

November 5th had always been a must-do celebration in Lancaster, and Lilly and I had enjoyed every one in the four years we had lived there. The days leading up to the big night were spent finding ways to make money with which we could buy fireworks. Brian and Peter had made Guy Fawkes out of old clothing supplied by their mothers, although I'm sure some of it was better than the clothes I wore and had worn for some time.

Standing outside a pub or on the corner of a street we would call out, 'A penny for the Guy,' but there was far too much competition from other kids; we had to come up with a better plan.

Woolworths in Penny Street had a counter full of fireworks and, after a gang meeting, it was decided, as I was the smallest, that it would be me who would try and take a few fireworks from the display. Whether the young girl behind the counter remembered me I didn't know, but my raid was a complete disaster. I'd no sooner reached for a brightly coloured banger, small enough to fit in my pocket, when, with a loud yell, the girl shot from behind the counter. Momentarily paralysed with fright and knowing that I was now in terrible danger, I took off like one of the rockets I'd been about to take. She was a good runner and might have caught me had I not, whilst legging it, taken the banger out of my pocket and threw it back over my head towards her; as I hoped, she stopped to pick it up. I made it.

The previous year had been a great Bonfire Night. I'd been with my gang and we'd been loaned a pushchair by Mrs Clark, friends of Brian's family; and Mr Clark had given us a devil's mask. One of the gang had been a very small boy called Robbie and he agreed to become our Guy. We sat him in the pushchair with an old coat over him, the mask on his face, an old woolly hat stuck on his head and some gloves on his hands. On threats of terrible torture if he moved a muscle or said a word we pushed him door to door asking for, 'A penny for the Guy.'

As the war was still on at that point, the streets at night were always in darkness, even though Lancaster had been bypassed by the Jerries; this meant nobody realised that our Guy was real. It was a great success; almost every house dropped a coin or two into our collection tin. We were even congratulated by some for having such a great Guy. We bought ourselves fireworks, lots of fireworks, and had money left over for cinder toffee and parched peas, neither of which was rationed.

This year, that wasn't going to be possible. I couldn't go to the bonfire with nothing and I knew Peter and Thomas would have some fireworks to take, so I'd have to take some apples instead.

My target was a large house with a large garden which had a number of apple trees, and it wasn't very far from the field where the bonfire was to be.

As I was just about to leave our house on Alfred Street, Lilly started crying.

'I want to come with you,' she sobbed.

'No, you're staying here.'

'But no-one's here and I don't want to stay on me own,' she said between tears.

'The old lady's downstairs; you're not on your own,' I pointed out.

'I'm gonna tell Mam when she gets back from Liverpool!' she started to shout, but I wasn't at all surprised the tears suddenly stopped when I told her I'd bring her back some cinder toffee, possibly some chestnuts and definitely some apples.

It was very dark and extremely cold when I left the house. Zipping up my windcheater, I headed off in the direction of my target. Peter and Brian were waiting in the lane alongside the house, talking in whispers with their hands buried deep in their pockets to keep warm.

We decided on a plan of action, and the pitch black of the November night would be a great asset to us. I climbed up over the garden wall and then up a tree I'd singled out when surveying the garden earlier. Peter and Brian were to keep watch, piercing eyes scouring the darkness for movement. When safely up the tree, I began to reach for the gloriously large apples I could just about see in the darkness. Suddenly, I was startled by a burst of light. Heck, they'd lit the bonfire early!

After a couple of minutes, sure that nobody had come out of the house, I continued to collect the apples. The light from the bonfire, though a field away, was so bright that I could now see the apples as clear as day. Stuffing the biggest and best ones into my windcheater until it could take no more, I was about to climb back down when the kitchen door opened and there, silhouetted in the light from behind her, stood a lady. I froze. She closed the door as quickly as she had opened it, to stop any further light showing.

I thought that was pretty funny as in Liverpool the lights were never ever shown in case the Jerries dropped a bomb on you. Up here, they'd never even heard a plane, never mind a bomb exploding; anyway, there was a massive bonfire just across the field, and any Jerry who couldn't see that surely shouldn't be flying the plane in the first place!

The lady had stayed outside; she'd seen Peter and Thomas in the light before closing the door.

'Hello lads,' she said, walking over to them. 'Going to the bonfire?'

'Er, yes,' answered Peter, uneasily.

'Got your fireworks, have you?' she went on. 'Bet you'll be glad to get there and warm up.'

'Oh heck!' I thought again. 'I can't move and she's going to talk all night! Not only that, she's dead right about the cold; I'm freezing up here.'

'I'll tell you what, boys, how would you like some apples?'

I saw Peter look at Thomas. 'Yes, please,' they said in unison.

'They're only drops,' she said, walking below me and picking up four apples off the ground. 'But you'll enjoy them, I'm sure.'

Up the tree I was trying very hard not to laugh, as I had about twenty of her biggest and best apples in my jacket. 'Oh yes,' I thought cheekily, 'We will definitely enjoy them!'

After passing the apples to the lads, the old lady finally went in out of the cold. Laden with my goodies, I climbed back down the tree and over the wall and legged it away with the other two, laughing all the way to the bonfire. Both Peter and Thomas agreed that twenty apples was a darn sight better than a few fireworks.

Six Land Girls, who worked at a nearby farm, had come down to see the bonfire. At the same time, some Yanks billeted in Lancaster had also come to join the fun; they'd brought bottles of beer and we watched as they talked to the Land Girls and shared their drinks. I tried to find somebody with cinder toffee, hoping to swap some apples for it, but nobody had any.

We soon got bored and went off up the field to set off Peter and Thomas's fireworks and play a game of soldiers. I was a Tommy and they were only Jerries, so I won.

Hearing loud cheers and shrieks of laughter from the bonfire, we raced back down the field; the Land Girls, lit up by the flames from the fire, were dancing around it. As they'd done at the end of war celebrations, they had taken off all their clothes and were making all the noise. The Yanks, and some of the locals, were clapping and cheering, whilst we just stared. It was November and we were all freezing; how could they take off all their clothes? Surely the fire wasn't that hot!

'I'll bet those Yanks have some gum or something,' I said suddenly.

'Well, I'm not asking them,' said Peter.

'Me neither,' Thomas replied.

I had a daring idea. 'Look, everyone's watching the girls and their clothes are over there; let's get some of them and hide them.'

'Why?' asked Peter.

'Just for a laugh,' I replied as we crept over to the pile of clothes. We quickly picked up a bundle each and ran into the blackness at the top of the field and put them under the hedge.

As we went back down the field, the fire was just red and green embers. The Land Girls were running over to get their clothes, followed by the Yanks. The girl in front of the others stopped before she got to the pile.

'Hey!' she yelled. 'Some of our clothes are missing!'

The others rushed up to the pile and started throwing clothes around and, as they were drunk, were swearing at every piece they picked up when it wasn't theirs. The Yanks stood laughing and clapping then, when one of the girls started to cry, they suddenly stopped.

One of them went over and I heard him say, 'Don't worry; we'll search around for them.'

As he went back to his friends, I walked over to them. 'Got any gum, chum?' I asked, as I'd heard that this was what you said to Yanks.

'No, buzz off!' said the man who had been talking to the crying girl.

'I saw some boys taking those girls' clothes,' I said. As they all looked at me, I whispered, 'Has anybody got any gum?'

They looked at me again; then all hands went into their jacket pockets and brought out packets of gum and some chocolate bars.

'Ooh, thanks!' I said gleefully, and stuffed it all down into my windcheater with the few apples that were left. 'They took all the stuff up there.' I pointed to the far corner of the field.

As they went to find it, all the girls came over to thank me and give me a kiss, some still with no clothes on. They were shivering and hugging themselves to keep warm, but I could still see their bodies. When the Yanks returned with the bundles of clothes, Thomas, Brian and I made a quick escape and ran off laughing. I could feel all the treats in my windcheater and couldn't wait to devour the chocolate.

When I got back home, Lilly was friends with me again as soon as she saw the chocolate bars, whilst Peter, Thomas and I were chewing gum for ages after that night.

THIRTEEN

Mam returned from Liverpool after being away for several days; Lilly was very excited as she had really missed her, but I was full of questions for her. How did it look now? Had she been to see our old bombed house? Which aunties and uncles had she seen? What were our cousins like now?

For some reason, Mam didn't seem too keen to give answers; no, she hadn't been to see our house but had been told that, along with all the other houses around it, it had been knocked down, as they were beyond repair. The city itself didn't look so bad, she said, though lots of buildings that had been bombed had still not been repaired. Mam had seen four of her sisters, all of whom had had more children, so we had more cousins than we had when we left. Fortunately, none of their homes had been hit during the Blitz so they still lived in the same houses. My favourite aunt, Auntie Lilly, had still not married and rented a couple of rooms in a house, and Mam said she was looking forward to seeing us. Uncle Eddie was still in the army waiting to be demobbed, so Mam hadn't seen him; in fact, she hadn't seen any of the brothers. As I hardly knew any of them, this didn't bother me in the least.

'Mam, when will we be going back to Liverpool?' I asked with trepidation.

To my relief, Mam replied. 'Oh, not for a while yet, Billy.'

I'm sure there was sadness in her voice when she said it, but then she added, 'I'll be home here most of the time until we go back, because I've given up my job.'

I was not impressed. When we were first evacuated and Mam had been working in Liverpool, Lilly and I had never received anything from her and it didn't really bother me, but I was always aware that my friends all seemed to get what they called pocket money each week. I was always envious, but as often as not they would share things with me that they'd buy at the weekends. Sometimes, if I ran an errand for someone, I'd receive a few pennies. When Mam moved to Lancaster and was working in Green Ayre Station, I'd started being given sixpence pocket money some weekends. Now it was fairly obvious that with Mam not working, that would end.

In no time at all, it was Christmas; we'd made some decorations with me and Frances cutting, painting and gluing chains and Lilly helping however she could. Mam wasn't there to help, as even though she was no longer working, she still went out at night. She didn't seem the same, paying very little attention to either Lilly or me, and she even allowed Frances to continue to put Lilly's hair in ringlets and to put her to bed.

When Christmas Day arrived, someone had bought me a toy bugle and Lilly a small doll. I was delighted to receive anything at all, but on seeing my friends' toys later, I pretended that my presents were too big to bring out - one of which was a very large toy castle, complete with an army of soldiers. When Thomas asked to see some of the soldiers, I said me Mam wouldn't let me bring any out. Later that day, the old lady, Frances, Lilly and I, plus a friend of the old lady's and Frances's brother, all sat down to dinner. Mam had gone out again.

When spring 1946 arrived, and the days grew longer, Peter, Brian, Thomas and I started to play further afield again and would venture to our big tree swing in Bluebell Woods. We resumed our games of Tarzan, taking it in turns to swing across the river all yodelling as loudly as we could, and often falling in fits of laughter onto the bluebells below. When *Tarzan and the Amazons* was shown at the cinema in Lancaster, with Johnny Weissmuller in the lead role, we were all so accomplished at bunking in that we did so with ease, watching with joy as our hero once again saved the day.

'In a few weeks we'll be going back to Liverpool,' Mam told me one morning.

'Why?' I asked, and when she didn't reply I probed again. 'When?' I asked quietly.

'Soon.'

It didn't seem to bother Lilly at all; she just wanted to be with Mam. I was distraught.

During the few weeks before being told we were leaving, it became more and more obvious to me that Mam wasn't well. As we slept in the same room with Mam and Lilly in the bed and me still on the settee, I noticed that she always seemed to be sick. I also wondered if Mam had been sneaking sweets from somewhere, as she was getting fat. I knew she'd been to the doctors because I heard her talking to Frances one day, but I had no idea what was wrong with her.

Then one afternoon, after I'd been scrumping apples, I was lying on the settee munching one whilst reading a comic when Mam started making a terrible racket. I jumped off the settee and stared at my Mam, and Lilly started to cry hysterically.

'Mam, what's the matter?'

'I'm OK, Billy,' Mam said as she let out another low moan. The old lady came running in and looked at Mam and then me.

'Out you go, Billy,' she said sternly. 'Out now and stay out for a good while. Take Lilly with you.'

As I went to get Lilly's hand, Frances came running in. 'Come on, Lilly,' Frances said. 'Let's go for a walk. The doctor will be coming to see your Mam.'

As worried as I was, I couldn't get out of there fast enough, and as I headed down the stairs, I heard Mam's moan become more of a scream.

I roamed the streets of Lancaster for hours wondering what the heck was wrong with Mam and hoping she was going to be OK. Hungry and tired, I eventually returned to Alfred Street, being greeted at the door by the old lady.

'Sorry, Billy, but you'll have to play out or go for a walk into town for a while longer yet.'

My hunger pains took over and I headed to some orchards near the moors, quite some distance from Alfred Street, where I gorged on plums and more apples. Later, when it was almost dark I headed home again. Frances was sat on the doorstep, waiting for me. As I got nearer she stood up and looked at me.

'Billy, you have another sister!' she said, a big smile stretching across her face.

I stared at Frances. 'What?' I exclaimed in horror. I refused to accept it; it was bad enough having Lilly!

'Come on, Billy, come and meet her.' Frances ushered me inside.

I climbed the stairs slowly and when I reached the top, Frances opened her bedroom door. I found Mam in the bed with Lilly on one side of her and a baby in her arms.

I ran downstairs to the settee and curled up in a ball, refusing to join Mam and Lilly or to look at the baby. How had this happened? Mam's illness must have had something to do with it, but why, just because she wasn't well, did I have to have another sister?

Lilly was calling to me to come up and see the baby but I ignored her; quiet tears ran down my hidden face. Eventually, Frances came in, took me by the hand and dragged me back up to the bedroom.

'What do you think?' Mam asked me. 'Isn't she lovely?'

I said nothing.

'We're going to call her June,' said Mam.

'Because it's June this month,' Lilly said excitedly. I was not impressed.

A week later, I overheard Mam talking to Frances, saying that a local train driver called Billy Bell was my new sister's dad. It didn't remotely interest me but knowing nothing about procreation and how it came about, nothing made sense. I later found out that he was married to another lady, but he had been ordered by a magistrate to pay Mam ten shillings a week for maintenance. He would have to pay it until June was sixteen; at the time I thought that was a huge amount of money, but then half a crown seemed a small fortune to me.

It was only a couple of weeks after June's arrival that we returned to Liverpool.

None of my friends had been around to say goodbye; however, Frances accompanied us to the station, holding Lilly's hand.

'You kids be good for your Mam,' Frances said, crouching down and pushing Lilly's hair away from her wet eyes. 'I'll miss you lot.'

'I'll miss you too,' Lilly whispered and wrapped her arms around Frances's neck.

'Come on, come on,' Mam said briskly, stepping up on to the train with June in her arms. I held my hand out to Frances but she grabbed me and pulled me into a hug; I fought back the tears I could feel springing in my eyes. Although it was hard to say goodbye to Frances, it was actually leaving Lancaster that made me so sad.

The train pulled into Liverpool Lime Street station and the whole of the city looked grey and dismal. As we walked through the city centre, we saw huge empty spaces where stores and houses had once been. It turned out we weren't the only evacuees returning to Liverpool, and our first stop was to the Lewis's store opposite the Adelphi theatre where the store had laid on a small party for returning evacuees. We were led to the basement where tables had been laid out with cakes and sandwiches and we were each given a small jelly in a paper cup, covered in cream. Lilly and I devoured as much food as we could.

We arrived at Mam's sister Dorothy's house on Liffey Street in Liverpool 8, another poor part of Liverpool. Small, with three bedrooms, a parlour and a kitchen, it was sure to be a tight squeeze. On being introduced to an aunt I was sure I'd never met before,

I was also introduced to her six sons and then, later that day, to her husband, Uncle Paddy.

Auntie Dorothy was a big woman with a young, pretty face and lots of blonde hair. She was Mam's younger sister after Auntie Lilly, and all her sons were younger than me; they met me with some apprehension and it took quite some time before we were all to become friends.

Lilly was the centre of attention. Auntie Dorothy assumed all rights to the little girl she'd never had, allowing Mam to give all her attention to baby June. This was fine by me; nobody seemed to care where I was and Uncle Paddy seemed to spend far more time out of the house than in.

Uncle Paddy, not long out of the army, was very good at going out and coming back with food he'd scrounged, pinched or obtained from 'God knows where,' Auntie Dorothy would say. Sometimes he'd be away for a day or two, but would always return with a triumphant smile on his face and a sack of supplies. Mam, Lilly and June slept in one the bedrooms and all us lads shared the small bedroom in two small beds. Some nights, as I lay top to tail with my cousins in the squeaking bed, I'd hear Uncle Paddy come home after being in the pub.

'What a bloody drunken sod you are!' Auntie Dorothy would shout. 'You'll be sleeping on the bloody couch tonight!'

We boys were always quite pleased when that happened, as the two youngest could then get into their mam's bed and we'd all have a lot more room. We older boys would always be the first to get up the morning after their dad had slept downstairs, as he always slept in his trousers and odd coins would have slipped out of his pockets and onto the floor. We would creep down the stairs and, stifling giggles, we would tiptoe up to him and quickly retrieve whatever coins we could find. It was always put to good use, after a clear vote with a show of hands regarding what to buy.

Around the corner from Aunt Dorothy's was Eden Street, where another of Mam's sisters, Auntie Eva, lived with her large brood of five. Unlike the Arrowsmiths with all their boys, Auntie Eva had three girls aged between three and twelve, and the two boys were somewhere in between.

My first visit to Auntie Eva's resulted in me not wanting to go again, but as I couldn't tell anybody why, I had no option but to pay other visits.

The reason was this: it was late autumn and everyone had gathered around the coal fire listening to the wireless. All the seats were taken, but room was made for me to stand between two cousins. Even though the cold air was settling in, I was still made to wear my short pants as I was still a few years short of fifteen. 'It's character building,' me Mam would often say. 'Now get outside.'

Whilst standing in the cramped parlour, listening to the wireless and watching my youngest cousin toddle around the room hitting his own head with a toy hammer, I got quite a shock to feel a hand go up my trouser leg and grab me. With a sharp intake of breath I looked quickly looked around and discovered it was the second oldest girl kneeling down by my legs with a great big grin on her face. The grin immediately vanished when I pushed her flat on her back.

'Oh, sorry, I didn't see you there,' I said panicked. 'I was just going home.'

I tried in vain to avoid Auntie Eva's house after that, but was always sent on errands there or told we were all going round to listen to the wireless.

On one occasion, I was stood outside the house when a girl of about thirteen ran up the street; she was being chased by a group of girls, one of which was my cousin. A few yards away from me, they caught her and pulled her to the ground, then laughing and shouting they pulled up her dress and pulled off her knickers and examined her. The girls paid absolutely no attention to me as I stood bewildered, wondering what kind of game it was. This, I was sure, was never played in Lancaster.

I quickly made myself scarce into Auntie Eva's house and, being young and unworldly, banished the memory from my mind. Later, as I got older and started to realise what girls were all about, that memory frequently returned, though I never discovered the reasons for what I had assumed was some kind of game only girls in Liverpool played.

Mam tried for some time to get me and Lilly into the local school but they weren't able to take us; we could have gone to different schools instead, but Mam was determined that I be around as much as possible to look after Lilly. Therefore, much of my time whilst at Aunt Dorothy's was spent looking for things to do, minding Lilly and running errands for just about everyone.

One day, I was sent to buy chips for the whole two families; not fish, though, as that was totally unaffordable. The chippy was a fair walk away in Lodge Lane, which obviously made it quite a walk back again. With chips in arms, I commenced the walk back to Auntie Dorothy's. The lovely smell wafting up from the newspapers filled the air around me; I could feel the warmth of the chips through the greasy paper. It was too much. Being a small boy with small hands, I made a tiny hole in the side of the paper and extracted a chip. Delicious. Nobody would notice if I just had one more.

By the time I reached Auntie Dorothy's, half the chips had gone. I plumped up the package so it still looked big and full, but as Mam took it from me it collapsed to half its size.

'You bugger!' she shouted, as she clouted me round the ear.

'What was that for, I haven't done anything!' I exclaimed as I saw my cousins slowly appear.

'You've eaten most of the chips, you little sod!' she yelled.

'No I haven't; that's what they gave me,' I replied, and everyone was silent.

Mam took one look at me then said, 'Come on, we're going back to that chip shop.' And so saying, she rewrapped the parcel and dragged me out of the house. As I marched along behind her, I desperately tried to think of what I could say or do when we arrived at the chip shop. One thing was certain; I would lie to the high heavens to avoid the battering I would get if I didn't.

I didn't have time to lie. The chip shop owner opened the newspaper at Mam's furious demands and agreed there were very few chips in there; he then set about examining the paper and more or less immediately found the small hole.

'Well, I'd say that's where the chips went!' he said to Mam, pointing it out.

I got what I'd known all along I'd get; a terrific belt round the earlobe with the promise of a lot more to come when we got home. Mam was true to her word and, having replenished the stolen chips, she made sure I didn't get a single one when everyone else tucked in to their dinner.

Though we had been in Liverpool for a few weeks, Mam still hadn't found us a school; actually, I wasn't convinced she'd even tried. A lot of the time Mam and baby June weren't around, and I always assumed that when things weren't going too well, she stopped with another of my aunts or uncles. Things were getting tough at Auntie Dorothy's and, although my aunt adored baby June, it was obvious that Mam, Lilly and I were becoming a burden on an already large family.

Whenever Mam was at the house, there was always bickering with my aunt about food or money, or the lack of it, or whether she'd found somewhere else for us to live. I tried to stay out of the house as much as I could, but I was always ordered to stay at home and look after James, Thomas and Alfie, the three younger lads, whenever Auntie Dorothy wanted to go out. Alfie always wanted to kick things around and anything that resembled a ball would be kicked from one end of the room to the other; I loved watching him play, but always worried that he'd break something of Auntie Dorothy's or Mam's and that I'd be the one to get the clout.

'You little sod! Why would you let him kick around in the house?' I could imagine Mam shouting at me. Many years later, Alfie's ball skills got him signed up to Liverpool football club where he became a local hero, scoring over twenty goals for the club.

Whenever I had the chance to play out I did, and eventually made friends with some other local lads; we'd go to Princess Park or Sefton Park to play football, usually with a tennis ball, or play hide and seek and just wrestle each other.

One day, a lad called Bobby told me he had an air rifle and a bike and was thinking of going to Mold in Wales to shoot squirrels in a wood known as Loggerheads; did I want to come?

The only problem was, I didn't have a bike. Uncle Paddy had one; no one knew where he'd got it from but one day he turned up with a battered old bike that was commonly known as a 'sit up and beg' bike. As I'd never had a bike, I'd never had to learn how to ride one.

'That's no problem,' Bobby said. 'You can learn on mine.'

After several hours of riding up and down Eden Street, and after many falls and scuffs to prove it, I became an enthusiastic cyclist.

When asked, Uncle Paddy was reluctant to lend me his bike, especially after Mam and Lilly told him repeatedly that I couldn't even ride one.

'Yes, I can,' I answered back, glaring at Lilly to mind her own business.

'No, you can't, you've never had a bike to learn on,' she replied.

'Yes, I have, Bobby has let me use his,' I proudly stated, happy I'd won that argument.

'Well, OK then, let's see if you can ride,' Uncle Paddy intervened. 'If you can, you can borrow it.'

Lilly couldn't wait to see me come a cropper and eagerly followed us outside, constantly reminding Uncle Paddy that I definitely couldn't ride a bike.

Inside, I was glowing; boy, were they in for a surprise!

Jumping on to Uncle Paddy's bike, I immediately made the mistake of thinking I was taller than I was, and instantly the bike and I both toppled over. Lilly started laughing, but I chose to ignore her. Uncle Paddy was annoyed that I might have damaged his bike, but as I got up I realised the seat was too high up for me to reach the pedals.

'Uncle Paddy, I just need to lower the seat!' I eagerly shouted, worried that that would be it and he wouldn't let me have another go.

Uncle Paddy disappeared into the house and moments later came back with a spanner and started to lower the seat for me.

'One more go,' he warned, and I managed a smug smile for Lilly.

Mounting quickly onto the bike, I rode off into the sunset, or at least to the end of the street, and returned triumphant. Neither Lilly nor Uncle Paddy was smiling now.

It was with great reluctance that Uncle Paddy kept his word and, with dire warnings of what I would get if any damage was caused to his rickety old bike, I was told I could use it.

Saturday duly arrived, with the sun shining brightly through the bedroom window. I jumped out of bed and quickly started to get dressed.

'Where are you going?' Alfie asked, sitting up in bed and rubbing his eyes.

'To shoot some squirrels,' I replied proudly.

'Ugh, yuck! Where?'

'At Loggerheads.'

'Where's that?' Thomas asked, now also sitting up in bed.

'Dunno,' I replied.

I met up with Bobby, who looked rather disdainfully at Uncle Paddy's bike; nonetheless, he was pleased I'd got the loan of it, so we jumped onto the bikes and headed for the Pier Head. I had no idea where we were headed or where Wales was in relation to Liverpool, so it came as a big surprise to find we had to cross the Mersey on a ferry. As luck would have it, Bobby was something of an expert at bunking on to ferries without paying as he'd done it a number of times, bike and all.

Looking at the large crowd of people waiting for the ferry to return from Woodside in Birkenhead, Bobby pointed to a group of cyclists and said, 'Right, come on Billy, try and get amongst them as they go on board.'

Nudging our bikes amongst the cyclists, it was obvious what we were up to, but grinning and making room, the men went along with our scam. As the ferry came alongside, there was a rush from the crowd to get on as quickly as possible to either get a seat or to go on to the upper deck. As the passengers getting off the ferry came down one ramp onto the pontoon and the crowds tried to get on, it was utter chaos; this helped our cause even more and we got onto the ferry with no problems.

'So, lads, where are you off to?' one of the cyclists asked us.

'Mold.'

'Ah, same as us,' was the reply.

Bobby took me aside and explained that he actually had no idea which way Wales was, so we decided to follow them.

Once off the ferry, we had no problem keeping up on the main road as buses, cars and other cyclists slowed the group down; however, as the road began to clear, their Hercules and Raleigh bikes began to pull away and we had to pedal like mad.

We managed to keep them in sight as long as we could, and when they turned off for Wales, we knew to take the same turning. By the time we reached the turning, they were well out of sight.

'Ah, no problem, Billy,' Bobby said. 'We'll just keep cycling until we get to Wales; it can't be far now.'

But it was. Mile after mile of gruelling pedalling, we kept stopping to rest our legs. Bobby, on a reasonably good bike, and with much more experience than me, was just as tired as me as he had the bag on his back with the air rifle in it. My 'sit up and beg' machine, which was old and weary and weighed a ton, convinced me I'd never make it and, even if I did, I'd never make it back again. It wasn't just my legs that were failing me but the damn old, no-spring, leather seat was playing havoc with my backside. After hours of pedalling, we arrived at Queensferry; we left our bikes outside a shop and went in to ask for directions.

'Bloody hell, lads, you're cycling all the way to Mold? From Liverpool?' The shopkeeper was incredulous. 'Well, you've got about another six or seven miles to go, lads; good luck!'

I couldn't have cared less if I never, ever got on a bike again, and I was certain that Bobby felt the same way. We were so tired, so hungry, so thirsty, so demoralised, and so without money.

'Why didn't you find out how far it was?' I said angrily to Bobby.

'Why didn't you?' he retorted.

'It was your idea; you were the one with the bike and the gun!'

'Well, if you didn't have that crappy old bike, we might have kept up with that group!'

'Don't be stupid!' I shouted back. 'Anyway, why didn't you bring something to eat or drink?'

'Why didn't you?'

Eventually, we ran out of things to shout at each other and, defeated, we sat down on a grassy bank contemplating our return. Also, for me, was the fear of seeing Uncle Paddy, as it was obvious it was going to be very late when we got back to Liverpool, if we ever made it.

After sitting in silence for quite some time, we fairly small, thirsty boys knocked on the door of a house on a side street and asked the lady if we could please have some water. Happily, the lady gave us a cup full each and after watching us gulp it down said, 'You boys are thirsty; where are you heading to?'

'Liverpool,' I sighed.

'Liverpool! On those bikes?'

'Well, they got us here,' Bobby replied petulantly. I nodded slowly.

'No wonder you're so hot and bothered! Wait here.' She rushed back inside and then returned moments later with a lemonade bottle full of water, some apples and two pieces of cake.

'These should help on your way back,' she said.

'Thank you, missus,' we both replied, grabbing the goodies from her.

Back on the grassy bank, we tucked into the cake and the apples and drank more water before we finally started our trek back.

It was evening before we reached Birkenhead; we used a similar trick as earlier in the day to board the ferry, but by now I really couldn't care if we got caught or not. Just sitting down on the ferry knowing it was inching us closer to home made me feel marginally happier.

Cycling in the dark back to Aunt Dorothy's, Bobby and I bid a tired and miserable farewell to each other at the end of Eden Street and, with trepidation, I made my way to the house.

'Where the bloody hell have you been?' Uncle Paddy shouted; I could tell by the look on his face and tone in his voice that he was madder than I'd ever seen him before.

Trying to explain that I'd been to Wales and back just seemed to make him even angrier, and his threats of what would happen to me if I ever got up to anything like that again whilst I lived under his roof scared the living daylights out of me.

Fortunately, Mam and June were staying somewhere else that night, else I would have got a hiding from her. Lilly, however, was home to hear it all and couldn't hide her delight at being able to do what she always did; tell Mam. I just gave her the usual thump to make it worth her while.

The next day, as expected, I got the usual hiding from Mam for 'yesterday's travels' and a bit more for thumping Lilly.

FOURTEEN

The summer of 1946 was a glorious summer with endless days of sunshine, made even better because I didn't have to go to school; I was as free as a bird. The only drawback was finding things to do.

Whilst playing in Princes Park one day with a couple of lads who were playing hooky from their school, they suddenly took off running as fast as they could to the park gate, without a word to me.

'Hey! Where you going?' I shouted after them.

I got up to follow them when a man approaching me demanded, 'Stay where you are!'

Puzzled, but not worried, as there were lots of other adults around, I stood whilst he walked towards me.

'Why aren't you in school, boy?' he asked.

'Don't go to school,' I replied.

'Which school should you go to?'

'Haven't got one.'

'Where do you live?'

'Auntie Dorothy's house.'

'Show me,' he instructed, and taking me by the shoulder we began the walk back to Liffey Street.

Within a couple of weeks of the school inspector meeting Mam, Lilly and I were placed in Granby Street School. Granby Street and Liffey Street were both in Toxteth, Liverpool 8, but were very different. Liffey Street was a typical, downtown, pretty rough area; Granby Street made Liffey Street look like a posh residential part, like Allerton. The people who lived there appeared to me to be from every country in the world, and their children all went to the school. There were Irish, Scots, Welsh, African, Indian, Chinese, Greek and Italian, and many more that I didn't know, and it seemed that they were all tougher than this five foot nothing ex-evacuee who had just joined them.

The school itself was the old, stern Victorian type built in the 1880s; it had a large playground with outside toilets and inside, a series of classrooms running the whole length of the building, each divided by a concertina wood and glass partition. When pulled back, which they were every morning, it made for a vast auditorium.

Each class, between each screen, was built up to the dark windows with a series of steps and fixed to each step was a school desk with a lift-up lid for storage and two benches for pupils to sit on. Between each set of desks was an aisle, up which the Master would stroll, looking down at the work in progress and occasionally cuff the back of the head of a boy who displeased him. A large blackboard on the opposite wall with a small table below for the chalk, and a chair, were the only other pieces of furniture.

I was now twelve years old and no longer in the junior classes, and though not quite a senior, the boys up to fourteen were my classmates; every single one of them was bigger than me.

On my first day at Granby Street School, I was told to sit at an empty desk three rows back, surrounded by boys who seemed to do whatever they liked. The Master seemed very young and also possibly very new, and appeared to have no control over the tough lads. A boy called Taggart, who was as tall as the teacher and had ginger hair, seemed to be the ringleader. No matter what the Master said, he ignored him. Another big lad, George Wayland, was in my class; he was black and sat a couple of rows away from me.

'Hey, you!' Wayland shouted at me. 'Why do you speak so stupidly?' I had picked up some of the Lancaster dialect and it stuck out back in Liverpool.

155

'Why have you got such a black face?' I replied.

Sniggers broke out around the room, then fell silent as George stood and walked round the desks. Despite the orders from our teacher for him to sit down, he blazed his way towards me. As I stood up to protect myself, he hit me right on the chin and knocked me out.

When I came round, the panic-stricken teacher was leaning over me. 'Are you OK, boy?' he asked.

I sat up and looked around the room. Wayland was sat back at his own desk watching, as though nothing had happened. In no time, I was back up at my desk with an aching jaw, fully expecting to see George heading straight for the Headmaster's study. Not so. The class continued as though this was an everyday occurrence. I later discovered that George Wayland was the Liverpool Boys' Boxing Champion; I suppose that played a part.

Two weeks later, Taggart was up to his usual tricks in the classroom causing chaos and disruption with his 'I'm such a comedian' routine. The teacher was screaming at him to sit down and shut up, but to no avail. Suddenly, the teacher rushed into the classroom next door and came back with a big thick cane; he shot up the aisle still yelling blue murder at Taggart. We all watched in horror as he set about Taggart with the cane, hitting him repeatedly on the head, face, arms and legs, anywhere he could reach. Taggart was reduced to a crying wreck; whimpering and sniffling on the floor. Triumphant, the teacher walked back down the aisle, into the other classroom, handed over the cane and then left the classroom. I never saw him again.

Shortly afterwards, our class was all broken up and we were placed in different classes; happily, neither Wayland nor Taggart were in my class, and I was able to get along quite nicely with most of my new mates.

Tommy Williams was the class joker; he was a black lad, Scouser through and through, and as thick as two short planks. Learning was not his forte, but he more than made up for it with a very funny outlook on life; the teachers would turn away to hide their faces when Tommy had cracked a side-splitting answer to one of their questions. Tommy became my best friend.

Sometimes, during the lunchtime break, we were allowed out of the school for an hour, and as Tommy lived close to the school, he would let me go back to his house with him. His mam was a lovely lady and a true Scouser too; she would make us Docker Doorsteps with lovely jam on fresh bread, then shoo us off back to school.

'Going for peanuts on Saturday,' Tommy said to me one day as we walked back to school; I looked at him, completely confused. I had no idea what he was on about, but was soon to find out.

Many of the Liverpool docks were concentrated in the south end of Liverpool, and outside of the docks was the Dock Road; it ran from the Aigberth area into the town, with deviation around the Royal Liver Building, Cunard Building and the Mersey Docks and Harbour Board buildings, and joined up at the Pier Head. Above the Dock Road, mounted on steel uprights, was the overhead railway which ran from the south end to the north end of the docks. Ships were always berthed in the docks, loading and unloading, and so the Dock Road was always busy with trucks and lorries. Along the road outside the dock walls were lots of silos used for storage; they were always covered with pigeons who lived off whatever they contained.

'We go down to the Dock Road,' Tommy explained. 'And stand somewhere near to The Seaman's Mission.'

'Where's that?' I asked.

'It's where the seamen sign on for a job on a ship; it's near the Pier Head. We wait for one of the peanut trucks to come from one of the silos and as it goes past we jump in the back.'

My eyes opened wide with interest.

'They're full of sacks, which are full of peanuts! Bring a bag and a knife with you,' Tommy instructed.

'What if people see us?' I asked.

'Nah, nobody takes any notice. It's a long walk from Liffey Street, though, Billy, so if you can borrow a penny, you can walk through to Upper Parly and get a tram most of the way to the docks.'

Saturday came and, armed with a penknife I pinched from Uncle Paddy's small toolbox, an old shopping bag and a penny I took from Mam's purse, I made my way down to Upper Parliament Street and found a tram stop. I boarded the rattling and very noisy tram and went upstairs, which was open to the heavens. I sat on the ancient wooden slats that served as benches and it was shake, rattle and roll all the way down to the docks. Now I knew why everyone called them 'bone shakers'!

It didn't take me long to find Tommy, and we walked back along the Dock Road and away from the Pier Head where we then waited. Other groups of lads were also hovering around, obviously all up to the same tricks.

'Let's move further along and get away from this lot,' Tommy said. 'They'll jump on the first peanut truck that comes along, slit the sacks at the back and take what they want. By the time the truck gets to us, we'll just need to run along behind, 'cos all the peanuts will be pouring out from the back!'

Sure enough, a short while later, as the lorry went past with a trail of peanuts all the way down the road behind it, all we had to do was run behind holding our bags open and filling them up.

Laughing gleefully, we found a spot under the overhead and gorged on the peanuts. As we wandered back to Upper Parly with the bags slung on our back, Tommy said, 'Quick, there's the bone shaker!' and ran to jump on. Having forgotten to bring a second penny with me for the return journey, I faced the long hard slog up the steep road and all the way back to Liffey Street bearing the weight of my bag of peanuts on my back.

Tommy and I did the peanut run on several occasions, and sometimes we went for coconuts. Mam, Auntie Dorothy and the rest of the family grew quite partial to the coconuts; I lied to them that Tommy Williams had an uncle who brought them over from Africa. Whether they believed me or not didn't matter, because they all ate them. Nobody ever seemed to ask me where I got the peanuts from.

Saturdays and holidays were the only chance we had to raid the lorries, so when one of my dad's brothers turned up at Liffey Street and introduced himself as Uncle George, I was very surprised and somewhat perturbed when he said he'd be taking me to a football match on Saturday. Though I enjoyed kicking a tennis ball around and having the occasional game with my class after school, I really wasn't at all keen on losing my Saturday by going to somewhere called Goodison Park with a man I didn't know.

Be that as it may, he turned up on the Saturday morning and presented me with a bell and said I was to ring it to support Everton, his favourite team. Off we went to Goodison where, because I couldn't see a thing still being so small, he lifted me onto the barrier rail from where I could see the match. As it turned out, I thoroughly enjoyed it, especially when one of the Everton players called Jock Dodds chased after an opposing player and purposely kicked him up the backside. The crowd were in hysterics, cheering and laughing wildly, and Uncle George explained proudly that this particular Everton player was as mad as a hatter.

It was only a short time later that I changed my allegiance from Everton to Liverpool FC, so every other Saturday found me bunking into the boys' pen in the Kop.

I was doing well in school, receiving good marks in English, Maths and Geography. This didn't go down too well with some of the other lads, who weren't getting the same praise from our Master that I and others got. The end result was being pushed around and being scoffed at during the break times. In Lancaster, I had been one of the toughest kids, where fights were usually nothing more than a wrestling match with the strongest being the winner. Things were definitely different in Granby Street. It was fists to the face right from the start with the aim to draw as much blood as possible, and my new-found enemies put me through it for several weeks.

During our break time after another lesson where my Master praised my hard work, one of the ringleaders started pushing me around. I retaliated. All of the built-up anger and loathing at allowing it to happen for so long exploded and I smashed him in the nose. Streams of blood ran from his nose but I didn't stop. I wrestled him to the ground and continued to hit him non-stop. None of the boys tried to stop me, but I suddenly felt the big hands of Mr Sullivan on my shoulders as he hauled me up and marched me to the Headmaster's study. The Headmaster was a fair man and I believe he had been told what had led to me losing control, but nonetheless I was to be punished the following morning in the usual way.

The usual way was for all the partitions to be pushed back so that the whole school could sit for assembly, say prayers and sing 'Jerusalem' or 'All Things Bright and Beautiful', and then the punishment of pupils was administered for the whole school to see. After small punishments had been administered to other boys, it was my turn. I was to receive six of the best on my backside from the Headmaster. I'd seen on previous occasions this punishment being received by some of the toughest lads, which had resulted in tears from them to the derision of the senior boys. I decided I would not allow this to happen. In the event, the strokes that landed on my short-trouser-clad backside were surprisingly soft, resulting in hardly any pain at all. I believe this was the Head's way of letting me know he knew what had led to my loss of temper. The rest of the school were not aware of the lightness of my punishment and the fact that there were no tears from me didn't harm my standing in school.

Around this time, another Master, Mr Hoolihan, better known as Pop, discovered I could swim. As well as his teaching duties, he also acted as Sports Master and was prepared to give his all in and out of school hours; he was worshipped by the lads, me included. He would take anybody to Princess Park who wanted to play football or cricket when school finished. He would train us and praise us, never losing his patience with even the worst students.

Of course, some of the boys were naturals, unlike me. One boy called Peter Downey was exceptional and, as far as everybody was concerned, was destined to be a footballer. After practices, we would set off for home; Downey lived somewhere near me but he wasn't the most sociable of lads and was a bit older than me. He had a peculiar, very athletic way of walking, which I tried to master as I walked behind him. I never achieved it.

It was during one after school kick-around that someone with a red pair of soccer boots accidentally kicked me in the shin; the boots had nailed-in leather studs and it was the studs that caused the injury. A flap of skin was lifted from my shin and with it came lots of blood. Pop was very concerned. 'You should have been wearing shin pads,' he chided as he wrapped his handkerchief round my leg. I was too embarrassed to tell him that shin pads, boots and any other piece of equipment were an impossible dream. I must have mentioned that it would stop me going to Lodge Lane Baths for a while because in school the next day, after being bandaged up by Mam with some torn up bed sheet, Pop approached me.

Firstly, he was concerned about my leg and after I assured him it was OK, he said, 'I'm going to start a swimming team; do you want to be in it, Billy?'

He would take us training, sometimes during school time, and it wouldn't cost any volunteers any money. Of course, I jumped at the chance and he was as good as his word.

On discovering I was quite a proficient, even fast, swimmer, he made me Captain, and happily my status in the school rose accordingly.

We took part in various galas against other schools, and though we were never champions, we always gave a good account of ourselves. One school in particular, St Bernard's, a Catholic school a few hundred yards away from Granby, raced against us. This school was the big enemy because we were always fighting with them. The fights were usually organised by the Seniors from school, with dozens and dozens of lads taking part, so when we eventually had to swim against them, we had to win – or face the wrath of our schoolmates afterwards. I'm pretty sure Pop Hoolihan was fully in the picture, although he never let on. Win we did, to everyone's relief!

Not long after, when the competitions seemed to come to an end, Pop organised a lifesaving course for anybody in the school who wanted to take part; as well as this, we could swim for certificates, for speed and for distance. I was delighted, because it meant that though the competitions had ended, I could still get in plenty of free swimming. I got all my certificates and became a qualified swimming life saver, eventually winning the Life Saving Bronze Certificate.

The summer of 1946 seemed to be constant sunshine - in Liverpool, anyway - and of course, the River Mersey was a big attraction. It couldn't be challenged, as I used to do in the Lune, but the dozens of ships from all over the world that were always coming and going were fascinating to me.

One day, my usual companion, Tom Williams, said, 'Let's go to the Cazzey and see what we can find.'

Once again, I had to ask, 'What's the Cazzey?'

As usual, he joked about my lack of knowledge about the important parts and places of the 'pool, and then he told me the 'Cazzey' was up Aigburth way. It was known as the Cast Iron Shore and all the banana boats passed it on the way to Garston. You could find all kinds of things washed up on the shore by the tide; some things were just thrown over the side by the crew of passing ships, but sometimes a banana boat would, knowing there were kids roving the shore, throw over great bundles of bananas.

I'm quite sure, up to that first time of going with Tommy to the Cazzey, I'd not had a banana since the night the soldiers had descended on our billet with the Johnson family in Aldcliffe, so it was with great joy that, along with some other kids, we found some large bunches of bananas. The fact that they had been in the Mersey didn't seem to have any effect on the taste at all and, after stuffing ourselves, Tommy and I took as many as we could carry on the long journey back home.

Mam, Aunt Dorothy and all the others were absolutely over the moon as they, like me, had not had a banana for a very long time. Tommy and I made many another visit to the Cazzey during my time in Liffey Street.

It was shortly before the end of 1946 that Pop Hoolihan decided he'd enter me in a diving competition, to be held in Dovecot Baths in a posh area of Liverpool, with the preliminaries at Lodge Lane Baths. I was quite apprehensive as, though I knew I could dive, I also knew I wasn't very good. Pop had seen me doing racing dives in the Galas, so assumed I could do just as well off a diving board.

So one evening after school, he and I went off to Lodge Lane to join the diving hopefuls from other schools. Watching some of the other boys put me in a total panic; they were doing swallow dives, back flips, somersaults and dives I'd never even heard of. I tried to tell Pop I couldn't possibly compete with them, but he wouldn't hear of it. So when my turn came round I thought I'd take a chance and try a swallow dive; how hard could it be?

It was a complete disaster! Everything went well until the moment I took up my stance on the top board, and then nerves and realisation of my complete lack of knowledge and experience took over. My dive caused a loud chorus of laughter from the other contestants, as I was still trying to stretch my arms out as I hit the water. Pop was just as eager to leave the baths as I was, and we made a hasty retreat. He was quite nice about it as we walked down Lodge Lane but, as it happened, I never swam for him again.

It was nothing to do with this diving charade, however, but everything to do with polio. The disease had sprung up all over the country and there were kids in 'Iron Lungs', as the breathing apparatus was called, in every town and city. Many would be crippled for life.

It was decided by the powers that be that public baths were probably one area that could spread the disease, so they were all closed. I couldn't believe it. Since my early days in Lancaster, the baths and swimming had been where I was most happy, and now it was gone. Pop disbanded the swimming team and a short time later left Granby Street for another job elsewhere. I never saw him again.

FIFTEEN

In Liffey Street, nerves were getting to be more fragile. Mam and Auntie Dorothy were constantly bickering, with Dorothy finally telling Mam she had to find somewhere else to live and Mam answering with, 'Don't think I'm not trying, as I'm was well aware we aren't welcome.'

Even at my age, I had seen Auntie Dorothy's pout when she'd taken us in; she'd had no idea that months and months later we would still be there. On some occasions, Auntie Lilly would call and would always bring fruit and sweets with her; obviously using her own sweet ration which, like everything else, was still needed at this time. Auntie Lilly would take some of the strain off Mam by taking Lilly for days out, and sometimes taking Lilly, Mam and June to stay with her for a few days in the one-bedroom flat she rented. As I was out doing more or less whatever I liked, this helped to reduce the tension, for a little while, anyway.

Suddenly, it was Christmas 1946, and I can't remember any part of it; not the celebrations, if there were any, nor the presents, of which I'm certain, in my case, anyway, that there weren't any. It seems as though I slept through it all and woke up in January 1947. That month, though, and the three or four months after, can never be forgotten.

The snow that hit Liverpool and every other part of the country was the worst winter of snow anybody had ever known. Drifts in every street, three or four feet high, caused terrible problems; works factories, docks and railways, just about everything closed down. Electricity and gas supplies were rationed to certain parts of the day and coal was in very short supply or couldn't be delivered anyway.

Uncle Paddy became a hero as he went out, ploughing through thick snow all the way to Tunnel Road where the train ran underground and went through it; it was at least two or three miles from Liffey Street. He would then walk along the railway embankments picking up pieces of coal which had fallen off the steam trains, and when he had enough, he'd walk all the way back through the heavy snow which was always falling, with a hundred weight of coal over his shoulder. As he had no work to go to, he'd be off again the next day to do it all over again.

Everybody would huddle round the open fire wrapped up in blankets and wearing any clothing they could get on. To complicate things further, food, which was still rationed, became even scarcer. Shops ran empty, ships could not dock with supplies because of ice flows, even in the Mersey, but somehow Mam, Auntie Dorothy and Uncle Paddy kept us fed. Nourished enough, as it happens, to trek through the drifts to the one place that I knew of that hadn't closed: Granby Street School.

Most boys wore short pants, whatever the weather, and kids like me usually only had two pairs, which were commonly well patched and sewn. I'd wear them all week, and then leave them to be washed on Sunday evening, putting on the second pair on Monday. I didn't have a coat of any sort, just a vest and shirt and darned socks and flaky shoes on my feet. Not quite the clothing for the snowiest, coldest winter on record.

I froze as I walked to school through the thick snow, hands in short pockets, shoulders hunched and chin pulled in, in an effort to stay warm; the fact that I had Lilly in tow didn't help, as she made for a much slower pace. However, she was always much better clothed than I, having a scarf and a coat with a bonnet on her head. I was never put out by this, as she was only a girl and, after all, she was my sister. I was somewhat compensated by the fact that somebody, possibly Mam, had knitted me a black balaclava so at least my ears were kept from dropping off.

Most days, reaching school was a blessing, as somehow it was kept heated despite the shortages; but during the almost four months of snow, supplies of whatever heating system was employed was occasionally turned off; most of the time was then spent in class just trying to keep warm.

At playtime, the school yard was a mass of boys hurling snowballs indiscriminately at anyone and everyone and it was here that one day I got my revenge.

George Wayland, who had knocked me out on my first day at Granby Street, was one of the enthusiastic snowballers, and because he was black and very tall he stood out in the mêlée. I had found a large stone and wrapped it in snow, making it the perfect missile. In Lancaster, I had always been quite good at throwing stones into the river or along the canal and today my aim was perfect. George was busy making another large snowball when mine hit him straight in the face; in the left eye, actually. I took great pleasure in hearing his yell and watching the tears of pain afterwards. Happily, it did no lasting damage, but it gave me great satisfaction.

As well as having the worst winter ever, there were other troubles in Liverpool at that time. There were several thousand Jewish people living here, mostly with businesses, shops, jewellers and pawn shops; some even had businesses in Granby Street and were friends of mine. Except for other kids saying things like, 'He's a Jew boy,' I'd never have known and, anyway, it wouldn't have mattered to me.

Unfortunately, I was aware of rumours going the rounds and had listened to conversations at home between the grown-ups; there was, it seems, a war going on in a place called Palestine between Jews from all over the world who were trying to set up home there, along with survivors from the holocaust, which I had seen on the news channels at the cinema.

I could never understand why here in Granby they were disliked so much. Many people were beaten up, shops were wrecked, businesses closed. I was on the top deck of a tram in Lodge Lane at the junction with Smithdown Road, when I saw a mob smashing in the windows of a jeweller's shop and dragging the people out. Nazi Swastikas had been daubed on the walls. I thought this was awful, as we'd not long ago been bombed by the Nazis. As I sat on the bus, I was remembering the pictures I had seen about the poor Jews and I was upset by our own Liverpudlians. I was ashamed. I learnt later that this thuggery was not confined to Liverpool; people were extracting revenge in many towns and cities, but it was being said that Liverpool was the most violent.

The winter showed little sign of ending and everyone was still suffering from the shortages and the cold; we were hearing more and more of the polio epidemic and more and more cases of another disease, once again exclusive to children. Tuberculosis, known as TB, or, in some places, consumption. It was a dreaded illness brought on by lack of food and the poor living conditions we were still suffering from after wartime. Pupils, some of whom I knew, were whisked away from Granby and sent to isolation hospitals in England and abroad; many died.

I was one of the fortunate ones and wasn't struck down with any of these horrors; I put it down to all the apples and fruit and coconuts and peanuts I'd eaten over the years, and I took advantage of the winter every way I could.

Sefton Park was a snowy, ice-bound wilderness, absolutely packed with kids having a great time on the weekends, after school and even, it has to be said, when we should have been in school. The park is one of the country's biggest and in it is a very large boating lake. It has islands full of trees in the middle and, as far as I know, is as big, if not bigger, than the London Serpentine. A path ran around the perimeter and alongside the path there were high banks of grass.

The lake was frozen with ice two or three feet thick and in any one day you would see hundreds of people sliding, skating and tobogganing on it. The ducks and other wildlife on the islands had obviously gone off to safer habitats as now we could no longer see them. My days there would be spent cadging a go on some other kids' sledge or sharing one with somebody else on board. We'd start at the top of a grass verge, zoom down across the path and on to the ice and across to the far side of the lake, yelling at people to move out of our way. We'd do exactly the same on the return. If I couldn't use a sledge, I'd just take a run from the path and slide as far as I could across the ice in my battered old shoes.

When extra snow came gusting down, there would be hundreds of snowball fights on the ice and bodies falling and sliding every which way. It was a fantastic time; I never noticed the wet and forgot all about the bad times. Mam sometimes insisted Lilly was to come with me and it became obvious to me that she was growing up; though I'd always considered her as 'my ugly little sister', some of the other boys of my age seemed to pay her a lot of attention. I couldn't understand it, but she loved it.

Throughout those awful, but exciting of times, when things were going from bad to worse in Liffey Street, to say we were no longer welcome would be the understatement of the year. The rows between Mam and Auntie Dorothy were more and more frequent and getting nasty. Auntie Dorothy seemed to be increasingly desperate as my cousins were all getting bigger, as were me and Lilly, and even June was now a toddler, and yet we were all still crammed into the same small space.

Poor Mam spent most of every day looking for somewhere else to live, carrying June with her, or pushing her along in a rickety old pushchair. What little money she had from the labour exchange was just about enough to buy food. I know there was nothing left to buy anything else. Places that we might have been able to move to always wanted rent of some sort, so were out of the question; there was even one occasion when Mam was told she could apply to the Workhouse near West Shirley Road. An awful Victorian building, it was the last residing place for the poorest of the poor and the dregs of society. Mam was having none of it. I know she visited Blackburn House, a housing organisation, on the corner of Dale Street and Scotland Road because we had, as it was termed, been bombed out. Mam applied for a council house but the list of bombed out applicants was endless and she always came away empty-handed.

I was now going on thirteen and had made a number of new friends, so I didn't see Tommy as much as I used to. One of the new friends was called Lenny, and he lived on a road that ran parallel with Granby Street.

The house was quite large, though I never saw the inside of it - I suppose I was too scruffy - and it had alongside it a large storage building with a loft above. The loft was used by Lenny and his friends as a playroom and above the trap door entrance, attached to the roof supports, was a large block with a single wheel, around which was wound a thick rope. The two ends of the rope were long enough to almost touch the floor below, and tied to them were two potato sacks stuffed with old clothes and stuffing of any sort to turn them into seats. One of Lenny's friends, Richard, was a very stout lad; it must have been a genetic thing as, like everybody else, we knew his family was just as poor. As well as that, we were still in rationing, and so he couldn't possibly get fat through overeating. The only other tubby kid I knew was Dennis Wing, whose dad owned a Chinese chippy.

Our favourite game for a while was hooking one end of the rope through the trap door and one of the gang sat in it; Richard would then jump in the sack still in the loft and as he came down the other chap came up. To get the heavy weight back up again, two of us in the loft would jump on the swinging sack together and so descending, would lift him back up.

A couple of weeks after becoming friends with Lenny, I had become an integral member of our gang and had the bright idea of giving us a name. I'd heard of other streets where gangs had a name, like a very notorious one called the Bunny Gang. I decided a good name was the Scar Gang. The name would necessitate all of us having a scar, so when I suggested using our hoist to achieve a scar, all were in favour.

We immediately put the idea into practice; Lenny nominated himself as Scar Gang Leader and, being leader, nominated me, whose idea it was, to be first. As I sat on the sack below the loft with my left arm bare, having rolled up my sleeve, it now didn't seem quite as good an idea as I had first thought, but I knew I would have to go through with it or lose face.

Our tubby lad took his place on the sack above and jumped through the hatch. I went up very swiftly and pressed my bare upper arm against the rope coming down; it immediately ripped some of the skin off and caused a deep painful burn, although without a lot of blood. It hurt like hell, but of course I couldn't admit it, and with a great deal of effort, I tried to appear completely nonchalant as I came back from the ladder.

When the rest of the gang saw my arm, the original looks of excitement had disappeared to be replaced with apprehension. I was in agony, but I'd done it - and I was going to make quite sure the others would, so I said, 'OK, who's next, Lenny?'

There were no volunteers, so a reluctant Lenny, being the leader, had to go himself. Like me, he managed to hide his pain, then he nominated two others. Both of these barely touched the rope with their bare arms and received only a red mark and the last had refused to be scarred that way. They were to regret their failure when I suggested we should get a small length of rope and each of the lads should hold out their arm and Lenny and I would pull the rope across their arms in a sawing motion, causing a rope burn. They did and it did. The most reluctant lad refused to do it this way or any other way, so he was thrown out of what had now become the Scar Gang. Not too long after this, the new way of entertaining ourselves became much more interesting; two girls came on the scene.

About the same time as this, Auntie Dorothy finally threw us out. She demanded that Mam pack up and leave, making it clear that whether or not we had anywhere to go, we were out. Even Auntie Lilly pleaded that Dorothy should give Mam a little more time, but it fell on deaf ears. Auntie Lilly went to her and Mam's eldest sister, Lisa, and demanded that she take us in.

Up to that point, I had never met Auntie Lisa, but I'd heard lots of stories about her from Mam, Dorothy and Lilly. She was considered the matriarch of the family, who felt she was a cut above all her sisters and for most of the time had little to do with them. She lived in a terraced house larger than her sisters in a much better part of Liverpool, which for some particular reason had suffered very little from the bombings, probably because it was much further from the docks.

Her house had a front parlour, a living room, kitchen, a bathroom and a separate indoor toilet. She also had an area in front of the house where she had large, well-kept flowerpots; the street was also well-kept and, at the top of it, was a park. Her husband, whose name I never knew, was killed in the war. Aunt Lisa's only son, Edward, was at least ten years older than me and lived with her; he worked somewhere a bike ride away, and although he seemed quite pleasant whenever I saw him, he had little to do with us.

Auntie Lilly, being the youngest sister and still unmarried, was Aunt Lisa's favourite, and was therefore able to convince Lisa that, if only for a short time, she had to take us in.

I wasn't too pleased with this turn of events as our new home was some distance from Liffey Street and Granby Street, and therefore some way from Lennie's house; the only compensation was that it was a bit nearer Anfield and the boys' pen in the Kop.

Lilly and I still had to be schooled in Granby Street and I had no intention of being separated from the Scar Gang so, much to Mam's annoyance, she had to give us 1d each a day for the bus or the tram. I still had to look after eleven-year-old Lilly, which initially made things difficult, but after convincing her that it would be a good idea to get up earlier and run the four miles to school, therefore saving our pennies, we would then have money to spend. Mam was not to know.

Not being familiar with Liverpool and knowing no different, Lilly and I took the longest route each day, which invariably made us late for school. Reaching Lodge Lane and turning down streets in the direction of Granby Street, we would be almost there when the massive buildings of St Bernard's Catholic School would block our way and we would have to detour a long way round it before joining up on the other side on Kingsley Road, then join Roseberry Street before backtracking to Granby. This made me the latest of the late, resulting in not one, but two strokes of the cane. The girls' school did not have the cane, much to Lilly's relief.

Another problem arose when I wanted to stay to play with Lenny and the rest of the gang after school; this was solved by me taking Lilly to the bus stop in Lodge Lane after school, giving her one of my pennies for the fare and then doubling back to Lenny's, where our new interest made it very worthwhile.

The two girls who had asked to join our gang were thirteen and, like most of us kids, were quite young and innocent. However, Richard was somewhat more mature and he started our learning process on the first day the girls turned up. We hadn't given a great deal of thought about giving the girls the scar treatment, thus making them fully-fledged members of the gang, and when it was put to them and shown how we did it, it was firmly rejected.

Richard had a brainwave. 'What if we let you join without a scar? When you climb up the ladder into the Den, you let us look up your dress to see your knickers instead.'

They both looked at each and, nonplussed, they both shrugged their shoulders and said OK. And that was just the beginning.

Richard then suggested another game, which was a new one to me, and, with the undisguised enthusiasm of the more forward of the two girls, we started to play Truth or Dare. We, in Lancaster, had been missing out on something far more exciting than Reallio with the occasional kiss. This game involved the girls undressing.

The rules were made up by the boys, so it was decided that the boys would ask the girls a question and if she couldn't or wouldn't answer it truthfully, the boy asking the question got to remove an item of the girl's clothing. If she answered truthfully, she would take off an article of her friend's clothing. They were in a no-win situation, but seemed to me to be more than happy with our rules.

One of the girls was much prettier than the other, so the boy asking the question would invariably pick her and ask questions she had no idea how to answer; he would then be entitled to ask another one, having removed a piece of her clothing, and then do the same again. Richard was an expert and most of the time, when it was his turn, he removed everything, including her knickers. He also made sure he touched her each time.

I was still quite shy and, when it came to my turn, I would tell the girl I'd keep my eyes closed as I undressed her, and I did; but as she would be stood naked when I had finished, I couldn't help but see her in all her glory. Though I pretended to be disinterested, in reality I thought it was the best game I'd ever played.

Things changed somewhat when the girls brought along another girl of about 15;

she was taller than all the lads and, after a game or two, she demanded a change to the rules. If we boys would not strip, the girls should be allowed to feel our privates. Naïve as I was, I declined, though Richard was very enthusiastic about this change of rule; the others initially slightly less so. After the first game, I left and never went back; how silly was I!

Whilst living at Auntie Lisa's, I came into money. I'd learnt a few things whilst living in Liffey Street from Tommy Williams and members of the Scar Gang; one of these was to find empty glass lemonade bottles, then take them to shops or pubs and in return get the penny or tuppence that was guaranteed by the companies to do so. In Liverpool 8, all the kids would scavenge far and wide, so they were in very short supply.

Jam jars were another source of revenue and when the rag and bone man came down the streets with his handcart, if you had any old clothes or empty jam jars, he would reward you with a ball or stick of liquorice, occasionally a penny or two. Rag and bonies never came to Auntie Lisa's street, but unlike Liffey Street there were quite a few shops on the adjacent main road. They all stocked lemonade and there seemed to be fewer kids round here. It was the simplest way of making my fortune.

All that was necessary was to go round to the alleyway behind the shops and help myself to some bottles or jam jars from the shop yard. Sometimes I'd have to climb over the shop wall, and sometimes I'd get lucky and the yard gate would be unlocked. I would then take my booty to another shop and collect my reward. The pub was very lax and proved to be my best source. All their empties were just stacked in crates at the rear, completely unguarded, waiting to be collected by the brewery lorry. Half a dozen at a time, taken singly from half a dozen different crates so as not to cause suspicion, would make sixpence each visit; a small fortune for me. It paid for my entrance into the boys' pen in the Kop.

The day the old Headmaster retired from Granby School was a sad one; the pupils, including all the 'hard-knocks', respected, even liked him, and the parting speeches from all the other masters and the rousing chorus of 'Jerusalem', followed by 'For he's a jolly good fellow', from the whole school, brought him to the verge of tears. Finally, he introduced the new Head, a much younger man, but nonetheless old to us boys, asking that we welcome Mr Coppack and aid him in his duties. It took only a week for practically the whole school to decide we didn't respect or like him; in fact, we hated him.

Coppack was instrumental in changing Lilly's and my direction of travel each morning on our school run. His first day as the new Head opened with him adopting the old Head's daily routine of prayers and singing with the late arrivals still kept waiting in a corridor outside. As always, I was late and joined the queue. Prayers and 'Jerusalem' ended and we filed in. Coppack stood with a face like thunder as the first lad approached the desk and was asked for an explanation, which was rejected. Then a long, very thin cane was produced from the side of the desk and the boy was given a stroke on each hand. Unlike the old Head, Coppack swung the long cane viciously, even raising one leg slightly to gain impetus and the boy involuntarily yelled with pain. There was a buzz around the assembly, quickly hushed, then a whisper down the line of boys waiting.

'Don't yell and don't cry,' was the sole message. They didn't and neither did I. More in fear of what my classmates would say or do if I made a sound. It was an hour or more before I could use my hands, and the fingers were so bruised they turned purple. Then and there I decided being late was no longer an option; we had to either use our pennies on the bus or find another way.

For a few days, much to Lilly's surprise and my frustration, we got the bus to Lodge Lane, then followed the old route round St Bernard's and on to Granby. It was only now, walking casually past the Catholic school, that I noticed boys going in through a small gate. I was determined to find where it led to on the way to putting Lilly on the bus home, but Lilly didn't want to be left standing at the bottom of Liffey Street in case any of our cousins went past, as we hadn't seen any of them since moving to Auntie Lisa's.

I ran with her to the bus stop on Lodge Lane, put her on the bus and then doubled back. By now, the St Bernard's kids had all gone and the gate was locked, but I could study the layout through a grill in the gate. Halfway across the school playground was a set of steps leading up to wooden doors with glass in the top half. I decided to go to the front of the school and peer through the main doors which were also glass; on running round to Kingsley Road and up the steps to the school and peering through the doors, I realised it was a long corridor that ran from the doors in the playground to the front of the school. Jubilation! Coppack problem solved and bus money saved. As St Bernard's was a mixed boys' and girls' school, they surely wouldn't notice Lilly and I using the gate as a shortcut.

However, the long, hard winter of playing through snowdrifts and sliding in Sefton Park, as well as all the strenuous exercise of the spring and summer months had played havoc with the only pair of shoes I had to my name, and they finally fell apart. Mam went out, with very little money, to find me a new pair and she returned to Auntie Lisa's with a pair of lace-up girls' shoes she'd found in a second-hand shop and were my size. Having given very little thought to my shoes other than to know they went on my feet, I had no idea that these were girls' ones and so went running off to school with Lilly, to try our new shortcut.

With my sister in tow, I walked casually through the back gate of St Bernard's, strolled up the steps, through the doors, down the corridor and out of the front doors. Success. Even Lilly was pleased and I was pumped up with success. The bubble was soon popped when we entered the Granby schoolyard and, standing waiting for the bell to ring for class, a boy standing nearby asked, 'Why are you wearing girls' shoes?'

Denying it vehemently only resulted in more boys gathering round and chanting, 'He's in the wrong yard; he should be next door with the girls!'

It finished abruptly when I, by now close to embarrassed tears, thumped the nearest lad then rushed around, arms swinging like a windmill, at the others. Eventually, the torment ended when it became boring, but it became known to somebody at St Bernard's, by one of the boys who was friends with him, and who also told him I used the gate as a shortcut.

The result the next morning was a gang of St Bernard's boys standing waiting in the yard by the gate. Lilly was panic-stricken, and I was not far off it either. However, my fear of Coppack was by far greater than my fear of this lot who, I consoled myself, we Granby lads always beat in our fairly constant raids on their school.

Telling Lilly to hang onto my jacket and swinging the shopping bag containing my school books, I rushed the gate, hitting some with the bag and barging the others aside with Lilly behind me, ringlets flying, and probably looking very pretty. I was safe from a rear attack and we made the steps and the corridor ahead. As much as the boys were hell-bent on hitting me, they would never have hit a girl, especially a pretty one, as I was beginning to realise Lilly was.

This routine was followed for a week or two with only the shouts of 'Girly shoes!' to anger me when yet another change of address ended the need to use St Bernard's corridor.

Girls' shoes or not, I became very keen on a girl from the girls' part of Granby Street School; I met Nancy whilst waiting outside the school for Lilly. She was thirteen with dark hair, a pretty face and was taller than me by a good two or three inches. She lived in a house on one of the side streets off Granby Street and I would run at top speed with Lilly to put her on the bus, then double back even faster to the end of Ponsonby Street, where Nancy would be waiting for me.

I earned her undying love when, one day, during the lunch break at school, I spent my last penny on a lemon from a greengrocer's opposite the school and presented it to her outside the girls' school gates; Nancy accepted it with blushed cheeks and a small smile on her face as the girls around her giggled. A couple of days later, I plucked up enough courage to ask if I could kiss her. To my surprise she said yes, but we couldn't do it here in Granby Street with other kids around, so after lots of thought, we decided a nearby jigger would hide us from public view.

Halfway down the jigger, Nancy stopped and leant back against a wall; holding her hands I attempted to kiss her. It was only then that I realised just how much taller than me she was, as I couldn't reach her lips. She tried bending her head down to me but I was having none of that. I'd seen how it was done in the pictures by my heroes, and that was how I'd do it. I left her against the wall and walked down the jigger, found two bricks and returned to Nancy. Putting them on top of each other and standing on them, I kissed her.

It was a lovely kiss, just as I'd hoped it would be, but seconds into it, whilst still holding hands, the bricks started to wobble. I wobbled too but continued to try to kiss her, as I didn't want the kiss to end. The uneven bricks wobbled again and I lost my balance, falling off; Nancy laughed.

'I need to go home now, Billy,' she said.

As I walked her back to the top of her street and said goodbye, I knew I wouldn't see her again. I vowed that day I would never try to court a girl taller than me again.

SIXTEEN

Things weren't going well at Auntie Lisa's by now; in fact, things were getting pretty stormy. She'd been loath to take us in, in the first place, and this gave her ammunition to be quite vicious to Mam. A lot of it went over Lilly's and my head at the time, but it came to its final conclusion after Auntie Lisa had heard me complaining for the umpteenth time about having to wear girls' shoes; she barged into the parlour and threw a pair of boys' shoes down on the table.

'These should fit Billy; now learn to look after your kids better, Bella, you lazy bitch!' and she stormed out of the room.

Mam and Lilly started to cry and they were immediately joined by June; I was too busy trying on the shoes, which just about fitted, to worry about them. Aunt Lisa had just gone up in my estimation, though my mam was certainly not a lazy bitch. She went further up in it the following Sunday when Mam, who had the use of the oven in the kitchen, boiled up a pan of cabbage and brought a large plateful into me saying, 'Here's your dinner, Billy; I'm taking June and Lilly out.'

She pulled out the battered old pram kept in the corner by the front window, put June in it and left the room; Lilly slowly followed, glancing back at me as she went. I sat at the table looking at my plate of cabbage, trying to decide whether to eat it or not, when the door opened and Auntie Lisa came in with a plate of Sunday dinner. She picked up my plate of cabbage, replaced it with her plate and, without saying a word, walked back out. I stared at the plate of roasted spuds, meat and vegetables, swimming in thick brown gravy. I ate every single bit, and there wasn't a scrap left on my plate at the end; I even wanted to lick the plate clean. It was the best meal I'd ever had.

When Mam returned, she'd no sooner dragged the pram up the steps outside and into the hallway when Auntie Lisa's shrill voice echoed down the hall.

'I want you out of here tomorrow, Bella! I've had enough of you; find somewhere else to stay and bloody well learn to look after your kids better!'

Mam was too distraught to even reply, but after she'd stopped crying, she started to gather up our few belongings. Lilly and I stood staring at her, not saying a word; June was oblivious to everything as she sat on the floor playing with her battered old teddy that Aunty Lilly had given her.

'No school tomorrow; we'll have to look for somewhere else to live,' Mam said wearily, not looking at us.

Lilly and I just shrugged; we'd been here so many times before.

The next day, with me pushing June in the pram, we walked up Cotswold Street, away from Auntie Lisa's without so much as a goodbye. At the top of the road, we turned down Gilead Street and rattled our way to Kensington, the main thoroughfare through Liverpool 6. Walking down the main street, we passed Jubilee Gardens then turned into Jubilee Drive. Jubilee Drive was a long, wide road with terraced houses on one side and the park on the other. The houses continued along the length of the road, with just the occasional one or two streets breaking off from it.

Fortunately, it wasn't cold or raining as Mam started at the first house, knocking on the door and begging the occupier to take us in. The response was the same at every house; a defiant no, with the slamming of the door. I was old enough to find it extremely embarrassing and looked the other way when Mam approached each house. Halfway along the street, at one of the scruffier looking houses, with an even scruffier looking woman inside, finally said yes; she had a spare room which could probably fit us all in if Mam could pay a small rent.

'I'll find the money,' Mam promised.

Inside, it was quite a big house with a long hall, off which, just as in Auntie Lisa's, was a parlour; there was also a sitting room and a very large kitchen, complete with a big black range with an oven and a big black kettle hung on a hook over the fire below. The lady explained that we would have to live in the kitchen during the day, which the family also used, and we'd have to sleep in the parlour. The only problem was that there were no beds so Mam would have to find some.

After putting the pram in the parlour, Mam left June with Lilly and me and went out to find some beds. We decided to put June back in the pram and take her for a walk in the Jubilee Gardens. Walking with June through the gardens, Lilly and I were totally agreed that this house seemed to be an improvement to Auntie Lisa's because of its closeness to the park and the fact that, on the way along Kensington, I'd spotted a public library which I was determined to use.

It was some time before Mam returned but she returned in a very good mood. She'd found some beds, she told us, and they'd be along shortly. Mam had gone back to Blackburn House where she was told yet again that she was a long way down the list, but being a 'bombed out' family, she was entitled to bits of furniture and cooking utensils and, yes, they would deliver them the same day. True to their word, a small truck arrived with two beds and mattresses, blankets and pots and pans.

Installed in the parlour, the beds were a great improvement on the sleeping arrangements we'd become used to since returning from Lancaster. Mam and June shared one bed, and Lilly and I the other. Somehow, Mam had also been allowed a small allowance of ten shillings to pay the rent. I hadn't seen her quite so happy for a long time.

The following day, Lilly and I had to return to school but there was no tram or bus service to Granby from our new home. This frustrated me greatly, as I knew that this meant we wouldn't get any tram fare. An older boy, who also lived in the house, knew where Granby Street was and gave me directions; it turned out we were much closer than I thought and, what's more, we by-passed St Bernard's so that I no longer had to fight our way out of their school yard.

It was whilst living in Jubilee Drive that I met Uncle Eddie again. Mam had been looking for other relatives and found out that Uncle Eddie had been sent to the Far East with his regiment in the war against the Japanese. He hadn't returned until almost a year after the European war had ended. Uncle Eddie lived in a 'pre-fab' with his family in the West Derby area of Liverpool. Mam had been to see them and Uncle Eddie asked how I was, as he remembered coming to see me in the hospital. He was looking forward to seeing me again.

Mam, Lilly, June and I took a bus ride to West Derby and had a pleasant reunion. Uncle Eddie had his own business, a cart with a small pony to pull it, and from it he sold fruit and vegetables which he bought from Liverpool Market in the early mornings. I thought it was fantastic.

'Hey lad,' Uncle Eddie said, after seeing my enthusiasm for his cart. 'Do you want to help me on Saturdays and before school?'

I couldn't say yes quickly enough. Since leaving Aunt Lisa's, I hadn't been able to carry on my money-making schemes, and I hadn't found a new way to make the pennies I'd become accustomed to. What I hadn't realised before saying yes, was how early the early mornings were!

With the exceptions of Sundays, any day I worked required me to be at the fruit and veg wholesale depot in the centre of town by 5.30am at the latest. After a piece of bread or the occasional bowl of porridge, I was out of the house and running to town by 5am; happily, the road into town from Jubilee Drive was all downhill. Uncle Eddie was always there before me and had always started loading up, so we were on our way by six.

The little pony would trot along with no effort at all, pulling along the cart loaded with potatoes, cabbages, carrots and, best of all, apples. Uncle Eddie was a big man, but the pony pulled us all along without complaint. Sometimes, I would be handed the reins, and I would be as proud as punch as we passed other kids who would eye me enviously as I tried to appear nonchalant and bored.

On reaching the area that had been chosen for that day, Uncle Eddie would ring a little bell to attract the good ladies who would come out of their houses and crowd around the cart. Uncle Eddie would call out the orders to me, and I would put the goods on the weighing scales using the various iron weights; he would check them, then say something like, 'And one for his nob,' and throw another spud or apple into the order whilst making a suggestive remark if she was attractive.

The ladies loved him and he could have gotten away with murder. Sometimes, I would carry the orders up to the house of the older customers and occasionally they'd give me a halfpenny or two, or sometimes just a farthing, but it always added up, and it was pennies earned that Mam knew nothing about.

Uncle Eddie paid me a shilling each day and Mam was aware of this and claimed half of it, sometimes all of it. I couldn't blame her, as wherever the money she received came from, there was never enough of it after the rent, food and clothes for us kids, and she would always go without. The pennies I received, which she knew nothing about, stayed a secret and allowed me to do things I'd be unable to do otherwise.

School was going well, and I was now in a higher form with a new teacher called Mr Robson, who was a tall, highly respected man in his fifties. He never seemed to lose his temper as others had; Mr Robson would never use a cane himself. If somebody misbehaved, he would be sent to the Head's study, the dreaded Coppack, and both would return to the classroom where the boy would be punished in front of us, usually with two strokes of the long thin cane.

As it was a boys-only school, all the teachers were male, so imagine our surprise when a very pretty, young, female student teacher arrived one day on a student training initiative! The first day everyone behaved impeccably; we were all in a state of shock as this had never happened before.

With things going so well the first day, a very relaxed student on the second day decided to read us an article which would not require the use of the blackboard. Mr Robson was sat in the only chair at the front of the class, so the girl asked two boys at the front to move to another desk, then climbed onto their desk, sitting herself on top of it with her feet on the seat, facing us.

What a joy! It was immediately apparent to us boys that we could see her knickers and stockings held up by suspenders. She started to read, completely unaware of the wonderful sight she was presenting to a class of red-blooded thirteen- to fifteen-year-old boys. She was only alerted when some of the boys not in viewing range tried to rectify the situation, causing several fights. Some wolf whistles rang out and the class descended into a cacophony of noise.

Our Master rose from his chair where he'd been making notes, realised the cause of the noise and helped the girl down off the desk, whispering an explanation and led her out of the room, her face crimson. Unfortunately, she never returned, but the dreaded Coppack did.

The whole class was caned, even those who had missed out on the lovely exhibition; Coppack must have been exhausted when he finished but he didn't show it. We never had a female student teacher again.

We had only been in Jubilee Drive a short while when Lilly finished at Granby Street. Mam had gotten her into a girls' school in Shield Road, which was a relatively short running distance along Kensington, or more often than not a short bus ride, when Mam could afford it. I was pretty pleased with this new arrangement, as I no longer had to look after Lilly, and she no longer slowed me down on my run to Granby. A further benefit was that I arrived earlier at school and could have a kick around in the playground before class.

When running down Roseberry Street, I'd noticed a very pretty girl a bit older than me leaving her house at the top of the street. She wore a college blazer, so was obviously at some posh school; I discovered later it was St Hilda's near Princess Park. One morning, running past her, I was part-way down the street when a piercing whistle stopped me in my tracks; looking back I saw the girl standing, laughing. Realising that the whistle was meant for me, I was both astounded and embarrassed, so quickly turned and continued my run, wondering why such a lovely girl would whistle at me. Girls didn't wolf-whistle, did they?

They did, or at least *she* did, because this continued as I ran past her house each day before school. After a few days, realising I would never have the nerve to stop and talk to her, I took a different, slightly longer route, and it was some time before I saw her again.

1947 was meandering towards its end when, one day, my class Master told me he had enrolled me in a boys' school choir made up of lads from different schools, who were to sing at the Liverpool Philharmonic Hall. He had realised I could sing, because there had always been a piano in one corner of our class and, on occasions when he had enjoyed a good day's teaching, he would finish early and play well-known tunes for us, inviting us to sing along.

I always loved singing and my voice hadn't yet broken, so I could reach the high notes other boys couldn't. When I realised people actually enjoyed listening to me and knowing that Lilly had a vastly better range than me, my brain went into overdrive. It was coming up to Christmas and there was money to be made.

In the lead up to Christmas, Granby, like most schools, sang a number of carols in the morning assembly, so we were word-perfect in everything from 'Silent Night' to 'Good King Wenceslas'. Lilly was very enthusiastic when I suggested carol singing round the local houses. It was always dark when we went out, and the street lights were very few and far between, but that didn't bother us in the least.

From early December right up to Christmas Eve, Lilly and I sang our hearts out, singing no less than three or four carols on each doorstep. Each house gave us what they could, even if only half a penny, but most were forthcoming both in generosity and their delight in our singing. We made what we thought was a small fortune. We had to keep it secret from Mam, though, because arriving home after the first night, we'd shown her how much we'd earned, whereupon Mam took the lot, giving us back only a couple of pennies each.

'That'll come in handy,' she said, putting the rest back in her purse.

Each night after that, before going home, we would split the takings equally between us, then halve it again to be able to claim to Mam that was all we had earned. The next day we'd buy Smith's crisps and lemonade and any unrationed sweets available, and sit in Jubilee Gardens eating and drinking our spoils. Lilly and I had finally started to become friends.

Christmas 1947 came and went, as so many Christmases had before. June got a new pair of gloves and a teddy bought by Mam with the carol singing money. Lilly and I each got a new pair of socks filled with some sweets from the ration book coupons Mam had saved up. Mam boiled some potatoes and cooked some meat, which she served with a small spoonful of gravy each; I devoured mine without stopping to speak. Afterwards, Mam asked us to sing our carols to her and June.

I had now taken to visiting more of my aunts, uncles and cousins that Mam had made contact with; I had so many cousins I was beginning to think everyone in Liverpool was a relation! My cousin John was called after his dad, Mam's brother, and his mam was also called Lilly; they lived in an old Victorian house on Canterbury Street, in an old part of Liverpool.

As soon as Aunty Lilly saw me, she said to Uncle John, 'There's no doubt who he is, eh, John? He's the image of Bella's fella.'

I realised she meant me Dad, and I felt proud. John and I got on well, especially as he had all kinds of toys to play with, so I visited him as often as I could; it was an easy running distance from Jubilee Drive and it was always worth the run to play with John's toys and have a slice of cake or a piece of pie from Auntie Lilly.

John and I would also visit Auntie Carrie, another of Mam's sisters, who had six kids, but her home was nothing like John's. Though just a few streets away from Canterbury Street, she lived in a circular tenement block with half a dozen steps up to the front of each terraced house. Each house had a kitchen and a parlour, both very small, and two very small bedrooms. The communal toilets were out in the central courtyard and the only water supply was from a communal, hand-operated water pump.

Despite this, my cousins always appeared really happy and we would all play together for hours. Auntie Carrie would always have jam butties, big thick doorstops filled with jam I'm sure she made herself. Auntie Carrie's kids were all younger than me, and I wondered how on earth she managed to keep them all clean. I couldn't imagine them standing at the water pump in the middle of the tenement block whilst Auntie Carrie washed them down. On asking my Auntie Lilly, whilst playing at John's house one day, she explained that, on a Sunday afternoon, Auntie Carrie would bring all six kids up here and three at a time they would use Auntie Lilly's bath.

In our house on Jubilee Drive, they did have a rather brown stained bath full of cracks, which Lilly and I were allowed to use once a week. I didn't have any problems with washing, though, as the polio scare had run its course and the baths had reopened. Lodge Lane and Dovecot baths were now well out of my range and so I'd started going to Steble Street in the Dingle area, with my new friend, Billy Armitage. The Dingle area was one of the poorer areas of Liverpool with lots of tenement buildings and rows of terraced houses.

Billy lived in one of the terraced houses on Foxhill Street and, much like myself, he was a quiet lad at school, interested in doing well and not interested in smoking, swearing and generally misbehaving as with so many of the other lads at Granby. Billy and I got on well and it wasn't long before instead of going home after school I was staying at his house, made welcome by his mam and dad.

Like me, Billy was an enthusiastic swimmer and Steble Street baths was only about a mile from his home. It was an old building with white tiled walls all around, with exactly the same white tiles forming the swimming pool; the only change of colour in the whole place were the wooden doors of the few changing cubicles surrounding the pool. The security on the front door was too good and so bunking in was not an option, but the fee was tuppence each, which was affordable for us both, and we got hours of fun after school.

Walking back to Billy's house along Northumberland Street, we would pass a chippy, and on the odd occasion we had a penny or two left over, we would ask the Greek owner for any scraps. He often had, so for a penny each, he'd give us a pretty big bag of well-fried batter that he'd fish out of his fryer. After hours of fun in the baths, it was food from the Gods to us two hungry lads.

Billy's dad kept a number of rabbits in various cages in his backyard. I never asked why, but I learnt the reason for it on one occasion when I was staying for tea; he served up rabbit and barley soup, followed by rabbit meat and boiled potatoes. I didn't ask which rabbit it was we were eating, but on going out to the toilet in the yard, passing the cages and failing to see my favourite rabbit, the penny dropped.

In Foxhill Street, none of the houses had bathrooms, so it was the old tin bath in front of the fire that was used by different members of the family on different nights of the week. Billy had a brother two years younger than him and a sister of eight years old, who all took their turns bathing in the tin bath. I was amazed one day when he said it was his mother's turn that evening and did I want to watch?

'We go round the back,' he said conspiratorially. 'Come into the yard and there's a small gap in the curtains; you can see everything as Dad scrubs her back and front.'

I couldn't think of anything I'd rather not see and said so in no uncertain terms. Billy just didn't understand and thought it was hilarious, though I think thereafter he gave up on it.

One day, after spending our usual hours in Steble Street baths, we returned to Billy's house to find his dad distraught. Someone had broken into his rabbit cages and stolen all of them, then wrecked the cages. I didn't think I'd ever seen somebody so upset. Strangely, he loved his rabbits, even though every so often he would cook one.

We never found out who stole the rabbits, but it wasn't long before Mr Armitage took up another hobby. He rebuilt one of the cages and started bottling onions. He had shelves full of them, all in his own spiced-up vinegar. Billy and I discovered that we really did like pickled onions, so whenever his dad was not around we would open several jars and take a few from each, hoping that they wouldn't be noticed, and sat back and enjoyed ourselves.

School was now going very well for me and my School Master encouraged me to aim for the School Certificate, as he felt I could certainly pass. I wasn't so sure; besides which, all grammar school kids in the area were known by the Granby boys as College Puddings, and were prone to being beaten up if they were foolish enough to cross into the Granby area.

However, I was still reading books and comics with stories of life at a boarding school and they filled my imagination; even reading some of the scarier happenings in *Tom Brown's School Days* didn't put me off. I knew there wasn't a snowball's chance in hell of ever going to a boarding school, but I accepted there was a possibility of a chance at a Grammar or Technical and so I spent more and more time, when not over at Billy's, going to the library in Kensington. I would take out two or even three books at a time, as the librarian knew how quickly I could read them and return them. I read most of the books in my bed at night by the light of a single candle; I would be tucked under my blanket with a burning candle in a Wee Willy Winkie holder resting on my pillow with one hand holding my blanket up and the other holding my book.

In class, I would write adventure stories featuring pirates and knights. Occasionally, the Master would be quite impressed and would read out my story to the class and, in doing so, would diminish my stature with most of them, instead of enhancing it, which I'm sure was his original intention. Naturally, more fights in the school yard followed; some I won and some I lost, but it just made me more determined to pass the next year's exams.

Most of my time out of school was spent swimming or at home reading or just wandering round the streets or parks with Billy. I'd lost interest in going to football training with the school, as it took up too much of my time after school finished at 4 o'clock, and I realised that I was never going to be a player of the calibre of Downey, who I had always admired.

Though I still watched Liverpool whenever I could, I knew I'd never play for them, so I spent more of my time at Billy's doing absolutely nothing and yet, bizarrely, enjoying it, except when Gladys was around.

Gladys was a quite pretty girl who, with her younger sister Dolores, lived opposite the Armitages' house. About the same age as Billy and me, on a couple of occasions Gladys attempted to enjoy our company, though neither Billy nor I were really that interested in girls; in fact, we were both very shy, so we rejected her. Gladys didn't like it one little bit so, along with Dolores, she would lie in wait for us, then follow us wherever we were going shouting, 'Baby face!' and, 'Why don't you get some long pants, you babies?'

The fact that the both of us were still in short pants hadn't, up to that point, bothered us, and still didn't bother Billy, but it certainly did me; as did being called 'Baby face'. Foolishly, instead of just ignoring her, we would set off at a gallop and would eventually outrun her and her sister. Her taunts continued for several weeks but finally she got bored of it and decided to move on to another target.

It was another year before I got to wear long trousers. It was 1948, and Billy and I decided to join the Air Training Corps as a step to joining the RAF in the not-so-distant future, not that it actually came to anything! I was still reading W.E. John's *Biggles* books and even his stories about the Women's Auxiliary Air Force and WAAF Flight Officer Joan 'Worrals' Worralson. I still had the impossible dream of being a fighter pilot; Billy just came along for the ride.

We decided to join 1366 ATC Squadron, which met once a week in a school in the Dovecot area of Liverpool, a more upmarket area of the city. From Billy's house it was a good two to three mile walk each time, but it was worth it, as after a couple of weeks they supplied us with our uniforms. How grown up and smart we felt when we got changed at

Billy's and walked past people we knew, including Gladys. Everyone, with the exception of Gladys, would give us a smile or a pretend salute; even some of the 'hard-knocks' we bumped into didn't bother us. Perhaps it was the abiding memories of the recent war, but whatever it was, people seemed to respect us.

After a few weeks of training, during which I learnt the Morse Code, I went up a notch in rank and was then offered, by one of the ex-RAF instructors, the chance to fly with him for a couple of hours one weekend. I was beyond excited. I was to meet him at Speke airport, which presented a bit of a problem because it was a long way from Jubilee Drive or Foxhill Street. Somehow, though, I managed to get the few pence for the bus fare and duly arrived at Speke.

The ATC instructor met me at the gate and we went over to an Auster, a two-seater plane where we were able to sit side by side. In my uniform, taking off over the Mersey, I felt like my comic book hero Rockfist Rogan. The heroic feeling quickly left me as my pilot, after giving me a sideways glance with a grin on his face, proceeded to demonstrate all the flying manoeuvres he'd learnt as a real RAF pilot. My stomach went from zero to 360 degrees and back again as he dived and dumped on an imaginary enemy, all the time watching me with the same grin on his face.

I knew he was determined to make me sick, as he'd given me a bag for that purpose when I climbed aboard. I was equally determined that I wouldn't be, and I wasn't, probably helped by the fact that, as on most days, I'd had nothing to eat since the evening before.

Flight over, he said, 'Well done, we must do it again sometime, son.'

'Oh no, we won't!' I thought as I set on for the extremely long walk home.

Billy introduced me to a lad he had gotten to know who lived near him, but didn't go to Granby Street School. Paul Wallace was a member of a church club which held meetings in an old house at the bottom of Lodge Lane, and he suggested that the next time he went, Billy and I should go with him and, if we liked it, perhaps join.

'No way!' Billy said. 'I ain't going to no church.' I nodded in agreement with Billy.

'You should come,' Paul replied. 'We're having a fancy dress party in a couple of weeks.'

'No,' Billy said bluntly.

'The parties are always good; we play games and there's loads of food.'

'I'll come!' I said instantly, easily persuaded at the thought of food. Billy just stared at me, but eventually he slowly nodded his head.

The following week, we turned up at the door of the old house and were welcomed in by the aging priest.

'Welcome, lads, come on in. Just join in any of the games that you feel like.'
I entered a large room where boys and girls were sat on the floor.

'This is a great game,' Paul said with a grin on his face. 'We all get a piece of paper with a number on it; here you go,' he said, handing Billy and me a piece each. I looked at mine; number twelve.

'Sit down and wait for your number to be called; it'll be a girl who calls it from behind that door,' he said, pointing to a door on the far side. 'When you go through to the other side, you'll get a kiss.'

I stared at him in amazement. As simple as that? I got my number called and would then get a kiss from a girl? Paul's grin was huge and even Billy was smiling at this new game.

It wasn't long before number twelve was called out from behind the door. After an encouraging slap on my back from Paul, I tentatively stood and walked over to the door, aware of all the eyes watching me. Slowly opening the door, I peered behind and got the most wonderful shock of my life. Standing there was the beautiful girl from Roseberry Street who had whistled to me as I ran past her house on the way to school!

'Hi,' she said, smiling at me. 'I'm Lorna Worthington.'

No words would come out of my dry mouth.

Leaning against me, she gave me a kiss. It was much longer and sweeter than the kisses we got when we played Reallio in Lancaster. At that point, I fell in love with Lorna Worthington.

When she let me go, I said, 'Thank you!' and walked in a daze back into the room.

'So, who'd you get?' Paul whispered as soon as I sat back down.

'Lorna Worthington.'

'You lucky sod! Most lads 'ere would kill for a kiss off her; she's going out with Joey Dooley though,' Paul replied sadly.

My world crashed. Joey Dooley was an older lad who lived near her house in Roseberry Street; he also wore long trousers. I thought things might change when Lorna saw me in my fancy dress costume the following week, when Billy and I wore our ATC uniforms, complete with long trousers, but it didn't.

The fancy dress party wasn't too bad, although Paul decided to come dressed as a girl with a Veronica Lake-style wig, dress and shoes. I got to look at Lorna from across the room, but, more importantly, I was able to help myself from the buffet table of food and ate so many sausage rolls and egg sandwiches that I thought I was going to pop! Suddenly, there was a loud commotion and I saw two lads pushing and shoving each other, and Joey Dooley was one of them. I saw the panic on Lorna's face as she followed the two rowing boys outside. A large crowd followed and soon Billy and I were swept up with everyone moving out of the building.

On the front lawn the two lads were fighting, fists flying and blood splaying, neither prepared to give up. What a fight! I kept seeing Lorna wince as a fist hit Joey's face, but then he would retaliate with a harder punch. Eventually, Joey threw a punch which landed the other boy on the ground. Surprisingly to me, Joey reached down and pulled the lad up off his feet. With bloodied faces, split lips and bleeding noses, the two lads shook hands and everyone cheered. Joey walked over to Lorna, put his arm round her shoulders and they went back inside.

SEVENTEEN

It was autumn when we upped sticks and moved again. Our time at Jubilee Drive had been one of our longer stints in a house since leaving Lancaster. I had become quite used to living there and looked upon it as my home. Now we were off again and I had no idea why. Mam just said we were going to a place with a lot more room.

We moved to a house on Schomberg Street, where one of dad's brothers, Uncle George, also lived, and who was probably instrumental in instigating the move. It was a better house than we'd had before, and the elderly couple, Mr and Mrs Ramsay, who lived there, gave us the run of the place. We were allowed to use the parlour and the kitchen and Mam, Lilly and June shared a bedroom, whilst I was given a bed in the garret.

Although I finally had my own area in which to sleep, the garret was a miserable place; cold and dark, it had no lighting and the steep steps up to it didn't have lighting either. Even during the day it was always dull. The eaves had a gap of about six inches on each side, which the wind whistled through most nights, and there were pigeons nesting in the corners.

My first night of climbing the rickety stairs with my Wee Willy Winkie candle holder in one hand and my collection of books in the other set the scene for future bedtime routines. As I climbed the stairs, I heard someone else behind me. Stopping and raising the candle to be able to see behind me, there was nobody there. Thinking I had imagined it, I continued up and so did the steps. Each time I stopped, they did. I ran up the stairs as quickly as I could without causing the candle to go out, got into bed, blew out the candle and pulled the blankets up over my head, breathing heavily. I held my breath and listened for any further sounds, but all I could hear was the cooing of the pigeons. I was too scared to relight the candle and so my days of reading for hours in bed were numbered. I never got used to the sound of the footsteps behind me as I climbed up to bed every night, but they were always there.

All the houses on Schomberg Street had a front garden; as June was now two years old and a precocious toddler, Lilly and I would have to spend a lot of our free time looking after her.

Schomberg Street was close to West Derby Road, which had a bus route that stopped at the junction of Shield Road, where Lilly's school was.

'How come she gets a bus fare to school?' I asked Mam, whereupon our usual row ensued, followed by the usual clout round my head. However, I'd learnt to catch Mam's hands before the second clout reached me. I was now stronger than her, and for the next couple of minutes she wrestled with me, demanding I let her go so she could clout me again. Eventually, I let go and then legged it out of the house.

I worked out a new route to school which took me through a vast bombed out area, but happily it was mainly downhill and still took me down Roseberry Street. Although she was still courting Joey Dooley, Lorna Worthington would still whistle and laugh as I ran past.

On my way home from school one day, whilst walking through the bombed out area, I noticed a small kitten. I bent down to stroke it and it happily let me, rubbing its face into my hand and purring. As I walked away, it followed me. I picked it up and put it back where I first saw it, but he kept following me.

'Bloody hell, cat, leave me alone,' I said to it, putting it back again, but he continued to follow me. Winding its way between my legs, in a moment of stupidity I picked it up and put it inside my windcheater. To my surprise, the old couple were happy for me to keep it, and so I named it Tiddles. For years to come, Tiddles was to become a millstone around my neck. From a kitten he liked nobody but me, and sometimes not even me; he was, in fact, insane. I suppose it was my fault as wherever I went, other than school, Tiddles would come with me, zipped inside my windcheater.

Mam hated him, Lilly also wasn't too keen, and June wasn't allowed anywhere near him. The two of us would often head off to New Brighton, walking most of the way and bunking onto a bus whenever I could, where Tiddles would roll around in the sand or ride with me on the roundabout which I managed to bunk onto in the fairground. Tiddles often thought of himself as our guard dog, and no other dog or cat would come anywhere near the house if Tiddles was sat in the front garden. If a visitor came to the house, Tiddles would run down the hall and attempt to scratch their legs.

Mam would kick the cat out of the way and yell at me, 'Lock that bloody cat away before I get rid of it!'

Tiddles would glare at Mam as I picked him up and carried him up to the garret.

The Ramsays had a radio and we were allowed to listen to various programmes with them in the parlour. Tiddles would be curled up on my lap as I sat on the floor listening to Arthur Askey and other comedians, howling with laughter. One of my favourites was 'Dick Barton – Special Agent', and I would sit engrossed in his stories, relieved in the knowledge that the war was over and that this was not for real.

Uncle George gave me a gramophone, which I was in awe of. Mr and Mrs Ramsay, Mam, Lilly and June all gathered around me in the parlour as I carried in the large wooden case with the huge trumpet attached. Uncle George had given me a record to go with it, so I wound up the long wooden handle as much as it would go, pushed the on switch which started the turntable rotating, and moved the arm which held the needle down onto the record. The 'Grenadier Guard's March' started to play loudly out of the trumpet speaker.

'Bloody hell, turn that noise down!' Mam said.

'I can't,' I replied, 'There's no volume control.'

Suddenly, the fine needle on the arm broke off; the arm jumped out of the groove and screeched loudly across the record.

'Billy!' Mam yelled. 'Turn it off!'

I quickly picked up the arm and turned the machine off; I turned to see everyone staring at me, then they all left the room until only Mr Ramsay and I were left.

'Billy, let's see if we can fix it,' Mr Ramsay said gently, and he set to work replacing the needle from the spares Uncle George had given me.

'Let's try the other side of the record,' Mr Ramsay suggested when he finished and he turned the record over, switched the turntable on, and gently moved the arm into place. Out of the large horn played 'The Teddy Bear's Picnic'.

I grinned at Mr Ramsay.

'There you go, son, enjoy.' And he left the room.

I played the music over and over again until even Tiddles got bored of listening and wandered out. It was the only record I had and, as I had no money to buy any more, Mam got sick of me playing it and a couple of weeks later she gave the gramophone to the rag and bone man. She said Mrs Ramsay had said it was either the gramophone or us; I didn't believe her.

Schomberg Street was fairly close to an area of Liverpool known as Everton Valley where the Lytton Picture House, or Saturday Bug Hut as we called it, was situated down a scruffy little street and it devoted every Saturday morning to showing kids' pictures. Outside the cinema you would always find a man with a handcart full of bags of past their sell-by date apples known as 'fades'. For a penny or two he would cut all the overripe parts from half a dozen apples, then cut the remaining bits into slices and put them in a paper bag.

We'd pay our penny entrance fee, usually begged from Mam, which I had to earn by minding June and running messages, then enter the tiny auditorium with my friends. There were four rows of wooden benches facing the big screen and as many boys as possible would be crammed in; there only ever seemed to be boys in the auditorium, and certainly Lilly never went with us.

We would sit in eager anticipation as the first couple of short films, usually comedies with Laurel and Hardy or The Three Stooges, were shown in grainy black and white and the place would fill with laughter. Then the main film would be shown, my favourites being the cowboy films with actors such as Johnny Mack Brown, Hop-along-Cassidy, The Durango Kid or Zorro. The silence in the auditorium was broken only by loud cheers as our heroes performed a supreme deed, or by even louder boos and cat calls as the baddies seemed to get the upper hand. This always led to scores of apple slices being rained at the screen, and if a bad guy was hit, the auditorium would cheer and jump up from the benches in satisfaction. At the end of the show, all the boys would file out, walking over a carpet of squashed apples, but nobody seemed to mind and the next Saturday it would be repeated all over again.

I didn't mind throwing my pieces of apple at the screen as I always returned home on a Saturday afternoon to a freshly baked apple pie by Mam; she seemed to make one every Saturday as she knew she was good at it. Mam would use the biggest dish she could find, line it with thick pastry and fill it with as many apples as possible. The smell of it baking in the oven would fill the house and Lilly, June and I would wait in excited anticipation of when Mam would take it out and tell us we could have some. It was the best dish she ever made.

The weeks went by with very little change. I still ran to school every day and continued to see Billy and also now Joey Dooley afterwards. Billy and I still went to Steble Street baths and we were regulars at the Saturday Bug Hut.

Shortly before Christmas, Lilly and I decided to start carol singing again, and, as we'd earned such good money the year before in Jubilee Drive, we decided to head back there. We went from door to door singing our hearts out and the pennies flew into the hat we held out. Returning home each evening, frozen stiff, Mam would be stood there waiting, holding out her hand for what we had earned, happily counting the coppers and wishing us well for the next evening. Little did she know that, also like last year, we only handed over half of what we made, sharing the other half between us.

I didn't spend it on lemonade or crisps or sweets this year, but instead kept it safe so I could pay for tickets to watch Liverpool matches at Anfield. Lilly and I also decided to buy Mam and June a present each for Christmas. Mam got a mixing bowl and wooden spoon so she could make even better apple pies and June got a new doll. Mam was so pleased and never asked where we'd got the money from.

A week before Christmas, I developed tonsillitis and my throat became septic. School was out of the question, even leaving the house was difficult, and I quickly became delirious. Mam said I couldn't possibly sleep in the cold and damp attic, even if I could have made it up the stairs. Despite being fourteen, I was still small for my age, and I fitted, unbelievably, although with my legs dangling over the edge, in June's pram, and that's where I slept for the next week. I couldn't eat anything, but I discovered sucking on a pink peppermint bar helped immensely. The bar was classed as a sweet but, as medicine was out of the question as it was so expensive, Mam used the sweet ration coupons to get me as many of the bars as she could; she even used Lilly's and June's coupons, much to their annoyance!

Billy came over one day to see why I hadn't been to school or to see him, but Mam wouldn't let him come into her room to see me. He told Mam that he would be leaving school after Christmas as he would be fifteen in January. I was really upset; I hadn't realised he was older than me. Some of the other boys that had been in my class who I knew were older had left in the summer. George Wayland, being one of them, went on to be a boxer, but Billy leaving too was a big surprise.

Recovering from tonsillitis took longer than we'd expected and I didn't feel up to going to school for a week or more after my throat recovered. Eating very little had certainly taken its toll; my already thin frame was thinner still and I was extremely weak. I also discovered I had developed a hatred of pink peppermint bars, much to mine and Mam's surprise!

Eventually, returning to school, with the usual daily runs there and back, I soon built up my strength and fell back into my old routine. With only a few months to go until I would sit my School Certificate exams, I threw myself back into my studies. I was determined to do as well as I could so that I could go to grammar school and attend the type of rich boy's school a lot of my heroes in books did.

I did well in my class at Granby, got on very well with my Form Master and made several enemies with some lads in class who saw me as a school swat. Billy was aware of my ambition, but thought it was a complete waste of time and couldn't wait to leave school and find a job and, with it, money. Unfortunately, Mam thought much the same and was forever telling me I would have to work when I left school and bring in the money. She was probably right, but I'd always had the dream of a better education, and I was determined to get there, come what may.

We boys in Senior Class discovered we had a new series of lessons to attend: Woodwork. We learnt how to make small wooden objects useful in the home and, by doing so, would automatically learn how to measure and about angles, and with it the ability to use a saw, chisel, hammers and mallet. The last time I had used anything like this was back in Lancaster making the go-cart, in a successful yet ramshackle way.

Our Woodwork classroom was based in a small building at least half a mile away from the school. No transport was provided and as the Woodwork instructor, Mr Williams, was based at the remote site, we had to make our own way there. The result was that by the time we reached the classroom, a third of our class had disappeared and the lad who'd been given the class list of names invariably was one of the missing ones. When asked where the list was by the teacher, we'd have to lie and say we'd never been given one. As this happened every time we turned up to class, the instructor seemed to accept our excuse without question.

The room we worked in had lines of woodwork benches complete with vices and rows of tools and we were each allocated an area to work in. Some of the class had handled tools before and were quite adept, but the majority, myself being one them, were quite bemused and, in being instructed to pick up a particular tool and use it, had no idea. Woody, as we quickly called Mr Williams, would choose a culprit and make him go to the blackboard behind the benches and write down the object's name as spelt out by Woody. He'd then rub it out and tell the lad to write it again half a dozen times; if any of the words were misspelt, the lad would receive a belt on the back of the head with whatever Woody was holding at the time. We all learnt to spell the names of the tools very quickly!

We realised, in a very short space of time, that Mr Williams was indeed as mad as a hatter; he would become enraged if somebody as much as whispered to the lad next to him when he should have been working. If Woody was holding piece of wood, a set square or even a tool, he would throw it at the lad and on one occasion he even threw a mallet. As well as watching what we ourselves were doing, we'd also keep a weary eye on Woody, and had all learnt to duck.

Woody showed us all how to saw a piece of wood with a long saw and one by one we all placed the bits of wood on the trestle and held it in place by putting our right knee on it. Whether he'd told us to actually move our leg out of the way as we sawed, or if I just hadn't listened, I'm not sure, but I yelled out as I managed to saw my leg above the knee. Woody panicked as he heard me yell and saw blood pouring from my leg, and he smacked me round the head and told me what a bloody idiot I was and then ran for the first aid kit by his desk. He yelled at everyone else to carry on with their work as he started to bandage my leg,

'And pay attention to what you're doing, unlike this bloody idiot!' he shouted.

Not long into the start of 1949, we were on the move again. Mam never explained why; she just told me to pack up my things and make sure I got Tiddles, as Mr and Mrs Ramsay did not want him left there.

Liverpool Football Club had been doing very well in the FA Cup and, not long after they beat Nottingham Forest 4-0 in an FA Cup replay, I found out we were to move into the street next to Anfield stadium. I'd virtually be a neighbour to my heroes! Now I could just walk round the corner to reach the boys' pen in the Kop.

The move to 60 Lothair Road was not too difficult, as we had very little furniture and belongings, but Mam and I struggled as we carried our two beds up to the attic room that had been allocated to Lilly and me; Mam and June were to share her bed in the basement room. Imagine my delight when I discovered that the bathroom upstairs, which we were allowed to use, overlooked Anfield's car park and that the players used it for training! I'd kneel on the toilet lid, peering out of the window and watch with avid admiration as the players wandered into the car park with their boots slung around their necks. The reserves and first team would stand in circles and have a coach throw a ball to them, which they would head back, and after several minutes of doing this, the ball would then be thrown to their feet and they'd kick it back. I could not believe how lucky I was to be able to watch my footballers train.

Shortly after arriving at my new home, I got even luckier. On the corner of our road was a small shop that sold anything and everything, including lemonade. I remembered my money-making scheme from Liffey Street and found that if I leant as far out of the bathroom window as I possibly could, I could see the backyard of the small shop where crates full of empty lemonade bottles were stacked. The main road at the other end of Lothair Road had a row of shops, one of which was a newsagent that sold lemonade.

The basement of the house had a small scullery off the front room where Mam and June slept; it had a working cooker which was solely for Mam's use and a door which led into the backyard where there was an outside toilet. The yard had a gate at the end which led onto the jigger behind all the houses and the small shop.

Once it was dark, when Mam thought I was using the outdoor closet, I'd sneak out the back gate, climb over the shop's back wall and put two or three bottles into an old bag I kept hidden in the yard. Unlocking their back gate, I'd do a couple of runs with bottles before re-locking the gate, climbing back over the wall and running back home. Hiding the bottles in the backyard, I'd then leave them until the next day, when I'd take them round to the newsagent; luckily they never asked how I came by so many empty bottles, just paid me the pennies which I'd hide in my room in a little tin under my bed.

Things got even better when the newsagent told me her usual paperboy had left and asked if I wanted the job! 'I pay 2/6 a week, Sundays included,' she said.

I jumped at the chance. I just had to find a way of explaining to Mam why I was getting up earlier each day, otherwise she'd take all my earnings.

'I've been picked for the school football team,' I told her one afternoon whilst she scrubbed her cooker clean.

'That's good, Billy, but I ain't buying you any kit.'

'I don't need it,' I said truthfully. 'But I 'ave to get up early every day, Mam, so I'll be leaving about half five each day.'

Mam didn't even notice.

I quite enjoyed getting up early when everyone else was sleeping and enjoyed it even more when I got to the newsagent's before 6am and, after going through their back gate, found crates of empty lemonade bottles. It was so simple to drop a couple of empty bottles into my paper bag, only to hand them in to the small shop at the end of the road, once I'd finished my paper round. Life was becoming very sweet.

Rich once again, I didn't tell Mam.

At this time, I was also studying hard, both at school and at home, as I was still determined to pass my School Certificate exams, which were not far off. Mam was still adamant that I'd be leaving school and getting a job, the pay from which she would then get. Even if I passed and got into Toxteth Technical Institute, my chosen school, Mam didn't have the money for my uniform, satchel and books, plus the bus fare each day, so my newfound way of gaining income allowed me to save up pennies each week, whilst still at Granby.

A month or so after starting my job, and with the help of my bottle returns, I had managed to save thirteen or fourteen shillings, and each time I added a few more pennies, I felt guilty at not helping Mam. I learnt from conversations I overheard between Mam and Auntie Lilly that Mam got money from 'Social Security' and 10 shillings a week from June's father in Lancaster, though that was never enough. I convinced myself that by passing my exams and going to TTI and learning a good trade, I would finally have a well-paid job and make it up to her. In the meantime, I would hang on to my earnings.

Then, disaster struck. Lilly spotted me delivering papers.

One morning, after I'd left the house early, Lilly was late for her school and was running to catch a later bus just as I finished my round and was returning to the newsagent's. I didn't see her, but she saw me, and on returning home that evening, Mam was waiting.

'How long have you been doing a paper round, Billy?' she enquired in that tone of voice which usually precluded a clout round the ear-hole.

'Not long,' I answered glibly. 'A week.'

'Liar!' she accused, following up with the expected clout, which through long practice I easily evaded.

'Don't you dare move when I'm trying to clout you!' Mam shouted and aimed a further clout at my head which, foolishly, I once again evaded; this made her even angrier. Now two hands were aimed at me, one for each cheek. This time I grabbed both her wrists and stopped their blows. Mam yelled even louder and tried to free herself; realising that I was now stronger than her, I just held on and, after a few moments of struggling, she gave up.

Letting go of her, I moved quickly to the side. 'They don't pay much but I've got two bob saved; you can have it!' I said, knowing I had two shillings in my pocket. Handing over the money to Mam calmed her down for a moment, before she dropped the next bombshell.

'I'm going round to see that newsagent tomorrow.'

Realising this would be the end of my paper round earnings, I said quickly, 'No need; I gave up the job this morning. She doesn't need me anymore.' And I stormed out of the parlour and up to my room in the attic where I wrote a letter for the newsagent, ending my employment.

Shortly after finishing my note, Lilly came upstairs, and she seemed contrite.

'I didn't realise telling Mam would cause so much trouble, Billy.'

I didn't believe her. Lilly never lost an opportunity to get me into trouble with Mam, but I resisted the impulse to give her a dig, which must have surprised her as much as it did me. I looked at Lilly and realised she was not a young girl anymore. At thirteen years old, she suddenly seemed much older. Although our relationship had begun to change, she still drove me nuts and still seemed to take great pleasure in it.

At bedtime she would always sit on the end of her bed and take as long as she liked taking out all the clips and pins in her hair, then stroll over to the mantelpiece and place each one individually on top, forming a straight line which she would meticulously check, making sure each one was just so. I'd be lying in my bed waiting impatiently for her to blow out the candle so I could sleep, but she seemed to enjoy winding me up.

I actually think we both dreaded going to sleep as ever since we'd moved into this house, our beds had become infested with bed bugs and we'd wake each morning to find red spots on our arms and legs where we had been feasted on in the night. Mam tried her best to kill them off by removing the bedding and pouring spoonfuls of paraffin into the joints and cracks in the wood frames, all to no avail because even if she did manage to kill them, others would soon take their place. We had no option but to live with it.

A further disappointment that hit me at much the same time was to find that my source of empty lemonade bottles came to an end when the corner shop, finally realising that bottles were going missing, had the entire wall surrounding the yard embedded with broken glass, making it impossible to climb over. On top of that, they also got a rather large dog who lived in the yard. To my dismay, Tiddles suddenly disappeared one night, never to return again. I wondered if the big dog next door had scared him away. The sweet life was over.

It was at this point that something I'd subconsciously understood, but had never previously accepted, was that Mam didn't really like me very much. Lilly was the apple of her eye and, of course, June would always be so. I decided our separation during the war years and my total freedom during that time had created a gap that could never really be closed. I knew in my own way that I loved Mam, yet I felt the feeling was never reciprocated by her.

My utter determination to better myself, to go on with my schooling when Mam insisted I should leave and go to work, created an even bigger divide between us. Deep down I worried she may be right, because she was my mam, but I couldn't accept it. After all, for most of my life, I had looked after myself and looked after Lilly as well. Now I wanted to realise my dreams and go to a real school with a uniform and an iconic school badge, just like my comic book heroes. My exams were my passport to my dreams and I worked harder and harder to achieve them.

I still bunked into Anfield on alternate Saturdays to watch my football heroes play, but when they hit a poor spell, I deserted them. It was the only time in my life that I allowed this to happen, and I felt ashamed that I did it, but my only consolation was that it allowed me more to study and it was time well spent, because finally I passed my exams and was awarded my School Certificate - my pass to the promised land.

Mr Coppack became a totally different person after my achievement; he was especially pleased that I wanted to join the TTI and gave me all the help possible. When asked what I wanted to study, it came as a bit of a surprise to me that I hadn't really given it much thought. School and lessons were all I'd ever considered. Now old Coppack came to those who had passed the exams with advisors from the Education Authorities to tell us what was on offer. I discovered that as well as learning about different trades, normal school work would continue but with the addition of a foreign language such as French added. I began to realise what I had let myself in for. This was not at all like the stories I'd read about my comic book heroes. It was with great trepidation that I agreed that I'd study architecture, including bricklaying and other skills.

Happily, I had the school summer holidays to come before starting at my new school. I spent the time visiting second-hand shops in the Anfield area and even further afield looking for a blazer to which I could sew a badge. I still hadn't told Mam that I'd passed my exams and that I would be going to the TTI, but led her to believe I was looking for a job. I knew that the day I had to tell her the truth, all hell would be let loose. To make matters worse, she'd want to know where the money had come from to buy a blazer and, more than that, it was essential that I have my bus fare money to school and back, as there was no way I could get to Toxteth doing my usual run through areas where my uniform would be like a red rag to a bull.

The day arrived that I finally found a blazer and a cap that fitted. I'd hoped to also get a pair of long trousers, but unfortunately the blazer and cap ate up all my hidden funds.

Mam, as expected, blew her top. 'You are the most selfish so and so in the world, Billy!' she yelled at me, throwing an empty pan across the parlour. 'After everything I've gone through since your father died to look after you three!'

Surprisingly, Lilly said nothing, when usually she would side with Mam. June just cried.

I did my best to try to make Mam understand that in the long run it would benefit all of us, but it was falling on deaf ears. She would not listen to me and I left the house disappointed that Mam couldn't be happy for me, just this once.

A couple of days later, Auntie Lilly paid one of her infrequent visits to the house and Mam wasted no time in telling her what a terrible son she had reared.

'Bella, what are you on about?' she exclaimed. 'You should be proud of Billy! In the long run, you'll be pleased he's done this apparently selfish deed!'

Mam wasn't best pleased with Auntie Lilly and, with only a week to go before starting at the TTI, we hardly spoke.

Whilst lying in our beds one night, I told Lilly what I expected the future to hold and, surprisingly, she was on my side, though she didn't dare tell Mam. I also told her how I'd have to buy a badge for my blazer and my cap, for which I'd saved the remainder of my secret stash; Lilly said she'd sew them on for me.

In the event, it was actually Mam who sewed them on, which I took to mean that Auntie Lilly had been instrumental in changing Mam's mind-set; she also told me the bus fare would be forthcoming.

On the morning of my first day of college, Mam presented me with an old school satchel she'd bought from a second-hand shop.

'You'll have to have something to carry your books in, Billy.'

I grinned at her as I positioned my cap proudly on my head and hung the satchel over my shoulder.

'Good luck, Billy,' Lilly said, as I headed to the door.

I felt proud as punch.

EIGHTEEN

Two or three months later, I decided the TTI wasn't for me. I hated it. All my long-held dreams of sport, adventure and wonderful pals from well-to-do families came to nothing. As a skinny, small new boy who still came to school in short pants, in shoes requiring urgent remedial work, and in what was obvious to all a well-worn blazer, I was not so much looked down on as totally ignored. This led, when I had tried to join in games or conversation, to hurtful remarks, which in turn led to the inevitable fights. Some I won, some I lost; however, if nothing else I earned some grudging respect, but no lasting friendships.

These attitudes were responsible for me hating to leave our little home each day and failing to absorb the learning I had once so enjoyed. I was supposed to be learning French, but our teacher's accent was a hybrid of Scouse with a great deal of 'hillbilly' Lancastrian as well, and he seemed to enjoy asking me to read a few words. The chortles of my classmates rang in my ears as I felt my face turn red whilst attempting to read the alien words scrawled on the blackboard. I wasn't the only one who was asked to read and found it difficult, but perhaps I was more thin-skinned than I thought. I just hated it. Learning the basics of architecture, my chosen subject, was torture. The growing hatred of coming to school just switched off my mind to learning and I must have been a total loss to the Masters.

I had taken to playing hooky, probably to the relief of the Master concerned. I'd take the bus to the Dingle, as usual, then roll up my blazer and stuff it, together with my cap, into my satchel; this did nothing to enhance my appearance when I donned them again to attempt a lesson that I liked - few and far-between that they were.

I was wandering along Aigburth Road whilst missing a lesson one day, when I came across three lads wearing my school's blazers and caps; they were shouting across to the other side of the road where a small, tubby lad was stood. As I got closer, I realised the boy had Down's syndrome, and the three lads were calling him all the nasty names they could think of. The lad just stood smiling and waving to them; I realised he thought they were friends. I felt my anger begin to rise and, before I knew what I was doing, I was charging towards the three boys with my fully-laden satchel swinging in my hand. I hit two of them square in the face with my satchel, producing copious amounts of blood. The third lad swung and punched me in the nose, then, obviously thinking that I was a lunatic, he turned and took off.

Realising that I had probably done more damage than I had intended, I ran off in the direction of Sefton Park holding my bloody nose. I was certain I was in big trouble; the three boys would be at school the next day, but would they recognise me? I hadn't had my blazer or cap on and there were so many boys in the school, I certainly wouldn't recognise them. On top of which, the other others had probably been too busy holding their bleeding noses and wiping tears from their eyes to see me. In the event, complete with crumpled blazer and cap, I returned to school the next day and the only person I had to answer to was my form teacher to explain why I hadn't been in class the day before.

I finally poured out all my sorrows to Lilly at night, who urged me not to tell Mam after everything I'd gone through to ensure I could go to TTI. On the odd occasion I saw Billy, I would moan about my troubles and he would tell me to pack it all in and get a job like him. I also spoke to his dad, as he had become somewhat of a father-figure to me; he commiserated but told me to stick it out, it'd all be worth it in the end.

I was sure this would never be the case, so on impulse one day I told Mam, 'I'm leaving TTI.'

She didn't get angry, she didn't say, 'I told you so,' she didn't show any emotion, she just said, 'Are you sure? You decided to go in the first place, so I guess it's your decision if you leave.'

I was both relieved and surprised by Mam's reaction. I had expected at least a sarcastic comment or two, if not a clout round the ear for wasting everybody's time, but I began to suspect that Lilly had already told her how unhappy I was. Now I'd have to find a job.

I had no idea where to start looking and neither had Mam. Billy suggested an Education Authority office in Dale Street, which had helped him when he was about to leave school. I made my way down to the office and was interviewed by a man who wanted to know what, if anything, I had been doing since leaving Granby Street. He seemed quite impressed that I'd passed my School Certificate exam, but obviously had no idea that I had gone to TTI, and I had no intention of enlightening him.

I told him a pack of lies about how Mam was in need of my help at home, how I had to look after my younger sister whilst Mam went searching for work herself, as well as continuously walking to Blackburn House, unable to pay for a bus fare, hoping each time she'd find she'd moved up the housing list. This part of my story was true, but only just.

The man looked extremely sympathetic and decided that, because of my educational approach, he felt I could do worse than take on a job he had on his vacancies list as an office boy with Manweb, the Merseyside and North Wales Electricity Board, which had offices in Derby House in Tithebarn Street. I was a bit dubious, but he explained I'd be starting at the bottom and that as it was such a good company the chances of promotion were very good, so I decided it sounded a good option and he arranged an interview for me the same day.

I had no idea what to expect. I was still in my short pants and wearing my blazer, which Mam had taken the school badge off, my school shirt but no tie, long socks and very scuffed shoes.

Arriving at Derby House, I was guided by an assistant to what I presumed was the top man's office and ushered inside, where a tall man with short grey hair stood. He sat down behind his desk and looked me up and down, then reclined in his seat.

'I must say, boy, I have my doubts, but seeing as you have been recommended to me, please take a seat.'

I quickly perched on the edge of the seat facing him and answered all the questions thrown at me. He then told me some of the duties an office boy would have to perform and finished by saying that if I wanted the job, I could start more or less straight away. I would be paid thirty shillings a week.

One pound, ten shillings! I was amazed. I'd never dreamt I would have so much money for running errands, filing papers and taking messages between offices.

'Yes, thank you, sir!' I said excitedly, and with a beaming smile I stood up to shake the hand he was holding out to me.

I was to start the following Monday.

Mam was over the moon.

'You'll have to wear a tie,' she said enthused. 'And we'll have to polish up your shoes until we can find you another pair. No more football in those! You'll be able to keep some pocket money,' she added, but didn't look too pleased when I told her I would be keeping five shillings to pay for football matches. Mam didn't reply.

Monday came and Mam gave me the bus fare to town without a moment's hesitation; my shoes shone where Mam had polished them with all her might and she produced a tie from somewhere. On reaching Derby House for the first time, I felt a little afraid, but on entering the foyer and explaining to the girl on the reception desk who I was, I was shown up to a large office full of girls and women who all sat at desks with typewriters. They looked up at me and stared with what seemed like cynical smiles. I felt like a fish out of water and was going to do an about turn when the receptionist led me to a small desk at the very front of all the other desks and said,

'This is where you work,' and then left.

The desk next to mine was occupied by a very pretty red-haired girl, who had a peculiar-looking typewriter in front of her, which I learnt later was a Comptometer, a mechanical calculator.

'Hi, I'm Laura,' she said.

'I'm Billy,' I replied, my voice shaking with nerves.

'I'll be showing you your job; it won't be long before you know it backwards,' she said kindly, and she was right.

One of my duties was to take piles of paperwork from my office to the office of a female manager who had an assistant called Jean. Both women were several years older than me, in their mid- twenties, and although Jean was pretty, the manager was strikingly beautiful, even though she wore glasses. I used to watch most of the men in the office trying to get her attention and talk to her whenever they could, and she would flirt with all of them. I saw more of her than any of the other men, though I was too naïve to appreciate my luck.

Whenever I went to the girls' office and Jean was in there too, she would stand alongside the manager with an empty chair next to her. As I closed the door behind me and waited to be given the piles of paperwork, Jean would lift one leg up onto the chair, raising her skirt to reveal her long leg, with bare flesh at the top of her black suspenders, and a flash of knickers. The two of them would watch me whilst pretending to be holed up in conversation, waiting for my reaction, which would invariably be a crimson face or a movement in my short pants which I could not control. Retrieving the paperwork and hastily escaping the office, I would hear peals of laughter from the two women as I walked down the corridor to my office, trying desperately to conceal my discomfort.

At this time, in the 1940s, a lot of boys my age knew nothing about sex. It was a taboo subject, never touched upon by adults in front of children and only partly learnt from snippets of information from more knowing boys. I'd kissed girls and I appreciated how pretty they were, but now I discovered, for reasons unknown to me, I was dreaming about them and having what I later learnt were wet dreams. I would wake in the morning mortified and scared, knowing Mam would discover what had happened when I changed my underwear, which wasn't too often. I would be at a loss to explain it.

Not long after it started, Mam said, 'What are you doing at night?'

I was horrified, exclaiming, 'I'm not doing anything; it just happens!'

The dreams kept on happening, though Mam never mentioned it again, and I was embarrassed to find that, in the main, my dreams were of Laura, Jean and her manager.

After a few weeks, I proudly went into work in a pair of long trousers I'd bought with some of my pay packet; Mam was not happy when she received a smaller amount from me that week, but I was finally in my first pair of long pants and I didn't care.

I was sent to Jean's office and, upon opening the door, saw both Jean and her manager standing by the desk with the empty chair alongside. They both looked at me but surprisingly Jean didn't lift her leg up onto the chair. I must have looked quizzical, because Jean grinned at me.

'I see you're wearing long pants now, Billy. I can't see your legs anymore, so you can't see mine.' And the two of them were still laughing when I was headed down the corridor, once again mortified at my crimson reaction.

Although I knew I would no longer be embarrassed going to the office, I was quite sad at the fact Jean wouldn't be showing me her bare leg again.

In the main, I was a great deal happier than I had been when going to the TTI, but my job was very simple, mainly filing documents, posting bills to the myriad of Manweb customers and running errands for my bosses, even occasionally for the girls in the office.

I seemed to spend more time out of the office than in it, which suited me fine as I was out in the fresh air, as free as a bird. I spent most of this time heading down to the Pier Head, just a short walk from Derby House, and on the way would pass the 'Sailors' Church' of St Nicholas which had, in the days of sailing, been surrounded by sailing ships from every sea-going nation on the earth. I had always loved the stories of Nelson's time with their great first-, second- and third-rate battleships, though my favourite had always been the much smaller Frigates.

Walking past St Nick's, as it was known, I would try to imagine such ships in their docks, now sadly replaced by roads running past the Cunard Building and on into the Dingle. The consolation was the Mersey was still there, that couldn't be replaced, and I could watch the big ships at anchor or proceeding up or down stream to faraway places, and for this I was being paid.

Mam and I were getting along much better since I had become a wage earner, and not long after I'd started work she had, as promised, bought me a new pair of shoes, and with them a pair of pumps too. On a Friday or Saturday night we'd even take Lilly and June to the pictures to see a new film, something June always got excited about, as a film meant sweets for her.

Suddenly I became aware that, despite living in a hovel next to Liverpool FC, life was good. I was earning a living, my family were all getting along pretty well, and even the Reds had come out of a poor spell and were getting back to their rightful position as one of the best football teams in the country. As I only had to work a five-day week, my weekends were my own, except for taking June for the occasional walk in the park or to the Pier Head to see the ships.

I was free to go to Billy's or attempt to see the old gang with Joey Dooley, in the hope of seeing Lorna.

It was on one of these visits to see Billy that Gladys was once again on the scene, this time without her sister. She was actually in Billy's house when I knocked on the door and, on opening it, Billy wasn't the most welcoming mate I'd ever had. I just walked in, as I always had done, with Billy hurrying behind me.

'Mam and Dad are not in,' he said.

Walking past the parlour, on hearing a noise I looked in to see Gladys in a state of semi-undress. She just grinned at me and said, 'Hi!'

Startled, I realised her knickers were on the settee beside her. I was in shock and couldn't believe Billy was here, in his own home, with Gladys, who had no knickers on. I turned to see Billy still behind me with a shallow grin on his face; I didn't know what to say.

'Come and sit down, Billy,' Gladys said, looking at me and patting the cushion beside her. Billy gave me a push but I quickly headed to the armchair by the fireplace, avoiding the settee.

Gladys wasn't in the least embarrassed, though Billy certainly was. As they sat side by side with me looking at them, still tongue-tied, Gladys was the first to speak.

'We were just having some fun, Billy. Have you ever done anything with a girl?'

I realised she was almost laughing at me, knowing I hadn't, and I became even more embarrassed as she continued, 'It's nice, isn't it, Billy?' she said, turning to my friend. He was nodding with a big grin on his face, but then decided to change the subject.

'You haven't been over for a while,' Billy said to me. 'I was going to come over to see you, to tell you I'm finishing work soon. I've signed to join the Navy.'

I found my voice instantly. 'You've what?' I shouted at him. 'What navy?'

'The Royal Navy,' Gladys answered for him and began to sing the first line of 'All the nice girls love a sailor'. I felt like answering, 'And some not so nice,' but refrained as Billy continued to explain.

'Yes, I'm going to be a stoker, a sort of engineer. I've got another two months to go before I get sent to a training school down near Plymouth called HMS Raleigh.'

Suddenly, sadness came over me; my best friend was shortly going to disappear out of my life.

It must have shown on my face as Billy added, 'Course, there'll be plenty of times I'll be home - they call it 'leave' - so I'll be seeing you then.'

'What about your mam and dad? I bet they're not happy, are they?'

'No, they're fine; they'll still have Bobby and Sandra here for a while yet, Billy.'

Billy was obviously happy about his future plans and was about to tell me more about it when Gladys piped up, 'He's going to have a going-away party, aren't you, Billy?' As Billy nodded, Gladys continued to me, 'In about six weeks; you'll come won't you, Billy?'

'Yes,' I replied.

Feeling dejected and rejected, I realised that the old adage of two's company and three's a crowd was, at this moment in time, very true.

Standing quickly, I said, 'Well, I've got some other things to do, so I'll be off.'

As I did so, Gladys stood up and came over, pressed herself against me and kissed me. 'See you then,' she said, and winked.

Billy followed me out of the parlour and at the front door whispered, 'She still fancies you, you know. Good luck!' And closed the door behind me.

Walking away, I thought about all our time as best mates, yet I had been superseded by a girl we had both detested in the past, though I had to admit she was now quite pretty and grown up. I also realised that Billy was older and more grown up than me and obviously more worldly, as far as girls were concerned. I was jealous and aware of my lack of knowledge. I was totally frustrated and had no one to turn to. I felt I was the only boy in Liverpool, perhaps the world, who was so lacking in knowledge of the fairer sex.

It was just a week or two before Christmas 1949, and Mam and I decided to take Lilly and June to Blackler's Store in town, where they had a Santa's Grotto and an enormous inflatable figure of Father Christmas, which stood from floor to ceiling. As we walked round, June gripped my hand scared, yet in awe, of the big Father Christmas, and Lilly loved looking at all the girlie things in the store. I was on Christmas holidays from Manweb and had received a Christmas bonus of five shillings, which helped buy some small gifts for Mam, Lilly and June, and some food.

    Christmas Day was rather uneventful, but Mam cooked up a small joint of meat with vegetables and gravy, followed by her amazing apple pie, and the four of us ate together in the kitchen. After tea, Mam asked me and Lilly to sing for her and June, and Mam reclined in her chair with a happy look on her face. I looked at Lilly and June, who were both smiling too, and realised it was definitely one of my best Christmases.

Leaving the 1940s behind and entering a new decade, we had now lived next to Anfield longer than we had stopped anywhere since 1942, and I had come to look upon it as home, bugs and all. Mam had become quite an expert as a bug destroyer, and her daily doses of paraffin had, for some of the time, done the trick and Lilly and I had fewer and fewer bites. I was still able to occupy the bathroom upstairs and watch my team train in the car park, though I always refrained from shouting or applauding as our landlady would not have been happy with me, and I was worried she'd stop me using the bathroom.

    Then, once again, disaster struck, caused completely by my own stupidity.

One of my jobs at work was to report each morning to Mrs Simpson, the tea lady, who had her own little kitchen in Derby House; she would send me out to a cake shop on Castle Street just behind our building. I'd collect six cakes and two bottles of milk for the Managers' morning tea break. Mrs Simpson would give me the money to pay for the supplies and I would duly return with them all, and the change. The cakes were always the same, absolutely delicious strawberry tarts with clotted cream on top, and if I had 2½p left from my wages, I'd buy one for myself. I'd sit on the wall behind the Town Hall and eat mine, savouring every mouthful.

Then, one day, I hadn't got any pennies of my own and, yielding to temptation, I bought myself one out of the change. I decided that if the shortage was discovered, I'd blame the cake shop for making a mistake. Returning with the shopping and change, I handed them over to Mrs Simpson, who just put everything on her table, and I left. I went back to my desk and waited to be summoned back to the tea room, but nothing happened.

The next day I went again and did exactly the same thing, enjoying my strawberry tart on the Town Hall wall. I waited to be summoned to the tea room, excuse ready to be spun, but again nothing happened. Blow me, I thought, she doesn't count the change. So another free cake was consumed the next day. No longer expecting to be sent for, it came out of the blue when I was called up to the Manager's office; I'd never been sent for by him, so I assumed it would be to run an errand. As I walked in, he pointed to the chair in front of his desk that I'd sat in for my interview.

'Billy, you've been stealing money out of the petty cash Mrs Simpson gives you for the cake shop run.'

I was shocked, and after finding my voice tried to bluster my way out of it, to no avail.

225

'We don't tolerate theft at Manweb, Billy. I've been in touch with the shop, and they've told me that for months they've supplied six cakes each day, exactly the same number every time, until recently. It's gone up to by one. Mrs Simpson then tells me that only six have been brought back by you. The only explanation is that you paid for a cake for yourself out of the money Mrs Simpson gave you, which she says she has noticed has been short for a few days now.

'Billy, you are, as of now, dismissed. Clear your desk of whatever is yours, and if you call at the pay office, you will receive whatever pay you are due, though you will find it will be short by the amount you owe Mrs Simpson.'

Doing as I was ordered, I was too ashamed to tell Laura why I was clearing my desk, saying I had taken a job elsewhere. I left the building, too terrified to go home and tell Mam, so I wandered down to the Pier Head and sat on a monument that overlooked the river for the remainder of the day.

Sure enough, on returning home and telling Mam, she blew her top.

'How could you just walk out of job you liked, Billy?' she shouted at me.

'It wasn't my fault, Mam,' I lied. 'I had a row with one of the lads from a different office, and it nearly ended in a fight but we were pulled apart. We were both dismissed instantly.'

'Did you start it, Billy?'

'No, of course not!' I retorted.

'Well, I have a good mind to go down to Derby House tomorrow and demand they reinstate you! How can they just get rid of you like that over a row?'

'It doesn't matter, Mam,' I said quickly. 'I think I've got another job; I've been looking since this morning. I've got an interview first thing in the morning.' Before Mam could answer I quickly left the parlour and went up to my room in the attic.

I spent the night in bed tossing and turning, wondering what the hell I could do. Lilly had been no help, constantly asking what I had in mind and telling me how silly I was to have had a fight at work; she wouldn't believe it was just a row, she knew me too well.

I was up and out of the house as soon as I could, as I'd decided to go back to the Education Office and hoped Manweb had not been in touch with the man I'd seen about my dismissal.

I saw a different man on my second visit and he didn't seem to know anything about my dismissal from Manweb. When he asked why I was looking for a new job, I told him I felt capable of a lot more than just filing and running errands. He studied my school reports and School Certificate results.

'I see you're quite good at Maths,' he said, and I agreed, although in reality it was my least favourite subject.

He pondered for a while, tapping his pen on the paper in front of him. 'You're a bit too small for some of the manual jobs available,' he finally said. 'So I understand why you were advised that an office job would probably suit you best. Have you any idea what you would really like to do?'

'I like ships,' I replied.

'Coming from Liverpool, that's not surprising; let's see what we're got,' he said and pulled out different files. After several minutes of flipping through the folders, he looked up. 'How's about a shipping company? I've got a job available in the offices of Booth Line Shipping in the Cunard Building. They want a boy who's quite smart and can do sums, mainly adding up.'

I jumped at it. Little did he know I would have taken anything to keep Mam happy, and he wrote a note for me to take to the Booth Line office stating that his office fully recommended me for the role of Office Boy, as I had some experience and should prove an asset.

As I entered the world-renowned Cunard Building, I was in awe of the architectural features, the staircases, chandeliers and models of famous ships in large glass showcases. I had no time to stand and stare though, so I headed straight for the gated lift that took me up to the third floor.

I found the big heavy doors with Booth Line engraved on them and slowly pushed them open. Peering in, I saw the long office was filled with high, dark wood desks that lined both sides of the room. Eerily quiet, there was no-one sat at any of the first desks, so I slowly walked down the centre of the room until I saw an old gentleman sitting at one of the desks.

'Excuse me,' I said quietly, 'I'm here about the Office Boy job.'

He just pointed to the door at the rear of the room and said, 'In there.'

I knocked on the solid wood door and waited.

'No, just go in,' the old man said.

I pushed the door open and found a small corridor with a further three doors in it; I knocked on the one that said 'Office' and heard a man's voice say, 'Enter.'

Another elderly man was sat behind his desk and he looked up as I entered. 'Yes?' he asked.

I stepped forward and handed him the note from the Education Office; reading it, he looked me up and down and then finally said, 'Sit there,' and pointed to a chair in the corner of the room. As I did as I was told, he stepped out from behind his desk holding a clipboard and pen. Handing it to me he said, 'Add that lot up.'

Looking at the page containing a long list of figures of pounds, shillings and pence, I was momentarily terrified. Realising I was being tested, I quickly concentrated but, scared of making a mistake, I took my time. Finishing it, I handed the board back to the gentleman and sat back in the chair, inwardly releasing a sigh of relief.

He perched on the edge of his desk and studied my answers. 'Correct, but you were slow. If you want to work here, you'll have to be much quicker than that.'

I was quick to answer that I could add much faster but didn't want to make a mistake; he seemed to accept my reply and added that I'd have time to check my lists if I got the job.

He went on to tell me how the business worked and what my duties would be as well as the ledger work, then finally asked, 'Well, Billy, would you like to work here?'

For a brief moment, I held my tongue and then quickly asked, 'What would I be paid?'

He smiled at me. 'Didn't I mention that? Is that important?'

I knew he was testing me. 'Well, yes, but I do want the job,' I replied.

'Good. Well, as an Office Boy, you start at the bottom of the ladder, so the pay isn't great, but here at Booth Line we like to think we do better than some companies. You'll start on two pounds and five shillings. So, do you still want the job?'

I couldn't believe it! Two pounds and five shillings a week working for a shipping company, possibly being sent on errands to their ships. I was ecstatic but tried not to show it.

'Yes, please, sir,' I said.

He stood up, shook my hand and said, 'Good, go and see John, he's at his desk; tell him you'll start on Monday and he'll show you the ropes.'

Going back into the main office, I was surprised again to see that John was the only person in there. Telling him I was being taken on as the new Office Boy, he said, 'We don't have Office Boys here; you'll be the Junior Clerk. When are you starting?'

'Monday,' I replied. 'What will I have to do?'

John showed me lists similar to the one in the Manager's office; they were lists of cargo and he explained that I would have to calculate the prices of all the items on each sheet. He must have seen the concerned look on my face because he said, 'You'll soon get used to it; it's quite simple, really, and you won't be doing it all day every day. We have another lad who works here and you'll take turns in and out of the office. He's out running errands to our dock offices at the moment.'

That cheered me up immensely; suddenly, things were really looking up.

Leaving the Cunard Building and virtually jumping for joy, I ran down to the river and wandered up along the Dock Road heading to Northumberland Street. Known as the 'Dockers' Umbrella', the Liverpool Overhead Railway passed some ten foot over my head. I saw several young boys jumping on the peanut and coconut lorries on the Dock Road, and I smiled as I remembered my jaunts with Tommy Williams. I was saddened to realise I was now too grown up to even think about joining them but watched with admiration as they continued the tradition.

Rather than go straight home, I decided to go and see Billy and find out about his going-away party arrangements and when he was actually going. It was a good thing that I did, as the party was to be on Saturday and he was leaving to join the Navy the following Monday.

'My dad's organised it,' he said. 'He sent an invitation to Lothair Road.'

'I never got it,' I said.

'Oh well, you know now, and more importantly, Dad's invited a few girls, although I only know Gladys and her sister!'

Billy and I sat by the fireplace in the parlour talking for several hours. I told him about my new job and he told me about the Navy, and then the conversation came round to Gladys.

'She was asking if you'd been in touch,' Billy said. 'I told her we'd written to you but hadn't had an answer.'

I wondered why she was asking about me and Billy read my thoughts.

'She said that she thought you were a bit embarrassed when you realised what she and I had been up to, but I told her you'd always been shy and naïve about girls and didn't know much about them.'

Of course, he was so right. Then he surprised me.

'She said maybe she could teach you. She thinks you'd like that.' Billy had a big grin on his face as I felt mine turn crimson. I left shortly after; Billy still had a grin on his face when he said, 'Looks like it'll be a good party. See you Saturday.'

Walking the three miles home, all I could think about, with some foreboding leading to excitement, was Gladys sitting on the settee with her knickers next to her and, though I was sure Billy had set me up, I couldn't wait.

Arriving home late that evening, Mam sat in the kitchen, with June on her knee and Lilly sitting next to her, waiting patiently for me to walk in. I sat down at the table without saying anything other than enquiring about food.

'Have you been in town all day?' Mam asked.

'No, I went to Billy's; his leaving party is tomorrow.'

Mam's face turned sour.

'What about the job?' Lilly asked me.

'Oh that,' I said, trying to sound uninterested. 'I got it. I'm going to be a Junior Clerk, not an Office Boy; a Junior Clerk for a big shipping company.'

Stern faces lit up with delight.

'What are the wages?' Mam asked.

I waited, savouring the moment, then said mendaciously, 'Two pounds a week, so I'll be able to give you thirty five shillings of it.'

Mam's smile got even bigger. 'I knew you'd get another job,' she said.

'That's smashing, Billy,' Lilly said, and June clapped her hands together. If only they knew that I'd now have ten shillings a week to spend!

I realised I didn't have a proper change of clothing for the party and, as I'd been wearing the same pair of long pants I'd bought with my one of my first Manweb pay packets, they were looking a bit tatty. Mam said she would wash and iron them when I went to bed, which would have to be pretty early as I had nothing to change into. Lilly thought this was hilarious; she'd never realised I had only one pair of long trousers. I did, however, have a couple of shirts and Mam said one of these would also be washed and pressed ready for the party. I'd never really given my lack of clothing much thought before, and I suddenly realised that both Lilly and June always seemed to have a change of frocks. I was determined to buy another pair of 'longies' as soon as I could.

By the time I arrived at Billy's, having walked all the way from mine in my newly pressed clothes, not having the money for the bus, the party was in full swing - mainly with half a dozen girls dancing to records played on Mr Armitage's gramophone. I was a bit disheartened to find there were only four boys there, Billy and me being two of them. His brother, Bobby, didn't count, as he was only eleven. I didn't know who the other two boys were and just nodded hello to them.

Billy's mam and dad had retired to the parlour to be out of the way but had left sandwiches and cakes, some bottles of lemonade and even, surprisingly, some bottles of cider. The other two lads were sat on chairs watching the girls dancing. Billy was pouring out glasses and as I walked over to him I was immediately handed a glass by Gladys.

'Have you tried cider before?' she asked. I shook my head. 'It makes you drunk. I like it,' she explained, and she took a big sip of her glass.

Having never been drunk, but having seen many adults who had, I wasn't overly enthusiastic but decided to try it, and after two or three glasses began to enjoy myself. Wild horses couldn't have pulled me up out of the chair for a dance, but Gladys did try. I'd never danced in my life. Then I was given no choice but to abandon my chair as a couple of girls demanded a seat. I stood with my glass and plate in hand with nowhere to sit.

'Let's sit on the stairs,' Gladys said to me and led me out of the room into the hallway. It was early evening now and the hallway was getting dark; Gladys climbed halfway up the stairs and sat down, and I followed. I finished my cider and sandwiches and put my plate on the step above me when Gladys suddenly pulled me towards her and kissed me. Enthusiastically, I kissed her back, hoping to high heaven that neither Mr nor Mrs Armitage would come out of the parlour. Then things got even better when Gladys suddenly pulled my arm and put my hand between her legs. I couldn't believe it, although I was sure hoping for something like that to happen. What I wasn't so sure about was when she did the same thing to me, and then I finally realised what it was all about.

For me, the party was a great success.

NINETEEN

Monday, bright and early, I was off to the Cunard Building, excited and just a little apprehensive, but confident that I would soon learn the ropes of my new job. I thought I was quite presentable in my well pressed trousers, clean shirt and a well-brushed ex-school uniform blazer from which Mam had removed the badge.

However, I was quickly deflated when John, the elderly clerk, looked me up and down and said, 'It's the policy of Booth Line for all office staff to wear a tie.'

'I've got one,' I said, thinking about the tie I wore at Manweb, which was now really too tatty to wear again. 'I'll make sure I put it on tomorrow,' I promised, not sure how I'd get hold of a new one by then.

For such a long office with lots of rows of desks, it was surprisingly short of people; with the exception of an elderly lady, there were just three other men in the room. One of which was a lad not much older than me. John introduced me to David and told me he was another Junior Clerk and would be showing me the ropes. I was given a desk next to David and, as I climbed onto the high chair with the large sloping desk filled with ledges and paperwork, I felt just like Bob Cratchit. If I hadn't been so worried, I'd have laughed.

'Don't worry about the tie thing,' David whispered to me. 'I've got loads and I'll bring one in for you tomorrow. Just get here a bit earlier.'

I smiled back at David and nodded.

After a couple of hours of David's explanations on the duties of my role, I found that it was quite simple, really. I'd always been able to add up and multiply and this was what all the paperwork was about, though it did have to be in ink and very tidily done.

David and I got on like a house on fire. He was only a year older than me and though I considered him quite posh, like some of the lads at college, he was a very nice chap. David explained the office was so empty as the company had been bought out by another company called Vestey, who also owned Blue Star Line. They had several different offices in Liverpool, some in the Royal Liver Building, others in the Mersey Docks and Harbour Board Buildings; this meant that a lot of time was spent taking messages and paperwork to different buildings. I was also entrusted with taking cheques to Martins Bank; walking through the doors I stared up at the huge glass ceiling and the incredible marble floors and décor. I'd never seen a building like it.

David and I would often take alternate days to run the errands but, as David became more inclined to stay with his paperwork, I'd happily take the dispatches. Most of these were usually to the docks, but occasionally I'd have to go further afield, which necessitated in the use of the Dockers' Umbrella; for this I'd be given the rail fare and, though it was only pennies, every penny counted for me, so if it wasn't raining I'd save the money and do what I'd always done, run.

A few weeks into my new job, I was saving up my leftover shillings each week to eventually buy myself a new pair of long pants. David and I had become firm friends, during office hours anyway, and one day David asked me if I'd ever been to Loggerheads in Wales? It rang a bell and I suddenly remembered my wasted journey a couple of years earlier when I'd borrowed Uncle Paddy's bike. Since then, I'd learnt that Loggerheads was where an outdoor pursuit camp called Colomendy was based; it was a place where children and deprived casualties of the war recovering from illness were sent during the war. Kids at Granby Street School who had been there told me what a wonderful place it was, and I always wished I would be sent there. I never was.

'We can travel by bus from Birkenhead,' David said. 'Changing at Mold.'

It would mean spending some of my trouser money, but I jumped at the idea; perhaps I'd finally be able to see what Colomendy was like when I got there.

'I was once meant to go to Loggerheads to shoot squirrels, but never made it that far,' I told David.

'Do you have a gun?' he asked me, eyes lighting up.

Of course I didn't, but it turned out he did; he owned an RSA 177 air rifle and a Webley air pistol, and we'd take them both with us.

The following Saturday, we set off early in the morning, meeting at the Pier Head and taking the ferry to Birkenhead, then boarding a bus for Mold. During our journey on the bus, I mentioned to David that I'd heard about the holiday place called Colomendy and was surprised to find he was an expert on it, as he'd been evacuated to the very place during the war. I couldn't remember any of the Granby Street kids ever saying they'd been sent there for the whole of the war, but it transpired that David had. David was from the Dingle area of Liverpool, which was much like my area of Bootle, and many of the kids from the Dingle were the very first to be sent away to Colomendy, some with their mothers. David had been there for about three years and loved it, though life was hard and food poor and scarce; he said that one day all the boys had rioted and caused a lot of damage over the food they were getting, and I wondered why they would riot, when they were actually getting food, unlike Lilly and me.

After two hours, and changing buses at Mold, we eventually arrived at Loggerheads. The woods were virtually on the opposite side of the road to the Colomendy camp and I was keen to see what I had missed out on by being sent to Lancaster. But David was far keener to go hunting and, as he had the guns, I didn't really have an option.

It was decided that I would have the RSA and he would have the Webley revolver. I realised, as he handed me a box of lead pellets, that David was going to do a lot more shooting than me as he could load his gun with a dozen or so pellets, where as I had to 'break the rifle', as David said, where it joined the butt, and insert a single pellet. I wasn't too bothered; I liked the feel of the rifle.

Off we went, guns primed, along one of the paths through the woods searching the trees above us for squirrels. We searched in vain for about an hour and then very shortly it all came to an end. I shot David.

Becoming bored, he had decided to have some target practice at my expense, as I became the target. I was so busy searching skywards for squirrels that I hadn't noticed he'd disappeared, until there was the crack of a pellet gun and a quick sting on my leg followed by another one on my arm. I yelled for him to stop but there was no answer and I had no idea where he was. I moved in, still shouting for him to stop when further pellets hit me.

'No squirrels, so let's shoot each other!' I heard David call.

'What?' I shouted back, desperately trying to locate David in the bushes around me.

'Let's shoot each other! It's only pellets!'

I tried to work out where his voice was coming from when suddenly his grinning face appeared above a clump of bush. Instinctively, I threw up my rifle and fired. There was a yell and a breaking of branches and then silence.

I ran over to the bushes and behind them lay David, eyes closed and silent; there was a small trickle of blood from his forehead. I'd shot him dead centre. I'd killed him.

Staring down at him, not knowing what to do, I was suddenly relieved to hear him groan. I knelt down next to him and helped him sit up; his face was as white as a sheet and he suddenly threw up. I was petrified! I kept saying how sorry I was, and that it was his stupid bloody fault and I had no idea the rifle was so powerful. We sat there for the best part of an hour before some colour came back to his face and he began to feel better. I was looking at the small pellet hole in his forehead and wondering whether the pellet was still in there, but was too scared to mention it. I was also feeling relieved that I hadn't shot him in the eye and blinded him.

We eventually made our way back to Loggerheads to wait for the bus back to Mold; happily, David and I were still friends,

'Where'd you learn to shoot like that, Billy? I thought you'd be shite!' David asked when we were sat on the bus; I told him about all the fairgrounds I'd been to when I was evacuated which had shooting stalls. I'd learnt how to shoot down small toys or sometimes coconuts which were suspended on a length of very thin string; the aim was to shoot the string, thus breaking it and receive the dropped toy or coconut. I became quite an expert.

Returning to Liverpool, David seemed like his old self and on Monday in the office he was none the worse for being shot, even joking about it; however, he still had the small hole in his forehead.

Telling Mam about our trip, although omitting any mention of the guns, I told her about David being evacuated to Colomendy and wondered why Lilly and I had been sent to Lancaster instead. She knew about Colomendy, saying she had heard of mothers and children being sent there but, as far she knew, that was right at the start of the war. After that, nobody had mentioned it to her and it was only after the Blitz of 1941 when our house, along with thousands of others, had been destroyed, that we had been ordered to evacuate. I still wished I'd been sent to Wales.

Life working for Booth Line was becoming routine, to the point of being boring. My job in the office wasn't challenging and certainly didn't put any strain on my brain; although I still enjoyed the freedom that delivering messages round the docks gave me. Having found many of the old buildings so awe-inspiring when I first started my job, I was becoming nonchalant when entering any new office.

However, when I entered the Mersey Docks and Harbour Boards offices, I was once again taken aback by the wonderful interior. It was a vast space with a circle of beautifully sculptured doorways leading into halls, which in turn led to countless offices. Its ceiling was a glass dome which allowed daylight to flood in. All around the frieze, between the dome and the doorways, in large letters were the words: 'They who go down to the sea in ships shall see the wonders of the world.'

I'd spend time sitting by the river thinking of Billy and imagining where all the ships were going, aware that some of those with the Booth Line funnel could be off to places like Manaus and Belem up the Amazon; they would drop anchor in Rio and other grand South American cities. Without realising it at the time, I was getting itchy feet.

At home, Mam and I were getting on very well, and she had even seemed quite happy when one day I had returned home with a new pair of long pants. Lilly was doing well at school, and she was in the school choir. Mam said she was certainly the best in it; I could quite believe it, knowing how good she'd been in our carol singing days. She was growing up too, and when I'd give her the odd shilling or two, she'd now spend it on socks, stockings or jewellery, not sweets like she used to. June was just four now and was quite demanding, insisting on being taken to the park or for a ride on the bus to the Pier Head, or on a trip with Mam to the cinema when she could afford it.

On the odd Saturday, I'd take June on the bus to Aigburth Road; from there we'd walk to my old haunt of Sefton Park where, now having money to spend, I'd hire a rowing boat and we'd row for an hour or so around the large lake, avoiding some of the usual hooligans playing in the boats, before walking around the park eating an ice cream.

It was at this time that it dawned on me that Lilly attracted a lot of attention from passing boys on the odd occasion that she came with us. Most of the time the boys were in groups or gangs which fed their bravado and they would whistle and shout compliments to her; Lilly would just blush and ignore them, though I'm sure she was always pleased. June would ask endless questions as to why they were calling to her sister, and this made Lilly blush even more, which gave me lots of amusement.

Whilst in the park one day, we bumped into my cousin Alfie from Auntie Dorothy's in Liffey Street. I hadn't seen him or any of his family since we had left. We chatted a while and it was later that I realised that, despite having such a big family from both my mother and my father's side, the only one of the family we ever saw was Auntie Lilly; it was sad to realise that from the day we'd left Jubilee Drive, they had all completely disappeared out of our lives.

Sometimes, after work, I'd call on Mr and Mrs Armitage to hear news of Billy and from there I'd go walking along to Kingsley Road, off which was Lorna's home on Roseberry Street, and hope to see her. I'd hang around until it started to get dark, but never saw her.

Life was quite pleasant, but dull.

Billy returned home on leave and it was to be two weeks of drunken debauchery, although on the second day he was home, when I left work and made my way to Foxhill Street to see him, I had no idea what was in store. I'd told Mam that for the two weeks of Billy's leave, I'd be spending a lot of time staying over at his house. Billy had made it clear that for two weeks, life, for me anyway, was going to be very different. I quickly discovered he was not the same person who had left to join the Navy.

Dressed in his uniform, Billy had grown up.

For the first time ever, I entered a pub. Billy led the way into The Grapes in Crown Street and ordered two pints of beer. We were in Crown Street, because Billy had learnt from a naval source that this particular pub was not too bothered who they served, underage or not.

We were welcomed with open arms, especially by two old ladies sitting at a table. 'Three cheers for the boys in blue!' they shouted as we entered and clapped Billy on the back, touching his collar for luck.

It was the start of a new life for me which I could never have foreseen. It was three or four pints of mild ale later that, egged on by Billy, I started singing. My pub audience were very appreciative and insisted on buying us more drinks. Shortly afterwards, I found myself in the pub toilet being as sick as a dog and vowing to myself never to touch alcohol again. The vow lasted until the following evening.

After spending the following day recovering at Billy's house, it was time to step out again. We headed off, not quite sure what to do, but one thing was certain - there was no way we were going back to The Grapes again! We did, however, try another pub near Granby Street, but the landlord politely refused to serve us because of our obvious young age. We decided to head to an off licence, buy some bottles of beer and take them home, hopefully finding a couple of girls on the way to share them with in Billy's front parlour.

Walking back to Foxhill Street we did just that, and two girls about our age were very happy to join us. As it turned out, Mr and Mrs Armitage were very broad-minded and gave us the use of the parlour without hesitation, even supplying glasses for the beer.

It wasn't long before the beers were consumed and the pretty girls were sat on our knees. Billy had turned off the only light on the ceiling with no objection from the girls; conversation had ceased because we had run out of questions and we knew just what Billy did or was being trained to do, and he had also regaled us with stories of what he called 'runs ashore' in Plymouth and the girls he'd met there. I'm pretty sure this was to prepare the girls for what was to come, and I believe they were as excited as I certainly was because, once again, I had realised how naïve and innocent I was regarding the joys of girls.

It was brought home to me when the girl on my knee started kissing me with her mouth open and tongue working. I'd kissed girls before but, even with Gladys, it was not like this. I responded enthusiastically and it wasn't long before events moved on and I had my hand inside her bra on two small breasts. Judging from the sounds coming from Billy and his girl, they were far more advanced than we were, so I moved on to her stockinged legs and up to her knickers.

Billy suddenly said, 'Why don't we change partners?'

My girl and I thought about it for a moment; realising there wasn't much we didn't now know about each other's bodies, we agreed. Another hour or so with my new partner went just as wonderfully as before, and I knew I would never be quite the same kid again. It all ended shortly afterwards, when both girls decided it was time they went home.

During Billy's two weeks' leave, I still had to do my daily stint at Booth Line and put in the odd visit to Mam and the girls, especially on pay day. Mam wasn't remotely bothered that I was spending all my spare time at Billy's; after all, it meant it was one less mouth to feed. I'm sure she would have felt differently had she known what I was getting up to, because it wasn't too long ago that having wet dreams was disgusting, as far as she was concerned.

Having little success at being served beer elsewhere, we did return to The Grapes on at least two further occasions, and each time were welcomed whole-heartedly. I had learnt my lesson and drank sparingly, terrified of being ill again; not so Billy. Once again, I would have to join a sing-song, refusing the offer of a pint now and again from some happy friend, whilst Billy tapped out the tune with his fingers and made some sort of drum noise from his mouth and accepting any drinks on offer. Fortunately, he could hold his drink much better than I could and we would still look around for some girls on the way home, and sometimes we got lucky. Mr and Mrs Armitage never turned a hair each time we came home with new friends, and the parlour was always available and was put to good use.

The time came for Billy to return to HMS Raleigh and I met him at Lime Street Station to say goodbye.

I didn't think he was in the least surprised when I said, 'I'm going to join the Navy.'

'Good on ya, Billy,' he said, smiling and patting my back. Then with a wink he added, 'You'll have some great runs ashore!'

Strolling home from Lime Street, it came home to me with a bang what I had just said, and I knew I'd get a quite different reaction from Mam. I didn't think they'd be too happy at Booth Line either, and doubt began to cloud my thoughts. I wandered slowly home, deliberating in my head, mindful of the fact I wouldn't just be leaving Mam but the two girls as well. I'd never had to make such a major decision in my whole life.

Mind finally made up, I ascended the stairs to the front door of 60 Lothair Road. It had been a few days since I'd been home due to the time spent cavorting with Billy and, feeling rather manky, I thought I'd put off the forthcoming row a little longer by having a bath. It wasn't to be; we no longer had use of the bathroom. There had been some sort of falling out with the landlady whilst I'd been at Billy's, and we were barred from using it.

Frustrated at not being able to have a wash and with the pressure building up inside me, I blurted out to Mam, 'I'm going to join the Navy!'

Only June laughed and clapped, too young to understand what I'd just said. Lilly looked up from the table, startled.

After a pause, Mam turned round to me and, looking angry, slowly said, 'No, you're not, Billy, you're too young. You're not even sixteen yet.'

'Billy's joined and he's only a bit older than me,' I pointed out.

'Yes,' she said, anger still in her voice, 'but if I remember rightly, you said he had to get his dad to sign a form.'

'Yes, he did,' I replied.

'Well, I'm your mother and I won't sign anything. You are not signing up.'

I tried to make her see reason but it was no good. Yet that wouldn't stop me. Come Monday I would go to the Royal Navy Recruiting Office in St John's Street.

Standing and arguing with Mam wouldn't solve my immediate problem, which was to have a bath and, as Mam was no longer talking to me, I turned to Lilly. She told me she'd found a bathhouse just off Walton Breck Road not far from the Kop and she, Mam and even June had been using it. The cost of using a bath for half an hour was a shilling with an extra three pence for a towel, and I was pleasantly surprised to find each bath was sat in its own private cubicle and was very clean and tidy; much nicer than the dowdy old bath in Lothair Road.

Come Monday, off I went to work, having made sure I was as well turned out as possible. Mam had assumed I'd resigned myself to giving the Navy a miss, for the time being anyway, and so was back to talking to me again as though nothing had happened. Lilly knew differently, though, as I'd confided in her what I'd proposed to do (after she'd promised with 'cross my heart and hope to die' that she wouldn't tell) and, as it turned out, she was on my side. The days of fighting like cat and dog were finally over.

Sitting at my Bob Cratchit seat in the office, I decided to tell David what I intended to do, as it was imperative that any errands to be done that day should be done by me. After he had sworn on his honour to keep a secret, I told him and the reason I needed to be the one to deliver any messages. Saying how sorry he was that I would be leaving, he agreed, and so I was free to do a detour from the docks to St John's Lane.

As it turned out, that particular Monday there were no letters, messages, bank visits or any other reason to leave the office and I would have been pushing my luck trying to get there and back in my short lunch break.

So, extremely frustrated, I returned home to be met by an excited Lilly, who was hugely disappointed to learn I was still a civilian; she actually thought I would have signed the necessary papers, as I'd told her I would, and come home a budding sailor.

The next day, smartly dressed again, or as smart as my well-worn clothes allowed me to be, I was early at the office, waiting expectantly for errands I was sure would be required after the quiet day the day before. I wasn't disappointed. Half a dozen or so different destinations at various docks and offices meant I had most of the morning to visit them. If I made good time and ran to most of them, I'd have plenty of time to visit the recruiting office afterwards.

The Royal Navy Recruiting Office in St John's Lane, with its medieval turret-roofed exterior enticed me to enter to see if the inside looked as much like a small castle as the outside. It didn't.

The Recruiting Officer, who I learned later was a Chief Petty Officer, was all humour and sincerity. Tall, thin and as straight as an ironing board, his greeting, as I was spun in by the revolving door, put me at ease.

'Hiya, Tiny Tim,' he laughed. 'I'll make sure you pass the height test; that was some entrance!'

Not knowing what he meant by the height test, I knew I was still on the small side, so I said nothing. I became less and less confident as I entered an office full of naval insignia – photographs, flags, models, and, most frightening of all, another man in naval uniform with rows of medal ribbons on his jacket.

I must have stopped in my tracks as the shorter of the two men said, 'Well, come on in.'

The Recruiting Officer followed me in and walked around his desk and motioned me to sit on the chair facing him. Sitting down, I felt even smaller as I looked across his neatly arranged desk. The desk itself was old and worn but beautifully polished, and I wondered, other than Billy Armitage, how many other lads like me had sat here looking across it. In the well between the two drawer sections of the desk, I could see the officer's perfectly pressed trousers sloped down to well-worn black shoes; shoes so highly polished I could see the underside of the desk in them. The whole fastidious, gleaming effect, obviously designed to impress potential recruits, was somewhat spoilt by the piece of chewing gum stuck under the desk and mirrored in his shoes.

The desire to point out the chewing gum was instantly dismissed as the officer said, 'Look up then, boy! OK, I'm a Chief Petty Officer; you can call me Chief or Sir, whichever suits you. What's your name?'

Lifting my eyes up from the magnetic shoes, I tried to sit taller; it was no use, he still looked down on me, even when leaning back. More disconcerting was the amused turn of his mouth.

'Billy, sir,' I answered nervously.

'So you're here to join the Navy, are you, lad? Tell me why you want to sign up.'

He waited as I collected my thoughts.

'I don't know,' I replied. 'I just thought it was a good idea. My mate's not long joined and he thinks it's great.'

The amused lip straightened but the voice remained cheerful and soothing.

'So, you fancy the uniform, do you, boy? Help you get the girls, wouldn't it? Well, you're right there,' he chuckled, as I said an unconvincing 'No.'

'Don't worry, that's why half the lads come in here to join up, and it's true ,you know; as the song goes, all the nice girls do love a sailor.' He paused and then added, his voice dropping an octave, 'And better still, so do the not-so-nice ones!'

I laughed, not quite sure of that last bit, but pretending that I did.

'Right, Billy, do you have any experience of the sea?'

'I work for Booth Line.'

'What, on a merchant ship?' he said, looking surprised.

'No, in the office in Cunard,' I said.

He grinned. 'Bit different in the Royal Navy, lad! Now, let's get down to business. I'll tell you what the Royal Navy has to offer; any questions, just pipe up straight away.'

My quizzical look stopped him instantly.

'Pipe up.' He laughed again. 'That means stop me and ask if you don't understand something I say. If you get in, you'll soon get used to that term.'

After some fifteen to twenty minutes, my head was spinning. I couldn't just be a sailor; I had the options of being a cook, a seaman, a stoker, an electrician, a steward, a sick-birth attendant, a signalman, a telegraphist or an artificer, amongst others.

As well as joining whatever 'branch', as he put it, I would have to take on other duties as required; cooks and stewards and the like would have to help supply ammunition to the guns in an action situation.

'Wouldn't have fancied that myself,' he went on, looking straight at me. 'I'm a seaman, with the added distinction of being a gunner. I'm a Chief Gunnery Instructor and I've never regretted it. They're the real sailors.'

'My friend Billy's a stoker,' I said.

'You can't be a seaman if you're a stoker,' he replied. 'They don't even know how to tie a knot!'

My mind was made up. 'I'd like to be a seaman,' I said.

'Good. Wise decision, lad.'

Satisfied he'd led me up the right path, he proceeded to baffle me even more; I could not be just a seaman, which, by the way, would take at least twenty years to learn; I would have to choose a second trade, the choices being a gunnery rating, an asdic rating, a weapons (torpedo) rating, a sail maker or a radar operator.

As I hadn't interrupted him, he'd hardly paused for breath, and now he did so. He looked at me, head to one side, and asked, 'What do you think; want to join?'

The triumphant way it was put to me could only be answered with a resounding, 'Yes, sir!'

'Good,' he said, his voice now a little sterner. 'Right, son, let's have your full name and address.'

The next ten minutes were spent on all my details.

'Age?'

'Almost sixteen, sir. On the 15th July.'

'Born?'

'Liverpool, sir.'

'Exams?' Hearing I had passed my School Certificate, he stopped to say I could, should I want to, enter as an artificer; not having the faintest idea what one of those was or what he did and being reluctant to ask, I told him I'd stick with my original choice.

'How tall are you, by the way?'

'I don't know, sir,' I answered.

Standing up, he called me over to a height chart in the corner of the office; with my back against the wall and standing as straight as I could, he looked above my head. 'You're five foot four and a half.' I must have looked worried because he continued, 'Pass all the other tests and we'll get you joined up. You'll soon grow more in Ganges.'

I had no idea what that meant and waited for it to be explained, but he moved me back to the chair. 'You'll be known as a Boy Seaman, should you qualify, but your father will need to sign a form allowing you to join first.'

'My dad's dead, sir, but my mam will sign.'

'That's fine,' he said, reaching into a drawer in his desk and pulling out a form and handing it to me. 'Bring this back next Tuesday when you'll have the other tests.' Then, shaking my hand, he led the way back to the entrance and thanked me for applying.

I set off back to the office at Booth Line.

David was keen to hear how things had gone, but we didn't have time to talk as we both had a pile of paperwork to wade through and it was an unwritten rule that we didn't talk when there was work to be done, so I just gave him the thumbs up.

When we finished for the day, David suggested a coffee at the small café at the Pier Head. Telling him how it had gone, I said the one snag was that Mam would have to sign a couple of forms giving her permission for me to join as my age was against me.

'How are you going to get around that?'

Placing the forms in front of me, alongside our cups of coffee, I said, 'Lend me your fountain pen, please.'

He handed it over and in two or three places I signed, 'Isabella Mansfield', then I gave it him back.

Later that night, whilst in our room in the attic, I told Lilly and showed her the forms; she was excited but concerned that Mam might find out.

'What if the Navy contact her?'

'I don't think so,' I said, but nevertheless spent a sleepless night worrying.

Knowing the next time I would be in the Recruiting Office I would have to pass a medical, which would probably necessitate stripping, I knew I needed to visit the bath house again before then, and in the meantime hid the recruitment forms under my mattress.

The following Monday, I asked John if I could leave an hour or so early as my mother needed me to look after my youngest sister whilst she went to see a doctor.

He was quite perturbed and hoped there was nothing seriously wrong and said, 'Of course you can leave early and give your mam my best wishes.' He was so sincere I felt quite guilty and wished I'd thought of some other excuse.

The guilt soon wore off as I made a beeline for a No. 27 bus near the Pier Head, which would drop me off alongside the road in which the bath house stood. Paying for my bath and towel, I was allocated a cubicle and in I went; closing the door, I turned to lock it and was stunned to see, hanging on the hook on which I would hang my towel, a gold watch. I'd never owned a watch in my life. Whether it was real gold or not, I had no idea, though it seemed pretty strange that its previous owner would be using a council bath house. I say previous owner, as I'd made the instant decision that I was the new one.

With only the slightest hint of guilt I placed it in my pocket and ran my bath, hoping that its last owner wouldn't return to look for it until I had left. I knew only too well that this made me a bigger thief than I'd ever been before; scrumping apples, stealing beer and lemonade bottles, even fireworks in Woolworths was nothing in comparison to procuring a gold watch, but I convinced myself with the old phrase 'finders keepers'. The problem was, what to do with it? I couldn't wear it, couldn't tell Mam or Lilly about it, and never gave a thought to selling it. It had to stay hidden until I joined the Navy because, after all, that wouldn't be too long, as my tests were the next day.

Arriving home, I went straight upstairs to my room and retrieved my forms from under the bed. I hung the watch from the springs under the mattress, knowing Mam would not be changing the bedding for a week or so, and folded the forms neatly into the inside pocket of my well-used blazer.

I was up bright and early the following morning, as usual, though I knew I wouldn't be going to the office that morning, or even possibly that day, depending on how things went at St John's Lane. I left as usual and hung around a phone box until I knew someone would be in the office at Booth Line and then rang up. Happily, it was the old lady who totally accepted, and promised to pass on my message to John, that Mam had to go back to the doctor and I would be in as soon as I could.

Entering the Recruiting Office through the revolving door, I was surprised to see a good dozen lads all sat around on seats in front of the Chief's office. I was asked for my forms, so duly handed over the paperwork with Mam's forged signature and was told to take a seat.

After a few minutes, the Chief Gunner came out of his office. 'Thank you for coming lads; I've got a list of names here and this is the order you'll have your medical, followed by a written examination.'

We all looked petrified; I looked around and whilst all roughly the same age, there was little doubt that I was the smallest. Seeds of doubt entered my mind; would we be selected on merit? Would they be selective on stature as well as health and intelligence? If so, I didn't stand a chance. Maybe I should have opted to be a stoker, like Billy; he was much the same height as me and he'd been selected.

Before I had time to change my mind, we were called in, two at a time, to a back room where a tall man, not in uniform, introduced himself as a naval doctor, then told us to strip off in one of two cubicles; I was so glad I'd gone to the bath house. Naked, except for underpants, we stood side by side in front of him.

'Right,' the doctor said. 'Who's Ashburner?' The lad, who was very tall, put up his hand, whereupon the doctor put his hand on his private parts and ordered, 'Cough.' Ashburner did so and the doctor then made a note on his form.

Then he did the same to me; I was perplexed, as I had no idea what that was about. Ashburner looked at me and I knew he was thinking the same.

The doctor then asked questions about illnesses and injuries we'd had whilst using his stethoscope on our chest and back; he seemed quite surprised when I told him about the illnesses I'd had during my time in the shelter, but said nothing. This only made me more nervous. Would my previous health problems count against me? Apparently not as, after getting dressed, we then had eye sight, colour blindness and hearing tests; after those, the medical was over.

Returning to the outer office and being motioned to sit down again after handing over my medical form, the Chief smiled and said, 'Good, A1, splendid. You're halfway to joining the Navy; just the intelligence test now.'

When everyone's medicals were completed, we were all led into another room where there were three lines of desks, each with a name on it.

'Right, you lot,' said the Chief. 'Sit down where you find your name; the questions are on the papers in front of you. You have one hour to complete them, starting now. Good luck.'

When I had finished I sat, not daring to move, surprised that I appeared to be the first to finish; I listened to the fidgeting and scribbling and waited for the others to finish. A quiet 'ting' of a bell signalled time was up and everybody sat bolt upright.

The Chief asked us to wait in the main office, saying he'd be with us soon with the results. We sat and introduced ourselves to each other in whispers. The lad called Ashburner confided to me that he thought he'd done quite well; not wanting to sound too confident, I said I was not too sure.

Eventually, the Chief came back in; he walked slowly behind his desk, his face quite grave. Spending a further few minutes studying the papers in front of him and thus prolonging our agony, he finally spoke.

'Right, you'll be pleased to know you all passed the medical.'

There was obvious relief all around the room.

'However, only two of you passed the intelligence exam.' He paused again, staring at us, obviously enjoying the various facial expressions he could see. 'Mansfield, Ashburner, you've just joined the Royal Navy,' and he came over and shook our hands.

Turning to the others, he took in their long faces. 'Now, don't be too despondent, lads, you're just the boys we need for the Marines.'

To me and Ashburner, he said, 'You two report to this office Monday of next week; you'll be going to Ganges.' Shaking our hands, he added, 'Welcome to the Navy, lads.'

As Ashburner and I left, I glanced back and saw a Royal Marine standing with papers in hand, talking to the lads who had failed the Royal Navy intelligence test.

TWENTY

During that week, I thought I'd pay a visit to Mr and Mrs Armitage, as I hadn't called on them since Billy went back off leave, and I felt the urgent need to let them know I was about to join him in the Navy. As always, they were pleased to see me and were more than pleased when I told them the news.

'I suppose you'll be joining him in Raleigh in Cornwall,' Mr Armitage said, and seemed a little disappointed when I said I was going to be a Boy Seaman at some place called Ganges.

'I'll know more on Monday; I'll come and let you know unless I am sent wherever it is right away,' I promised.

On leaving their house, I saw Gladys on the other side of the street.

'I saw you going into Billy's,' she said, crossing over to me. 'So I've been waiting for you to come out.'

The last thing I wanted was to be caught up with Gladys so I spoke quickly, 'Hi, Gladys. I've just passed my naval exams and been drafted into the Navy. I'm on my way home now to pack.'

'Me mam's not in,' she said. 'In fact, nobody's in, come in and have a cup of tea.'

'Just had one,' I replied. 'Thanks, but I've too much to do; I haven't even told me mam yet.' And off I ran.

I wasn't looking forward to getting home; I was going to have to tell Mam that I had joined the Navy and come Monday I'd be off to serve Queen and Country. There was going to be an almighty row. In the event, I decided to tell Lilly who, if I didn't come home on that Monday evening, could then tell Mam. At the first opportunity, I would write a letter from this place called Ganges explaining everything and apologising.

Lilly was having none of it. 'You have to tell Mam,' she said, firmly. 'I'm not going to do it for you!'

I offered her the last few shillings I had in my pocket, but it was still a definite no.

'The best thing I can do then is to go to St John's Lane and report to the Chief and then come back on the bus to tell Mam exactly what was happening.' Of course, I had no intention of doing so, but I knew Lilly would tell Mam what I'd done when I didn't come home on Monday.

On the Sunday, I wrapped my very few belongings up in the smallest bundle I could and put it under my bed. I then retrieved my watch from the bed springs and put it in my pocket; I would wear it as soon as I left in the morning. I spent most of the evening playing with June, feeling guilty, and even sad, that I would be leaving her for a while. I knew I had to phone Booth Line and let them know I was leaving, but I'd decided to do it after I'd kept my appointment at the recruitment office. How fortunate it was that I'd decided on all these arrangements before I went off the next morning with my concealed bundle under my arm.

I said 'goodbye' to Lilly, in case I didn't see her when I supposedly came home to tell Mam, and made my way to the Recruitment Office, where I was welcomed with a smile from Ashburner.

Then my world almost collapsed when the Chief said, 'Right, lads, you'll be joining HMS Ganges, which is what's known as a Shore Frigate, a Frigate being a small Destroyer, but rest assured there's nothing small about Ganges. You will each be known as 'Boy Seaman' and you will be at Ganges for the best part of a year; by the time you leave, you will have learnt a trade, of which you will have a number of options, and you will be sailors. You will receive from this office a letter at your home telling you when to muster here for the journey to Ipswich.'

I was shell-shocked. Here I was, possessions on the seat next to me, wrist watch sparkling on my arm, and nowhere to go.

'Any questions?' the Chief asked.

Ashburner, who seemed as puzzled as me, asked, 'When exactly will we be going, sir?'

'Not sure,' was the answer. 'There will be recruits from other offices in the north coming to Liverpool; you'll all be travelling together, probably in September. The letter will tell you everything you need to know.'

All I could think was, 'Good job I didn't tell Mam,' and 'Good job I didn't ring Booth Line,' and 'Good job I hadn't convinced Lilly to tell the tale!' Now I had the best part of three months to wait before I would have to do it all again.

Then a horrible thought struck me. The letter; I had no idea when it would be sent and no way to intercept it. I wasn't going to have to tell Mam; the Navy would do it for me, and I would be the one to suffer the consequences! On top of that, I had to set off at the gallop to the Cunard Building, dreaming up a damn good reason for being late; what a start to my new career!

I continued working for Booth Line, although my heart wasn't in it, conscious that I still needed to earn a wage and keep Mam happy. I also wanted to save my shillings so I'd have some to take with me when the time finally came. As each day passed, I returned from my chores at the office expecting an explosion of rage from Mam, but it never happened.

It was September 1950 when the letter finally arrived in its very official envelope and Mam opened it. Lilly told me that Mam had told her that she'd cried when she read the contents but wasn't totally surprised. Mam had listened when Lilly confessed that she'd known for some time, but I'd sworn her to silence. Lilly begged Mam to accept it and not have a row, as it was done and dusted, and there was no way back.

Strangely enough, there was no row.

'You should have told me, Billy,' was all she said.

I was to report to Lime Street Station on 10th October, where I would be met by a Naval Petty Officer and put on a train for London. I would be met by another at London Euston station, who would then join us on a train to Ipswich, where I would board a bus for a place known as Shotley, where HMS Ganges was.

In the weeks leading up to my departure, I decided to spend my spare time with June, taking her to the Pier Head, Sefton Park and even to the pier at New Brighton. Mam, Lilly and I had decided to tell June that I would be going away, assuming that it would make her less upset when I did go, but it didn't work. Apart from when I was at work, June wouldn't let me out of her sight. I didn't mind, as it was only for a short time.

Lilly was suddenly grown up. Turning fifteen that month, she was almost ready to leave school and get a job. She was already earning money of her own putting her singing voice to good use at a working men's club once or twice a week. Mam was both pleased and proud, especially as there was yet more money coming in, most of it spent on Lilly herself, and some on June. I no longer felt guilty when I thought of leaving them.

The great day arrived, and after all the waiting I was suddenly anxious, worried even, that the life I had always known was about to end, and a new life, about which I knew nothing, was about to unfold.

The last weeks had been, in the main, very pleasant. Mam and I had got along very well, and it had become pleasurable to come home and sit and talk with her and Lilly, with June listening in, about what the adventure I was about to embark upon held for us all. I'd left Booth Line on good terms and had even been given a bonus of a few pounds, which I had offered to Mam.

She'd refused it saying, 'You'll probably need that if you don't like the place you're going to. You'll have the money to come home.'

None of us knew that, once in the Navy, especially at Ganges, it was only if the Royal Navy didn't want you, that you could ever leave.

With hugs and kisses, tears from Lilly and June and fond farewells from Mam, I boarded the bus on Walton Breck Road to Lime Street, where I was met by the Chief. About a dozen other boys from various northern towns were milling around, some looking excited, some looking nervous. As I scanned the large concourse, I noticed Ashburner stood off to one side; I smiled my hello and he smiled anxiously back at me.

This was it. We were off to start our new life.

Printed in Poland
by Amazon Fulfillment
Poland Sp. z o.o., Wrocław